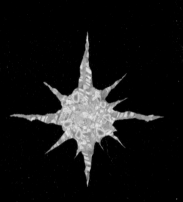

PLANETARY:

WARREN ELLIS — Writer

JOHN CASSADAY — Artist

LAURA DePUY AND DAVID BARON — Colorists

RYAN CLINE, BILL O'NEIL AND MIKE HEISLER — Letterers

JOHN LAYMAN — Editor

ALEX SINCLAIR, JOHN CASSADAY, AND ED ROEDER — Logo and Book Design

PLANETARY CREATED BY WARREN ELLIS AND JOHN CASSADAY

PLANETARY: THE FOURTH MAN
Published by WildStorm Productions. Cover, design pages and compilation © 2001 WildStorm Productions.
Planetary and all related characters and elements are trademarks of DC Comics. All Rights Reserved.

Originally published in single magazine form as PLANETARY #7-#12. Copyright © 2000, 2001
WildStorm Productions, an imprint of DC Comics. Editorial Offices: 7910 Ivanhoe, #438, La Jolla, CA 92037.
Any similarities to persons living or dead are purely coincidental. PRINTED IN CANADA. ISBN # 1-56389-776-8

DC Comics, a division of Warner Bros. - An AOL Time Warner Company.

THE FOURTH MAN

DEDICATIONS

For Stuart Green, Dave Elliott, Marie Javins, and the memory of
Archie Goodwin. Without these four, I wouldn't be writing this.
So now you know who to blame.
And for Niki and Lili, because they've put up with me in
the long trip from there to here.
—Warren

During the year in which this art was built, I experienced a great
spectrum of personal peaks. Page for page, this book will always remind
me of that year and its towering highs and abysmal lows. And what I
found along the way. So thank you for it, Lisa. Thank you for it all.
I'll miss you.
—John

JENETTE KAHN President & Editor-in-Chief   PAUL LEVITZ Executive Vice President & Publisher
JIM LEE Editorial Director – WildStorm   JOHN NEE VP & General Manager – WildStorm
SCOTT DUNBIER Group Editor   RICHARD BRUNING VP – Creative Director
PATRICK CALDON VP – Finance & Operations   DOROTHY CROUCH VP – Licensed Publishing
TERRI CUNNINGHAM VP – Managing Editor   JOEL EHRLICH Senior VP – Advertising & Promotions
ALISON GILL Executive Director – Manufacturing   LILLIAN LASERSON VP & General Counsel   BOB WAYNE VP – Direct Sales

INTRODUCTION BY Joss Whedon

Planetary haunts me.

It haunts me like a dark, low-budget science fiction movie from the fifties, seen on a black and white TV when I was still too young to deal with it. It haunts me like a visionary short story from those pocket-sized magazines with words like Amazing, Astounding or Asimov on the cover. Like a history class that's so good that for a moment you realize people actually *lived* that stuff, and you're right there with them. Like a Leone western. Like James Bond, if he were actually as cool as we remember him.

Look at the covers. The logo. No two alike. Every issue its own short, dazzling tale that would bind the reader even if they had no idea it was part of a larger whole. I first picked it up at issue #8, the second chapter of this volume. I was stunned by the imagination, the darkness, the *scope* of the thing. Plus, hey, giant ants. Going back and buying the first seven issues was an instant necessity, as was waiting droolingly for every issue since. What kept blowing me away was how different each piece was. There was more imagination and originality in every issue of *Planetary* than in practically any movie you're gonna see this year. Warren Ellis draws inspiration from so many cultural wellsprings that his work truly does become a sort of history of the twentieth century as it exists in popular fiction. But this is no mere pastiche — Ellis both subverts and elevates the elements he takes, making them fit perfectly his own epic vision. No one who loves comics can get through issue #10, "Magic and Loss," without a true thrill of childlike dread.

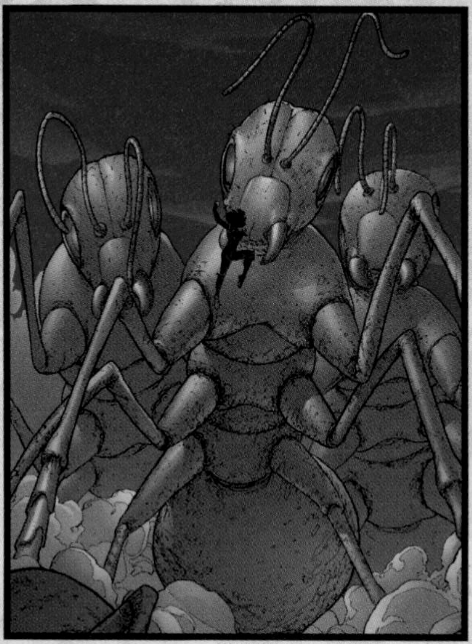

Ellis's love of literature and history, filtered through his own strange vision, puts him alongside contemporary Alan Moore in more than just quality. One could easily see their universes entwined — Tom Strong and perhaps Miss Mina Murray bumping into Elijah Snow and Jenny Sparks of The Authority. While so many comics are rebooting, Ultimating and Year One-ing themselves into a masturbatory frenzy, these two are creating universes as rich and strange as any we could hope to encounter; eerily familiar and totally new. The two stand right now as the pillars of modern comics. (Or possibly the "intimidating British guys with intense facial hair of modern comics," but "pillars" is easier to say.) What separates them is that while Moore's pages overflow with visual information, his panels crammed with explosions of life and lore, Ellis gives us a sparer, more cinematic frame. He takes his time. He waits.

Then the giant ants.

Or the rocket, the well of ghosts, the pattern of ice in a grassy park. His sense of pace, of *space*, is truly epic. He is aided in this by the extraordinary John Cassaday. Capable of extreme detail but never giving more information than needed for the moment, Casssaday is the perfect match for Ellis' vision. Ellis clearly wants to let the visuals tell his story (another nearly lost art in comics), and Cassaday rewards us with breathtaking vistas alternating with quiet, wry moments of humanity. He puts us in giant alien chambers, and we are *there*, puts us up close in moments of appalling violence, and we are *there*. He captures. Plus, Jakita Wagner: wicked hot.

Jakita's hotness aside, it's really Elijah Snow that this book belongs to. It's in this second volume that pieces of the puzzle begin to come together, that Elijah does more than just excavate. The whole begins to take shape and what would have been perfectly fine as an unrelated series of short stories begins to reveal itself as something much more complex and rewarding. Snow is a great character to walk this world with. The "creepy old goat," as one bystander calls him, is a man who's done too little, seen too much, and finally had enough. He's terminally cranky, and I admire that in a hero.

So go with him. Go back for a second trip through the warped scape Ellis and Cassaday have woven, and see if it doesn't haunt you a little bit. The game's afoot. Enjoy.

Joss Whedon

1/1/01

Joss Whedon is the acclaimed creator of *Buffy The Vampire Slayer*.

WILDSTORM

WS

CHAPTER
SEVEN

PLANETARY

ELLIS • CASSADAY • BARON

...unwavering faith, a
...ular piety towards
...s a veneration the
...und for all that apper-
...e beauty of the courts
...rd, an imagination
...ith the glories of the
...mbined in impelling
... of this memoir to
...his heart and soul
...re for the restoration
...otten faith and for
... in the land of its
...gnificence in art and
...e.

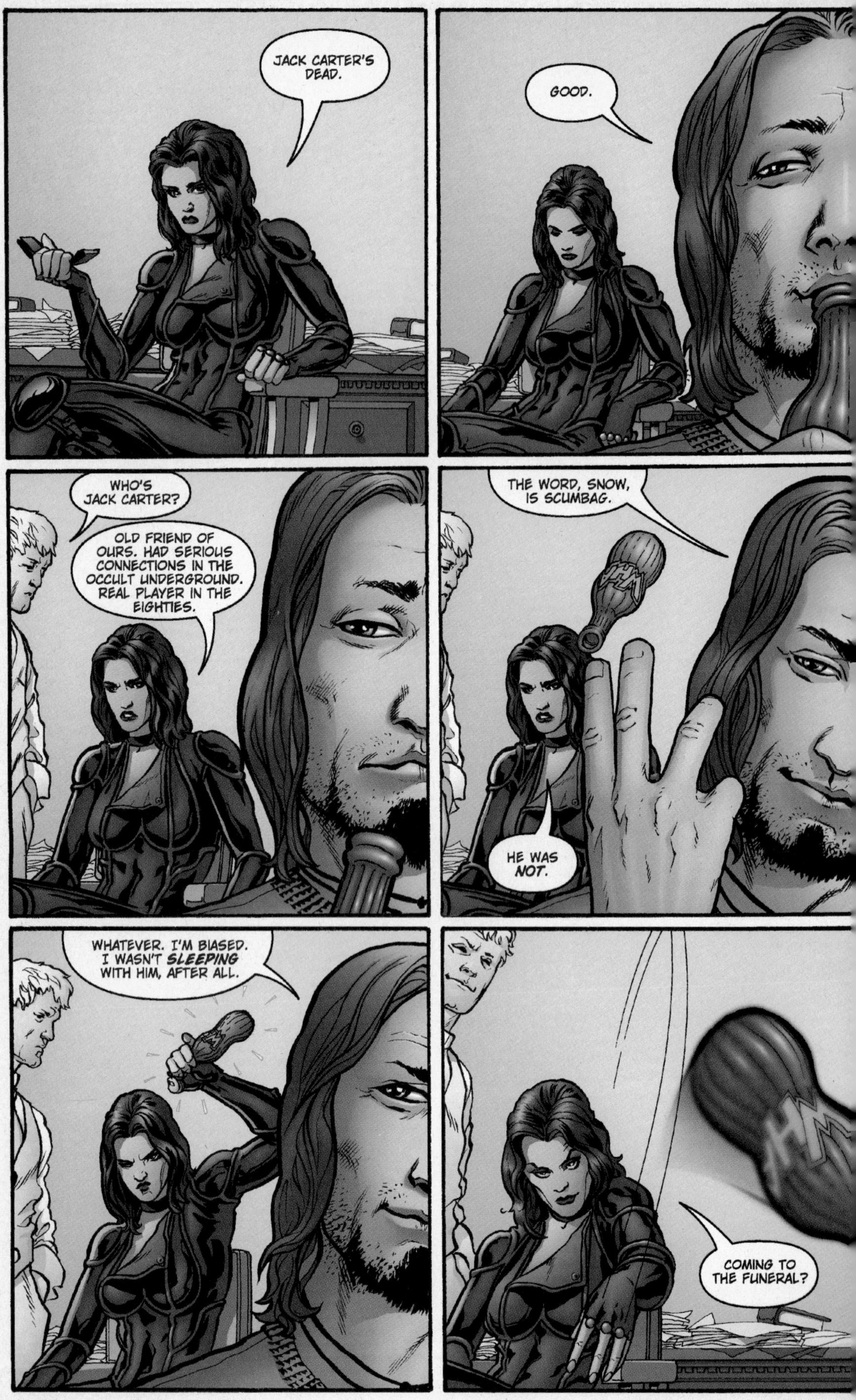
JACK CARTER'S DEAD.
GOOD.
WHO'S JACK CARTER?
OLD FRIEND OF OURS. HAD SERIOUS CONNECTIONS IN THE OCCULT UNDERGROUND. REAL PLAYER IN THE EIGHTIES.
THE WORD, SNOW, IS SCUMBAG.
HE WAS *NOT*.
WHATEVER. I'M BIASED. I WASN'T *SLEEPING* WITH HIM, AFTER ALL.
COMING TO THE FUNERAL?

"To Be In England, In The Summertime"
a tale of the planetary

WARREN ELLIS ~ THE SCRIBE
JOHN CASSADAY ~ THE ILLUSTRATOR
DAVID BARON ~ HUES AND PIGMENTS
with thanks to Laura DePuy
RYAN CLINE ~ CALLIGRAPHY
JOHN LAYMAN ~ THE SPONSOR

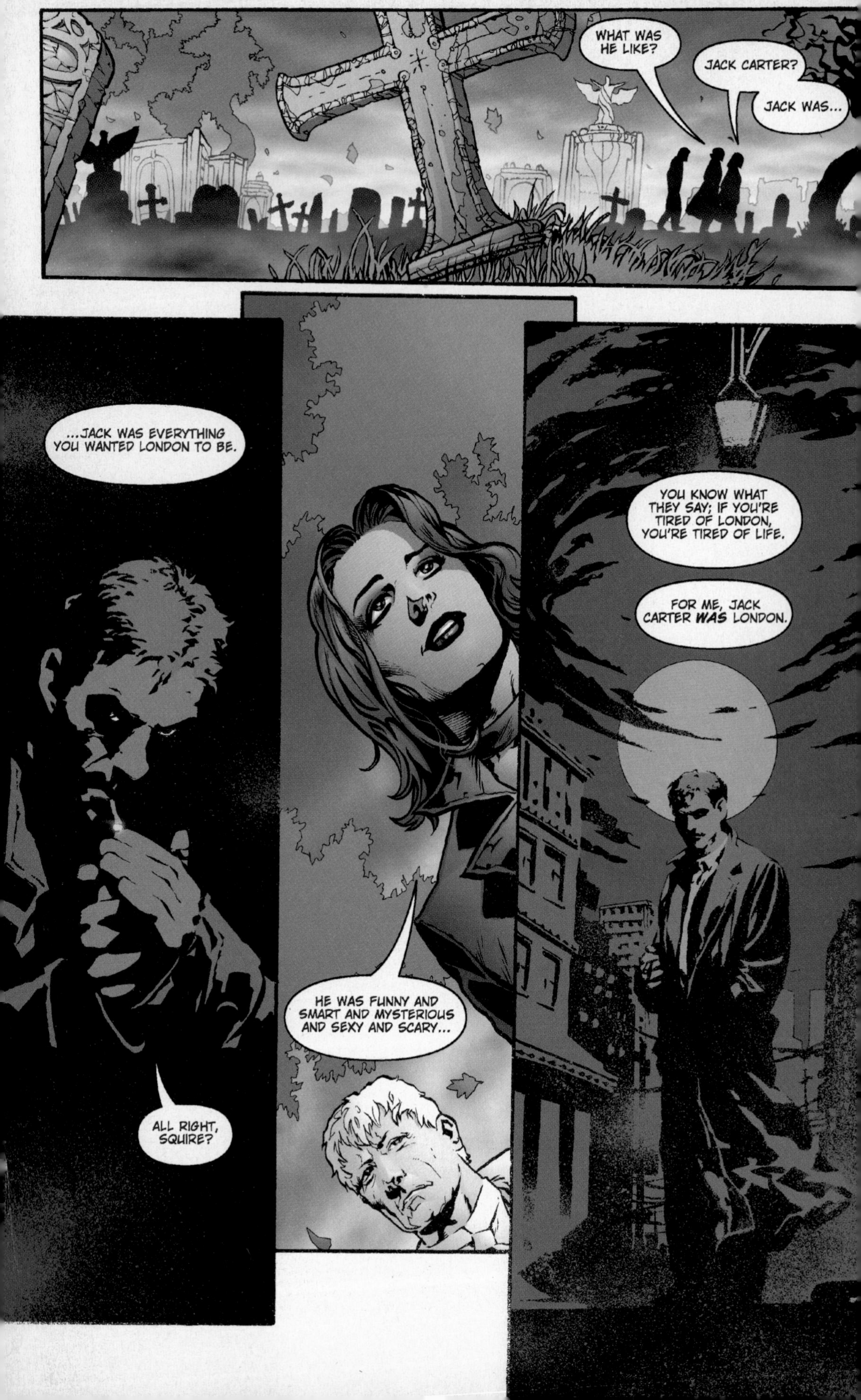
WHAT WAS HE LIKE?
JACK CARTER?
JACK WAS...
...JACK WAS EVERYTHING YOU WANTED LONDON TO BE.
HE WAS FUNNY AND SMART AND MYSTERIOUS AND SEXY AND SCARY...
ALL RIGHT, SQUIRE?
YOU KNOW WHAT THEY SAY; IF YOU'RE TIRED OF LONDON, YOU'RE TIRED OF LIFE.
FOR ME, JACK CARTER *WAS* LONDON.

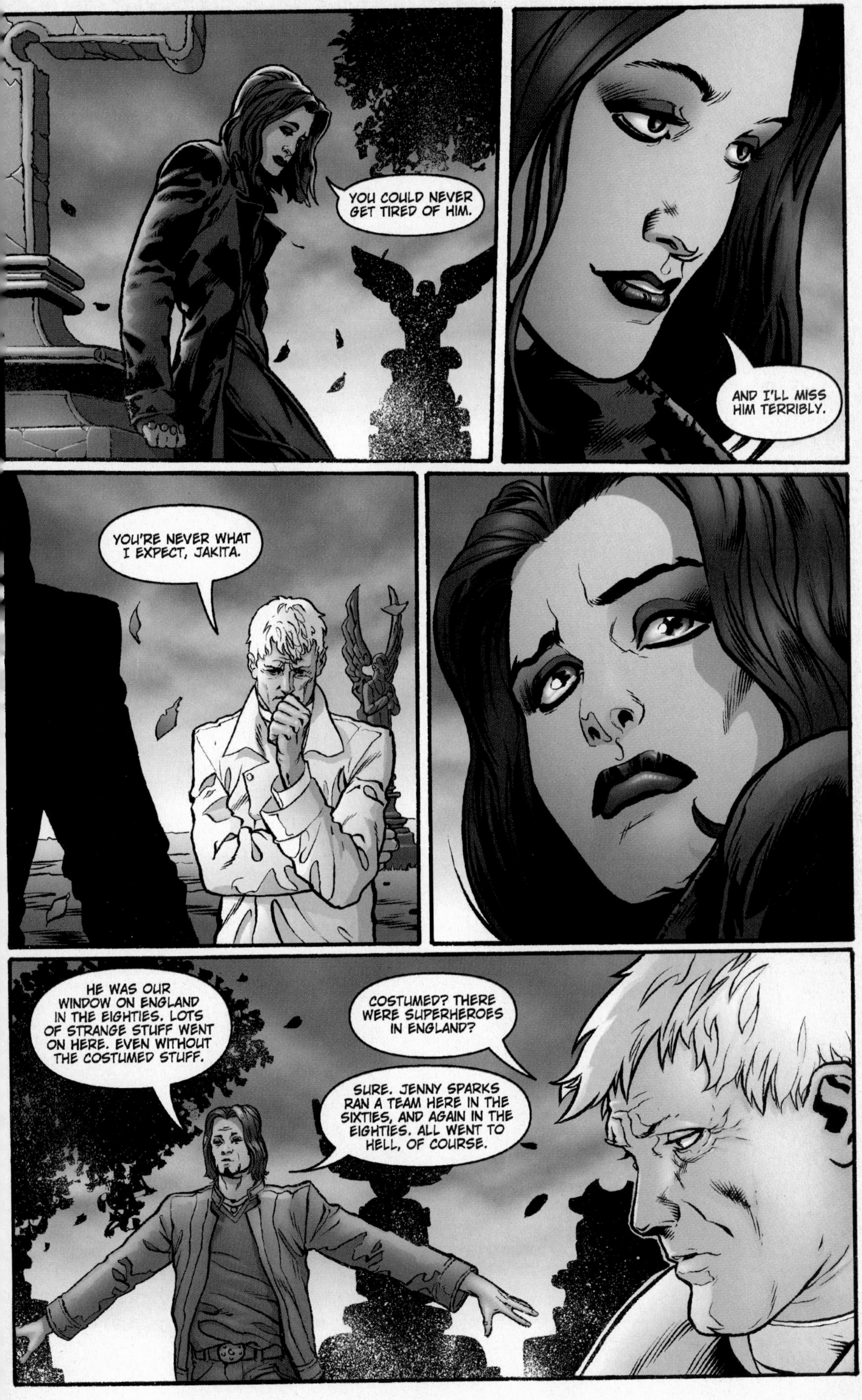
YOU COULD NEVER GET TIRED OF HIM.
AND I'LL MISS HIM TERRIBLY.
YOU'RE NEVER WHAT I EXPECT, JAKITA.
HE WAS OUR WINDOW ON ENGLAND IN THE EIGHTIES. LOTS OF STRANGE STUFF WENT ON HERE. EVEN WITHOUT THE COSTUMED STUFF.
COSTUMED? THERE WERE SUPERHEROES IN ENGLAND?
SURE. JENNY SPARKS RAN A TEAM HERE IN THE SIXTIES, AND AGAIN IN THE EIGHTIES. ALL WENT TO HELL, OF COURSE.

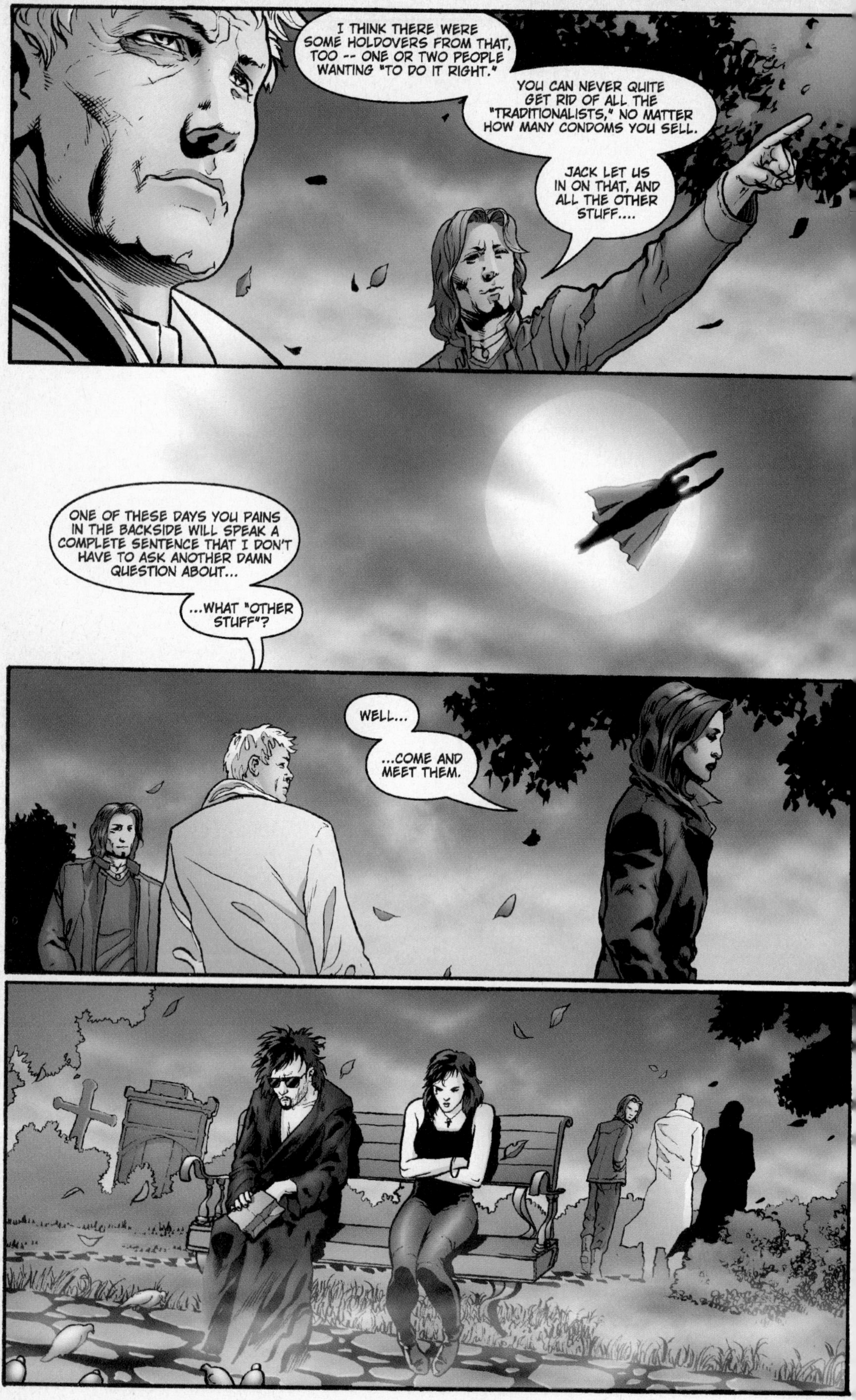

I THINK THERE WERE SOME HOLDOVERS FROM THAT, TOO -- ONE OR TWO PEOPLE WANTING "TO DO IT RIGHT."
YOU CAN NEVER QUITE GET RID OF ALL THE "TRADITIONALISTS," NO MATTER HOW MANY CONDOMS YOU SELL.
JACK LET US IN ON THAT, AND ALL THE OTHER STUFF....
ONE OF THESE DAYS YOU PAINS IN THE BACKSIDE WILL SPEAK A COMPLETE SENTENCE THAT I DON'T HAVE TO ASK ANOTHER DAMN QUESTION ABOUT...
...WHAT "OTHER STUFF"?
WELL...
...COME AND MEET THEM.

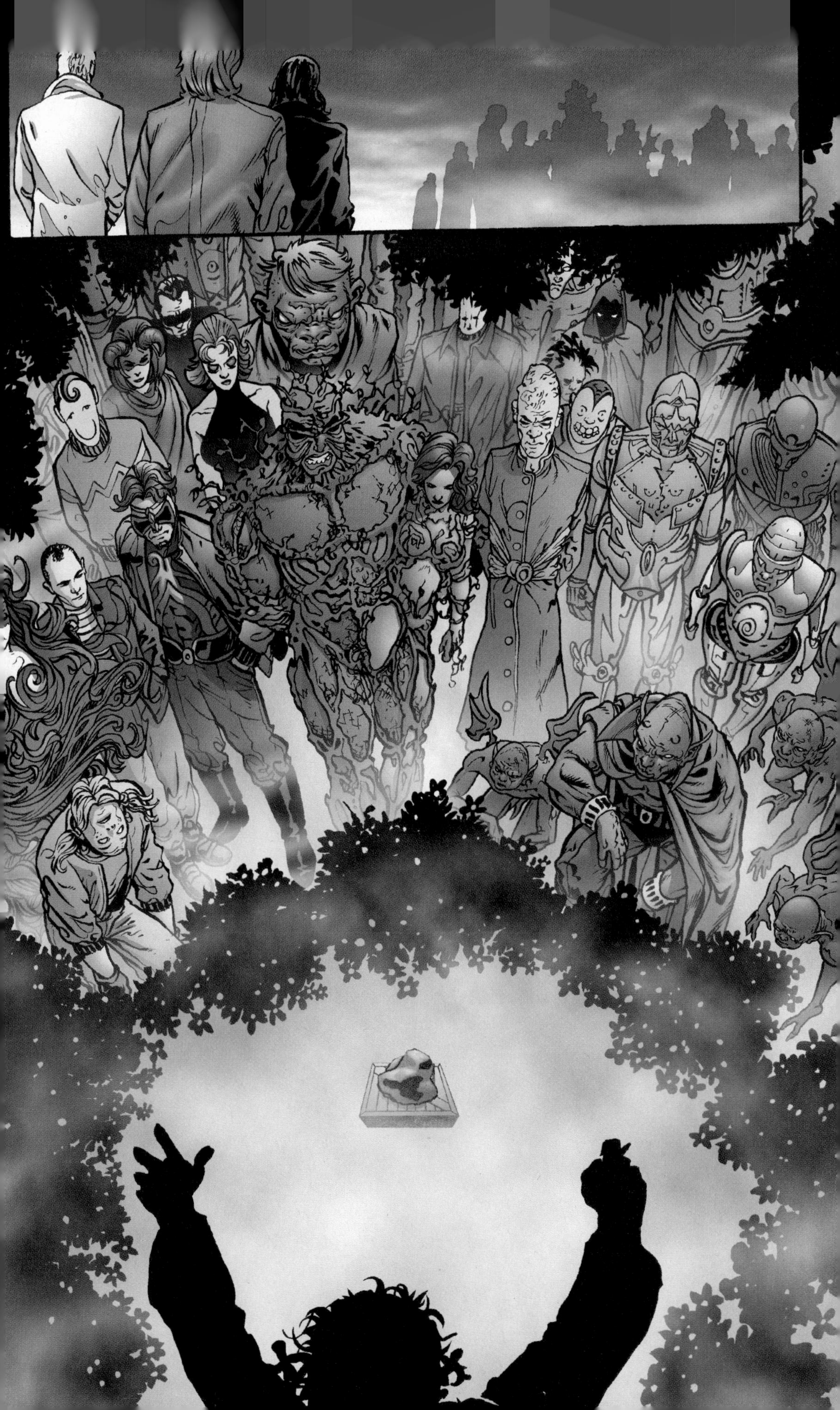

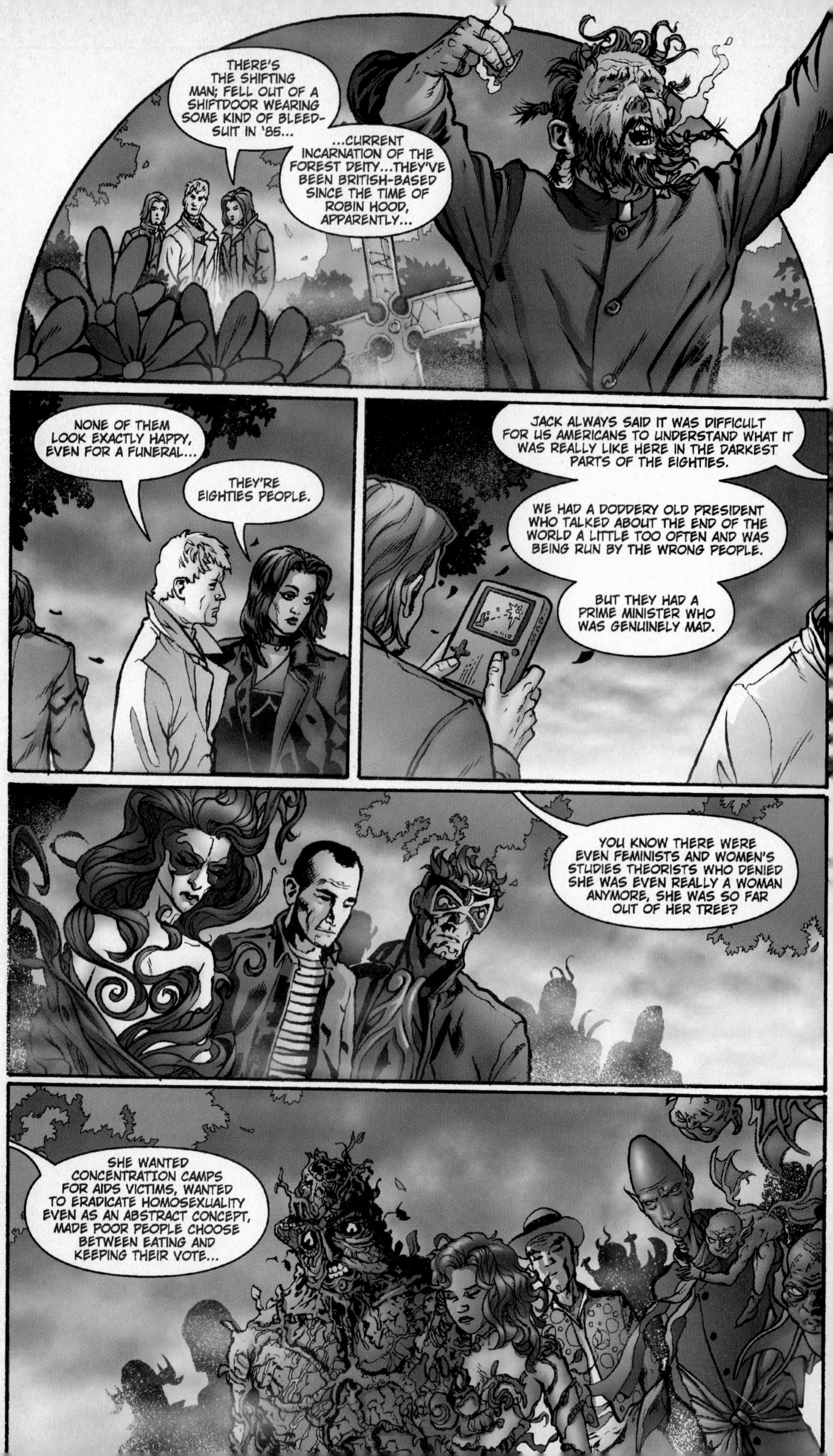
THERE'S THE SHIFTING MAN; FELL OUT OF A SHIFTDOOR WEARING SOME KIND OF BLEED-SUIT IN '85...
...CURRENT INCARNATION OF THE FOREST DEITY...THEY'VE BEEN BRITISH-BASED SINCE THE TIME OF ROBIN HOOD, APPARENTLY...
NONE OF THEM LOOK EXACTLY HAPPY, EVEN FOR A FUNERAL...
THEY'RE EIGHTIES PEOPLE.
JACK ALWAYS SAID IT WAS DIFFICULT FOR US AMERICANS TO UNDERSTAND WHAT IT WAS REALLY LIKE HERE IN THE DARKEST PARTS OF THE EIGHTIES.
WE HAD A DODDERY OLD PRESIDENT WHO TALKED ABOUT THE END OF THE WORLD A LITTLE TOO OFTEN AND WAS BEING RUN BY THE WRONG PEOPLE.
BUT THEY HAD A PRIME MINISTER WHO WAS GENUINELY MAD.
YOU KNOW THERE WERE EVEN FEMINISTS AND WOMEN'S STUDIES THEORISTS WHO DENIED SHE WAS EVEN REALLY A WOMAN ANYMORE, SHE WAS SO FAR OUT OF HER TREE?
SHE WANTED CONCENTRATION CAMPS FOR AIDS VICTIMS, WANTED TO ERADICATE HOMOSEXUALITY EVEN AS AN ABSTRACT CONCEPT, MADE POOR PEOPLE CHOOSE BETWEEN EATING AND KEEPING THEIR VOTE...

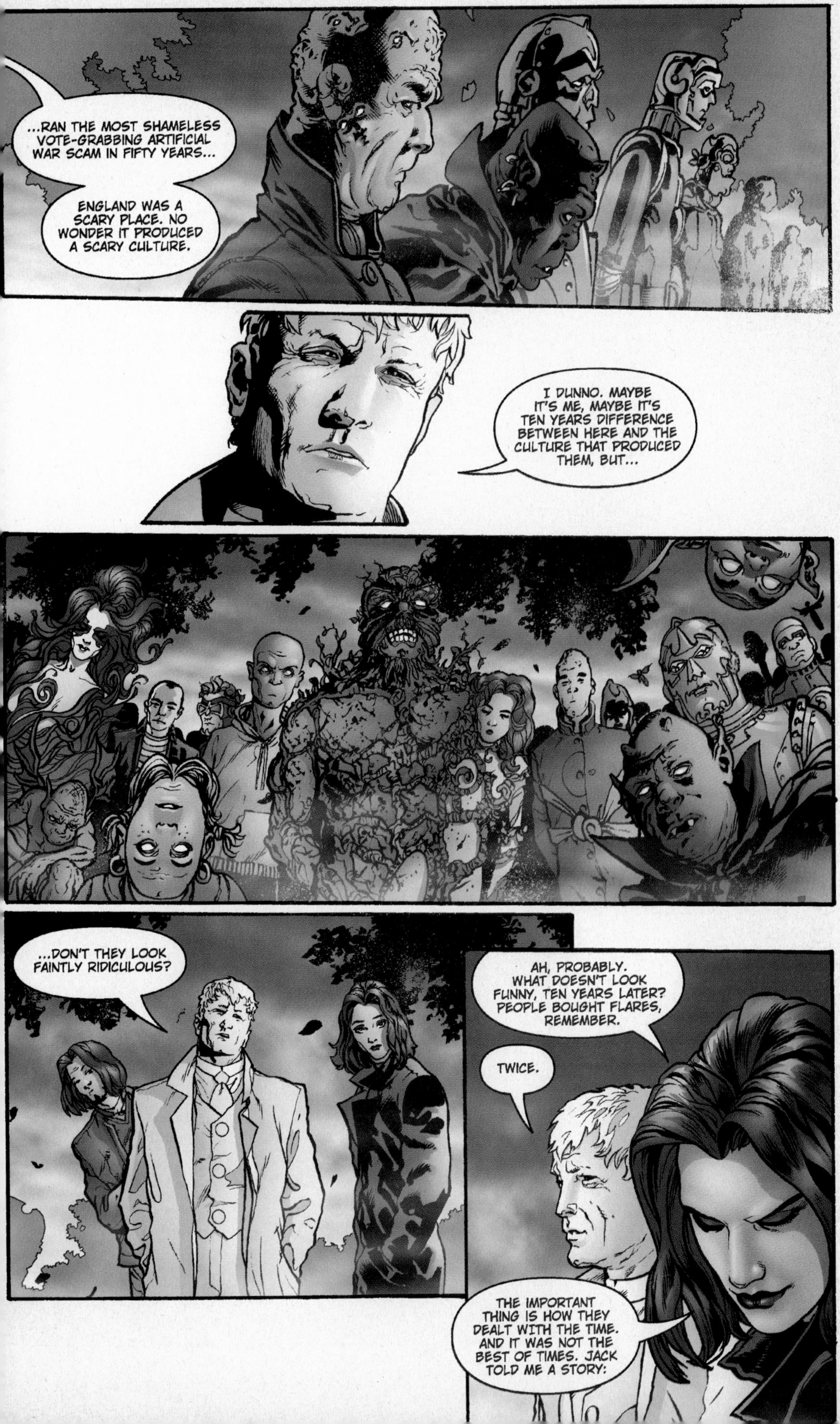
...RAN THE MOST SHAMELESS VOTE-GRABBING ARTIFICIAL WAR SCAM IN FIFTY YEARS...
ENGLAND WAS A SCARY PLACE. NO WONDER IT PRODUCED A SCARY CULTURE.
I DUNNO. MAYBE IT'S ME, MAYBE IT'S TEN YEARS DIFFERENCE BETWEEN HERE AND THE CULTURE THAT PRODUCED THEM, BUT...
...DON'T THEY LOOK FAINTLY RIDICULOUS?
AH, PROBABLY. WHAT DOESN'T LOOK FUNNY, TEN YEARS LATER? PEOPLE BOUGHT FLARES, REMEMBER.
TWICE.
THE IMPORTANT THING IS HOW THEY DEALT WITH THE TIME. AND IT WAS NOT THE BEST OF TIMES. JACK TOLD ME A STORY:

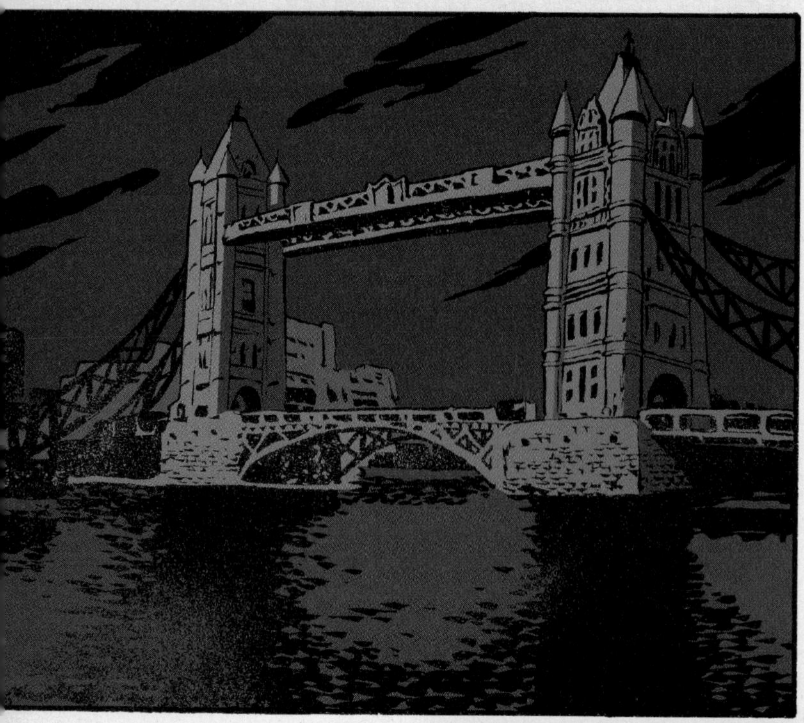

1987

SOME NIGHTS, IT NEVER SEEMS TO GET PROPERLY DARK IN LONDON. CLOUD COMES OVER AND BLANKETS THE TOWN, AND THE ORANGE GLOW OF THE STREETLIGHTS SUFFUSES IT, SO THAT LONDON LOOKS LIKE IT'S TRAPPED IN AMBER, AND US WITH IT. AND WE ALL LOOK UP AND NOD LIKE OUR MUMS AND DADS AND PARROT THE OLD "WELL, IT'D BE COLD WITHOUT THAT CLOUD COVER," AND DON'T FOR A MINUTE THINK ABOUT BEING SEALED IN LONDON WITH NO ESCAPE.

THE SKY WAS BLACK AND ORANGE WHEN I LEFT MAD LINDSAY'S GAFF ABOVE THE SHOE SHOP IN CARNABY STREET. I DIDN'T LOOK BACK. I KNEW SHE'D HAVE HER CHOPS PRESSED TO THE WINDOW, SCREAMING HER GUTS OUT AND PULLING WEIRD FACES. SEALED IN BRICK AND GLASS. THERE WAS A RIPPLING SOUND, LIKE WAVES BREAKING, JUST ABOUT AUDIBLE FROM HERE ABOVE THE TAXIS. IT WAS HER OWN STUPID FAULT. EVIL MOO. I DID ME ZIP UP INDISCREETLY IN FRONT OF A BLOKE OF THREE HUNDRED COLLECTING FOR THE SALVATION ARMY AND MADE HIM GIVE ME TWENTY QUID BEFORE ANGLING OFF CARNABY INTO BEAK STREET, WALKING UP INTO SOHO'S TANGLES.

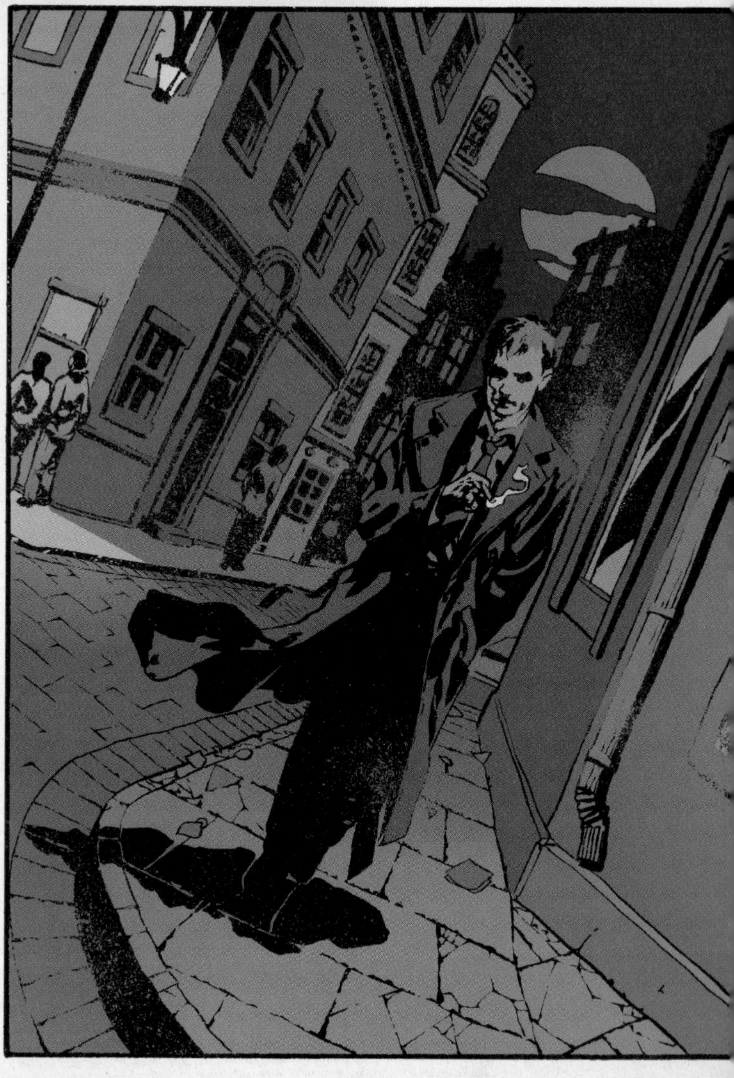

CHRISTMAS NEVER DOES BUGGER ALL TO SOHO. IT'S GREY AND DOOMED AND HOPELESS AND LIFE-SUCKING ALL YEAR ROUND. EVEN THE BEAUTIFUL GIRLS, NEW TO THE LIFE, EAGER OR CALCULATING, ADD TO THE MISERY BY IMPLICATION. YOU KNOW HOW THEIR STORIES WILL END.

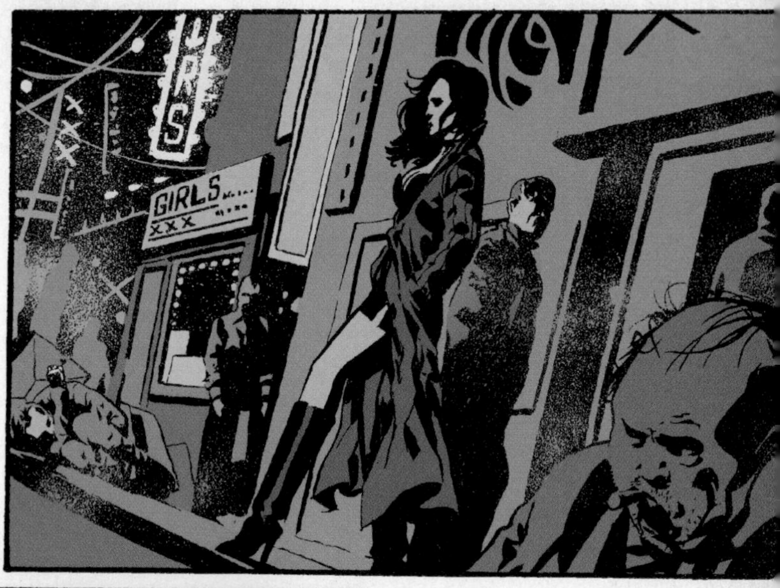
GIRLS
XXX

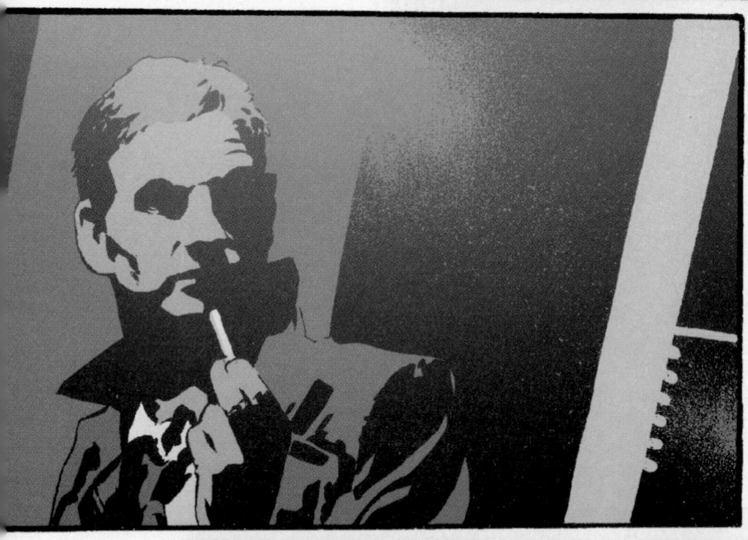

I WAS JUST FANCYING A PINT AT THE COACH AND HORSES WHEN I SAW A MAN WHO WASN'T THERE.

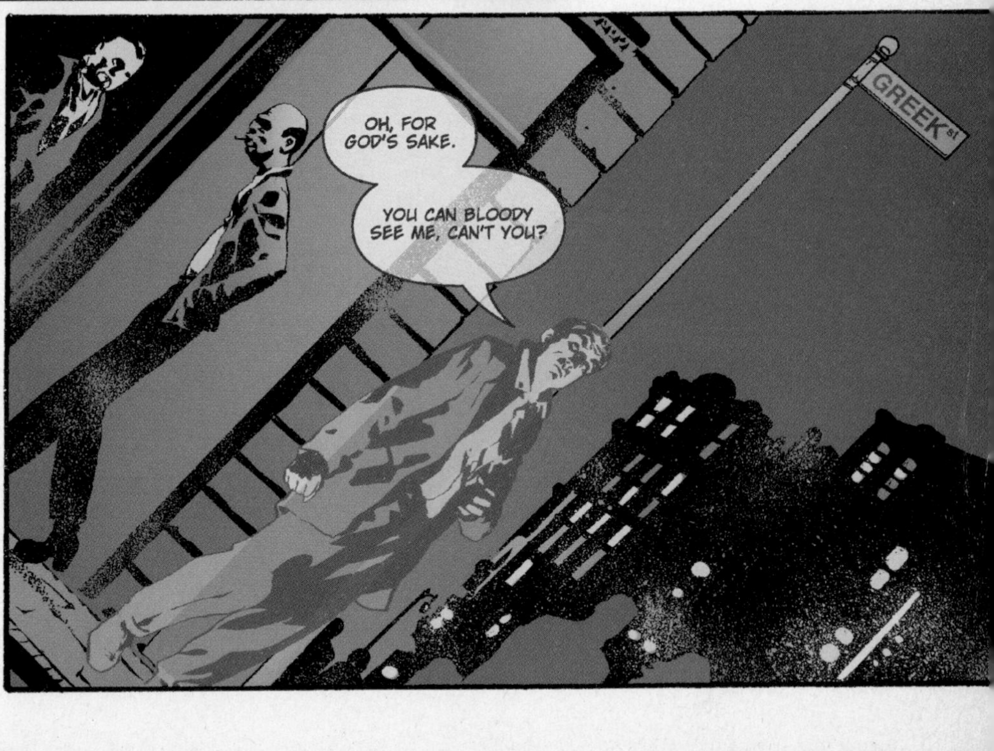
GREEK St
OH, FOR GOD'S SAKE.
YOU CAN BLOODY SEE ME, CAN'T YOU?

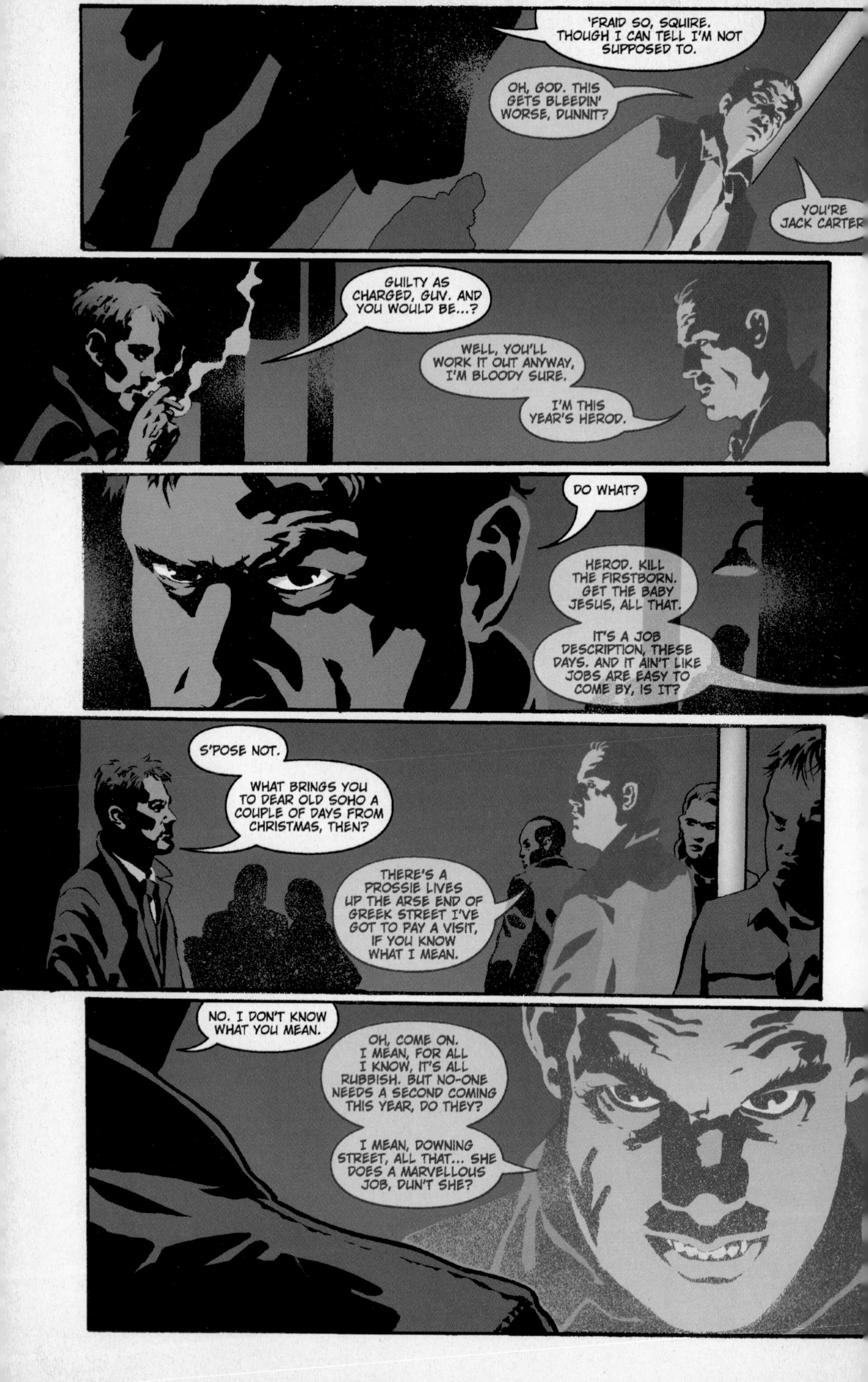
'FRAID SO, SQUIRE. THOUGH I CAN TELL I'M NOT SUPPOSED TO.
OH, GOD. THIS GETS BLEEDIN' WORSE, DUNNIT?
YOU'RE JACK CARTER
GUILTY AS CHARGED, GUV. AND YOU WOULD BE...?
WELL, YOU'LL WORK IT OUT ANYWAY, I'M BLOODY SURE.
I'M THIS YEAR'S HEROD.
DO WHAT?
HEROD. KILL THE FIRSTBORN. GET THE BABY JESUS, ALL THAT.
IT'S A JOB DESCRIPTION, THESE DAYS. AND IT AIN'T LIKE JOBS ARE EASY TO COME BY, IS IT?
S'POSE NOT.
WHAT BRINGS YOU TO DEAR OLD SOHO A COUPLE OF DAYS FROM CHRISTMAS, THEN?
THERE'S A PROSSIE LIVES UP THE ARSE END OF GREEK STREET I'VE GOT TO PAY A VISIT, IF YOU KNOW WHAT I MEAN.
NO. I DON'T KNOW WHAT YOU MEAN.
OH, COME ON. I MEAN, FOR ALL I KNOW, IT'S ALL RUBBISH. BUT NO-ONE NEEDS A SECOND COMING THIS YEAR, DO THEY?
I MEAN, DOWNING STREET, ALL THAT... SHE DOES A MARVELLOUS JOB, DUN'T SHE?

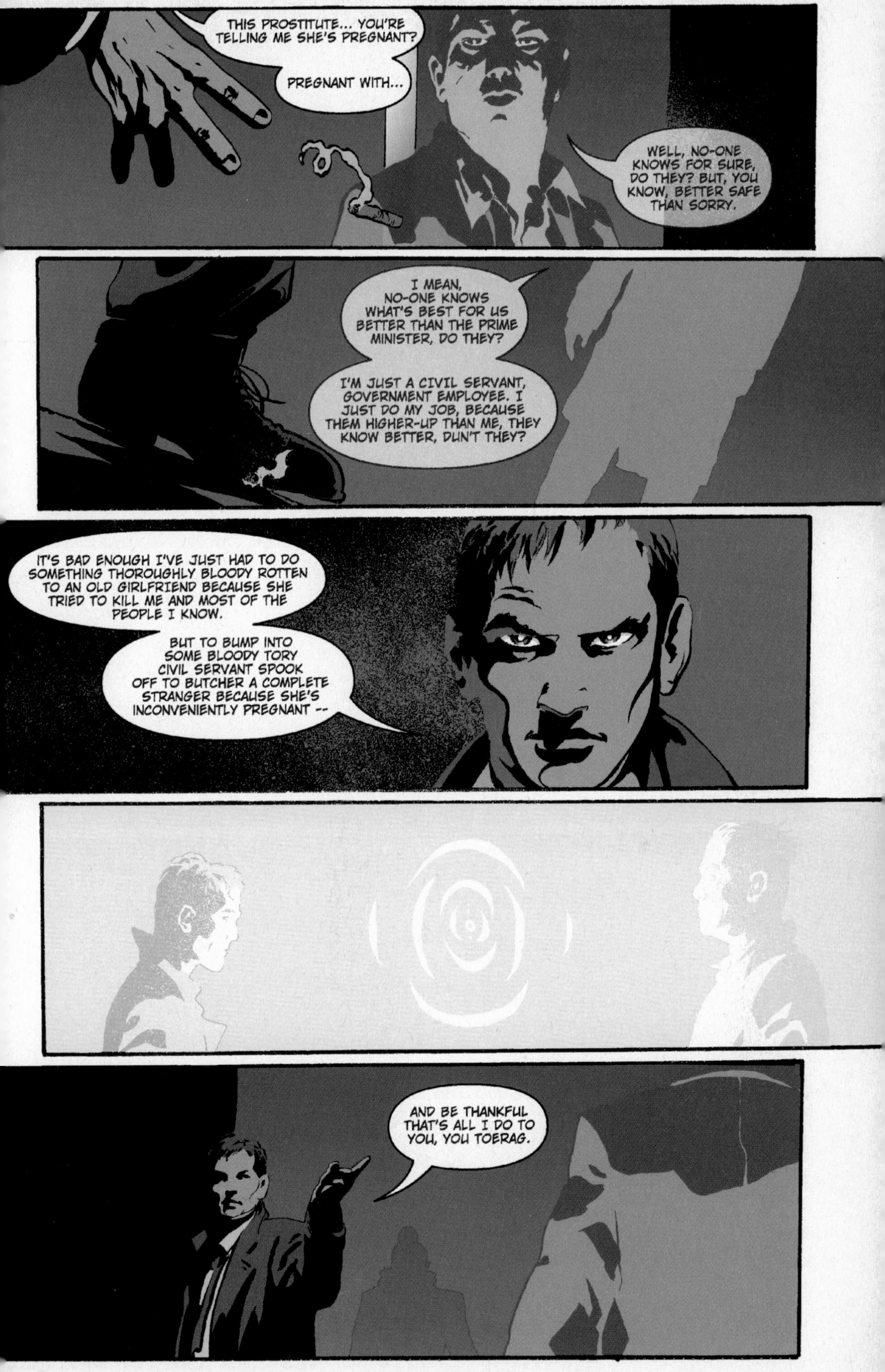
THIS PROSTITUTE... YOU'RE TELLING ME SHE'S PREGNANT?
PREGNANT WITH...
WELL, NO-ONE KNOWS FOR SURE, DO THEY? BUT, YOU KNOW, BETTER SAFE THAN SORRY.
I MEAN, NO-ONE KNOWS WHAT'S BEST FOR US BETTER THAN THE PRIME MINISTER, DO THEY?
I'M JUST A CIVIL SERVANT, GOVERNMENT EMPLOYEE. I JUST DO MY JOB, BECAUSE THEM HIGHER-UP THAN ME, THEY KNOW BETTER, DUN'T THEY?
IT'S BAD ENOUGH I'VE JUST HAD TO DO SOMETHING THOROUGHLY BLOODY ROTTEN TO AN OLD GIRLFRIEND BECAUSE SHE TRIED TO KILL ME AND MOST OF THE PEOPLE I KNOW.
BUT TO BUMP INTO SOME BLOODY TORY CIVIL SERVANT SPOOK OFF TO BUTCHER A COMPLETE STRANGER BECAUSE SHE'S INCONVENIENTLY PREGNANT --
AND BE THANKFUL THAT'S ALL I DO TO YOU, YOU TOERAG.

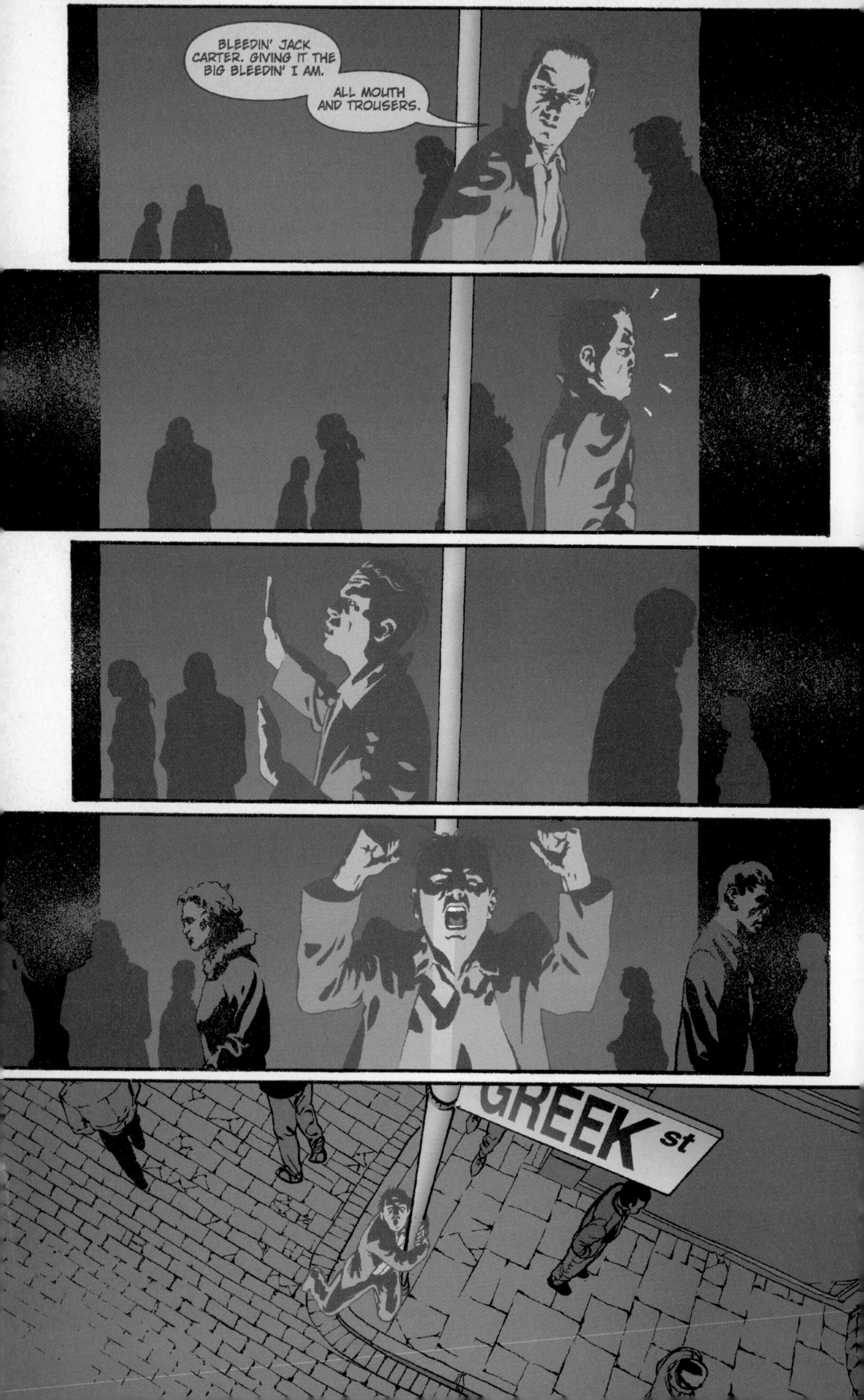

BLEEDIN' JACK CARTER. GIVING IT THE BIG BLEEDIN' I AM.
ALL MOUTH AND TROUSERS.
GREEK st

MEMORIAL SERVICE WITHOUT A BODY. TERRIBLE THING.

IT WAS ONLY A DAMN CREMATION, SNOW.

WHERE ARE WE GOING?

I WANT TO SEE WHERE JACK DIED.

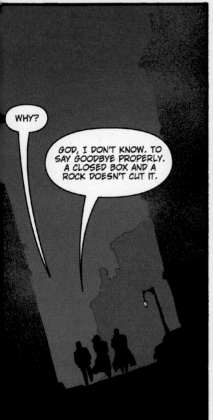

WHY?

GOD, I DON'T KNOW. TO SAY GOODBYE PROPERLY. A CLOSED BOX AND A ROCK DOESN'T CUT IT.

SEE?

CRAP. JAKITA, HE WAS A CON MAN WHO PULLED A SCAM ONCE TOO OFTEN.

NO-ONE LIKED HIM AND EVENTUALLY HE PISSED OFF SOMEONE WHO WASN'T AFRAID OF THE SPOOKY BAD MAGICIAN REP.

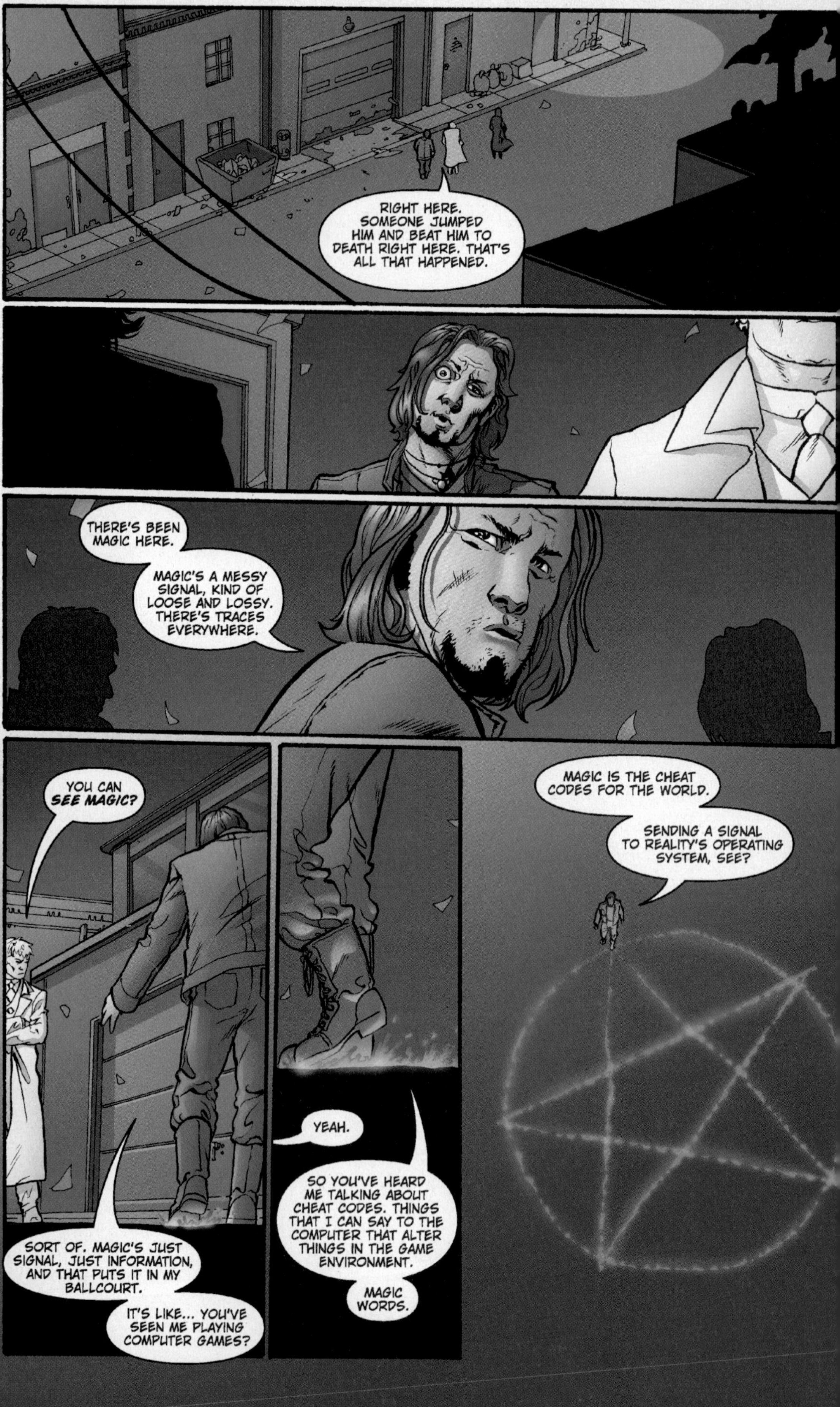
RIGHT HERE. SOMEONE JUMPED HIM AND BEAT HIM TO DEATH RIGHT HERE. THAT'S ALL THAT HAPPENED.
THERE'S BEEN MAGIC HERE.
MAGIC'S A MESSY SIGNAL, KIND OF LOOSE AND LOSSY. THERE'S TRACES EVERYWHERE.
YOU CAN *SEE MAGIC?*
SORT OF. MAGIC'S JUST SIGNAL, JUST INFORMATION, AND THAT PUTS IT IN MY BALLCOURT.
IT'S LIKE... YOU'VE SEEN ME PLAYING COMPUTER GAMES?
YEAH.
SO YOU'VE HEARD ME TALKING ABOUT CHEAT CODES. THINGS THAT I CAN SAY TO THE COMPUTER THAT ALTER THINGS IN THE GAME ENVIRONMENT.
MAGIC WORDS.
MAGIC IS THE CHEAT CODES FOR THE WORLD.
SENDING A SIGNAL TO REALITY'S OPERATING SYSTEM, SEE?

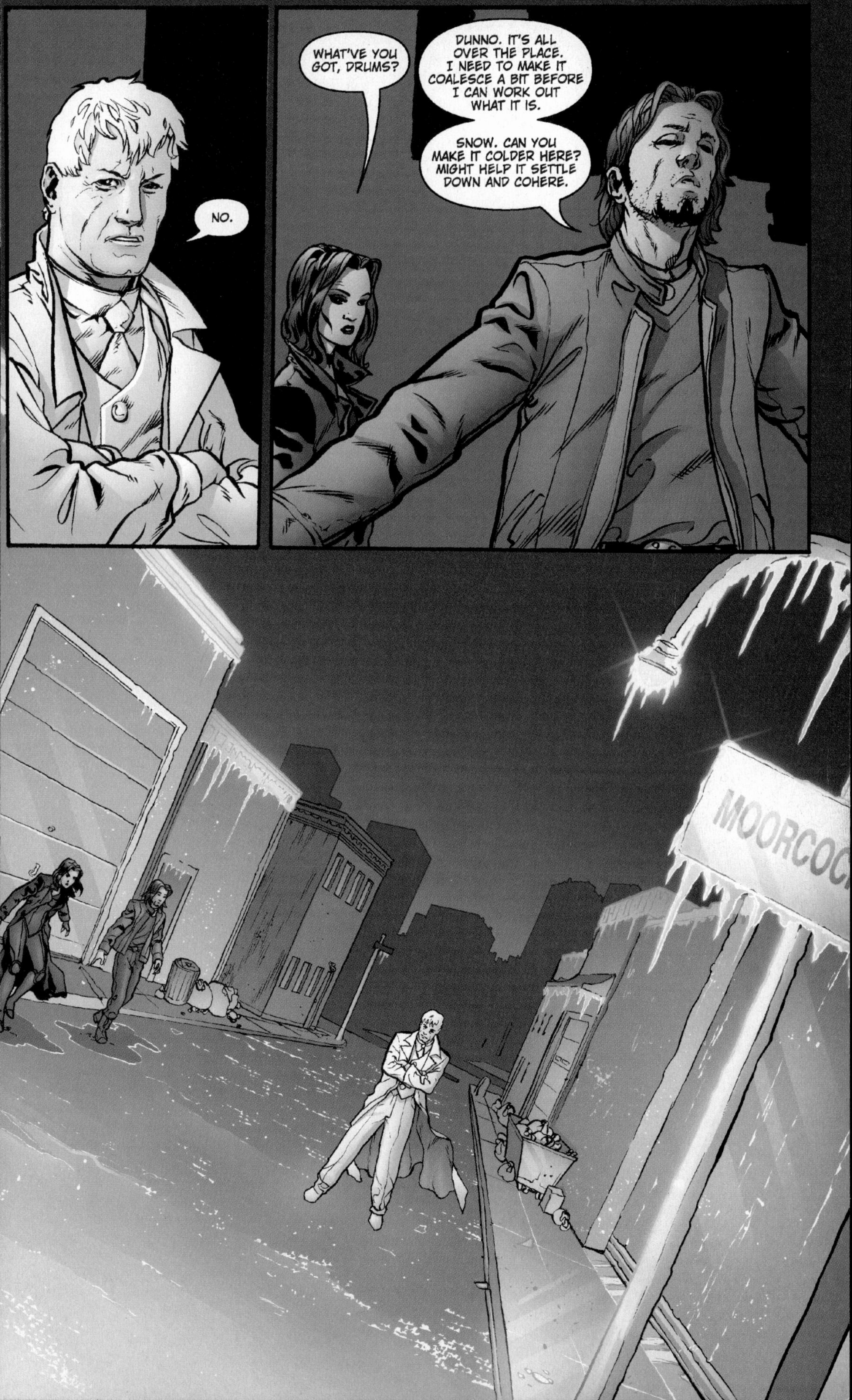
NO.
WHAT'VE YOU GOT, DRUMS?
DUNNO. IT'S ALL OVER THE PLACE. I NEED TO MAKE IT COALESCE A BIT BEFORE I CAN WORK OUT WHAT IT IS.
SNOW. CAN YOU MAKE IT COLDER HERE? MIGHT HELP IT SETTLE DOWN AND COHERE.
MOORCOC

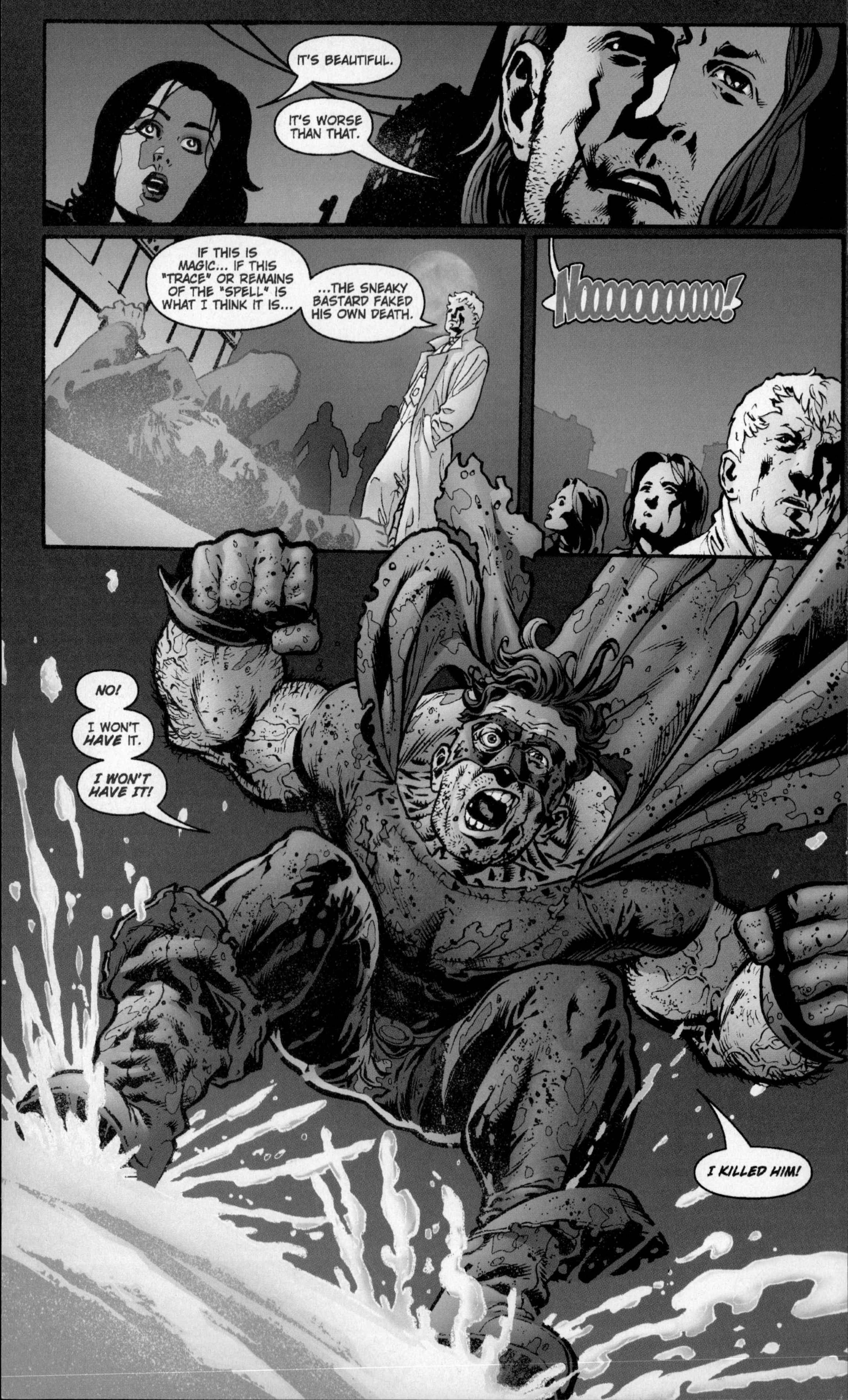

IT'S BEAUTIFUL.
IT'S WORSE THAN THAT.
IF THIS IS MAGIC... IF THIS "TRACE" OR REMAINS OF THE "SPELL" IS WHAT I THINK IT IS...
...THE SNEAKY BASTARD FAKED HIS OWN DEATH.
NOOOOOOOOOOO!
NO!
I WON'T HAVE IT.
I WON'T HAVE IT!
I KILLED HIM!

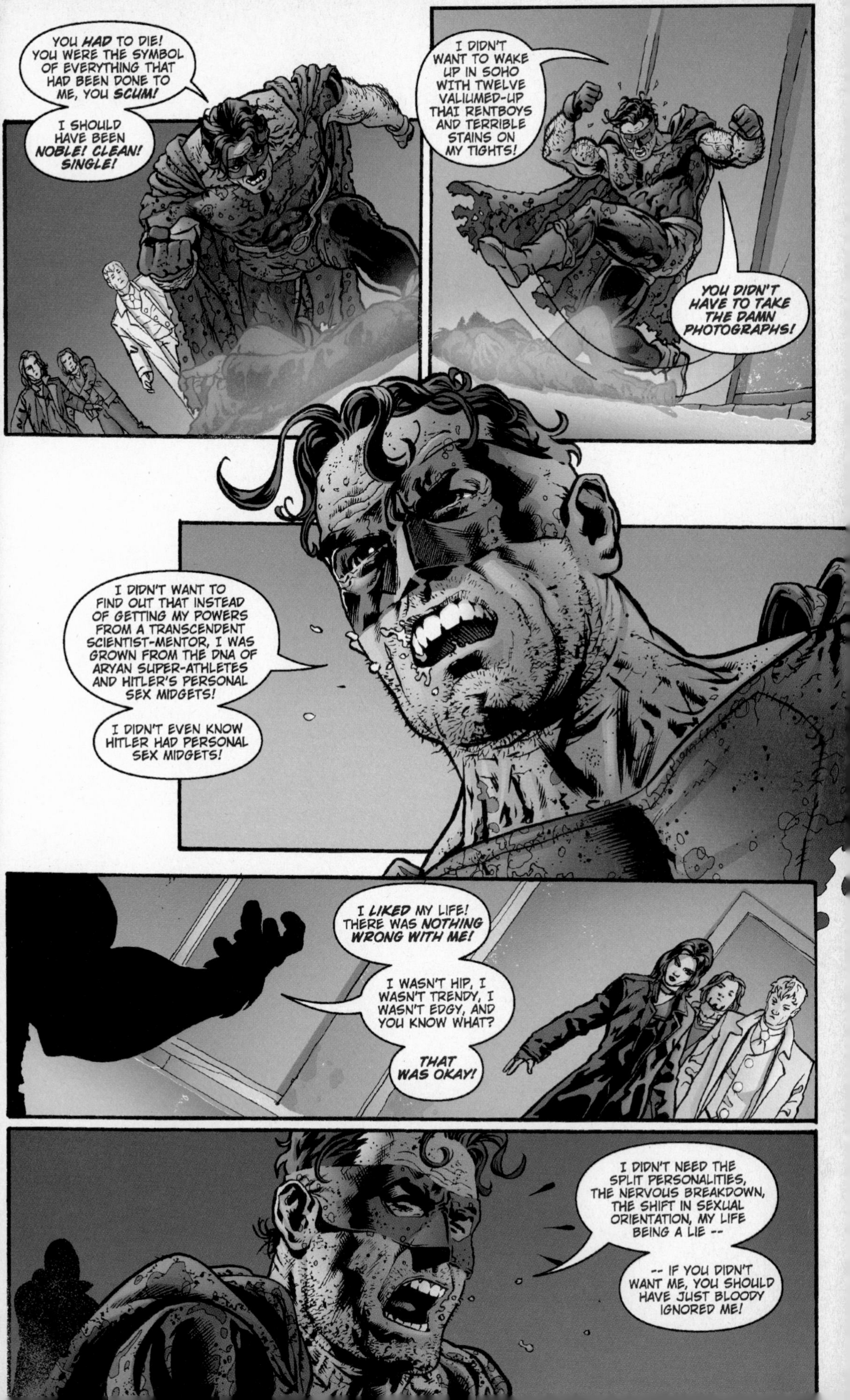

YOU HAD TO DIE! YOU WERE THE SYMBOL OF EVERYTHING THAT HAD BEEN DONE TO ME, YOU SCUM!
I SHOULD HAVE BEEN NOBLE! CLEAN! SINGLE!
I DIDN'T WANT TO WAKE UP IN SOHO WITH TWELVE VALIUMED-UP THAI RENTBOYS AND TERRIBLE STAINS ON MY TIGHTS!
YOU DIDN'T HAVE TO TAKE THE DAMN PHOTOGRAPHS!
I DIDN'T WANT TO FIND OUT THAT INSTEAD OF GETTING MY POWERS FROM A TRANSCENDENT SCIENTIST-MENTOR, I WAS GROWN FROM THE DNA OF ARYAN SUPER-ATHLETES AND HITLER'S PERSONAL SEX MIDGETS!
I DIDN'T EVEN KNOW HITLER HAD PERSONAL SEX MIDGETS!
I LIKED MY LIFE! THERE WAS NOTHING WRONG WITH ME!
I WASN'T HIP, I WASN'T TRENDY, I WASN'T EDGY, AND YOU KNOW WHAT?
THAT WAS OKAY!
I DIDN'T NEED THE SPLIT PERSONALITIES, THE NERVOUS BREAKDOWN, THE SHIFT IN SEXUAL ORIENTATION, MY LIFE BEING A LIE --
-- IF YOU DIDN'T WANT ME, YOU SHOULD HAVE JUST BLOODY IGNORED ME!

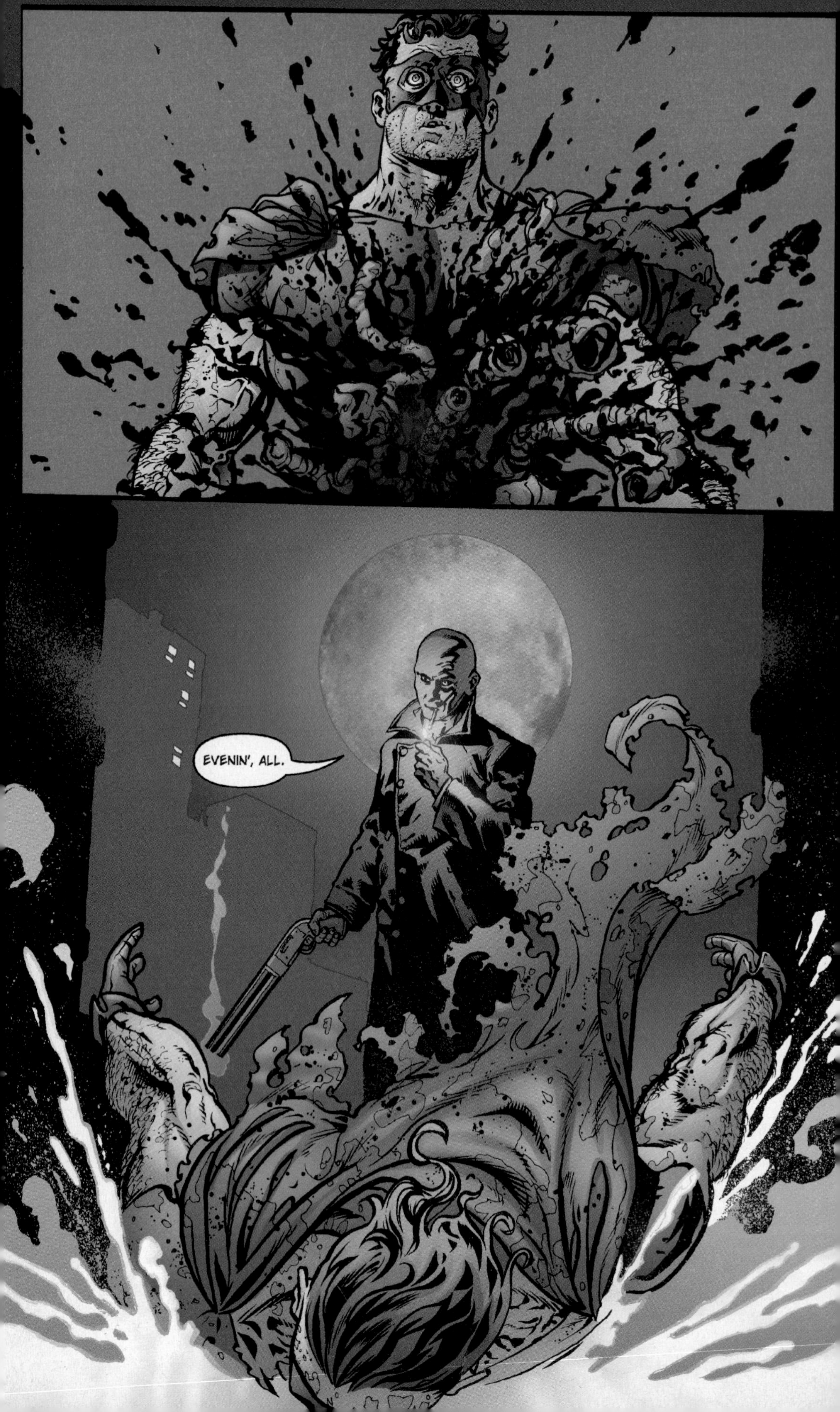
EVENIN', ALL.

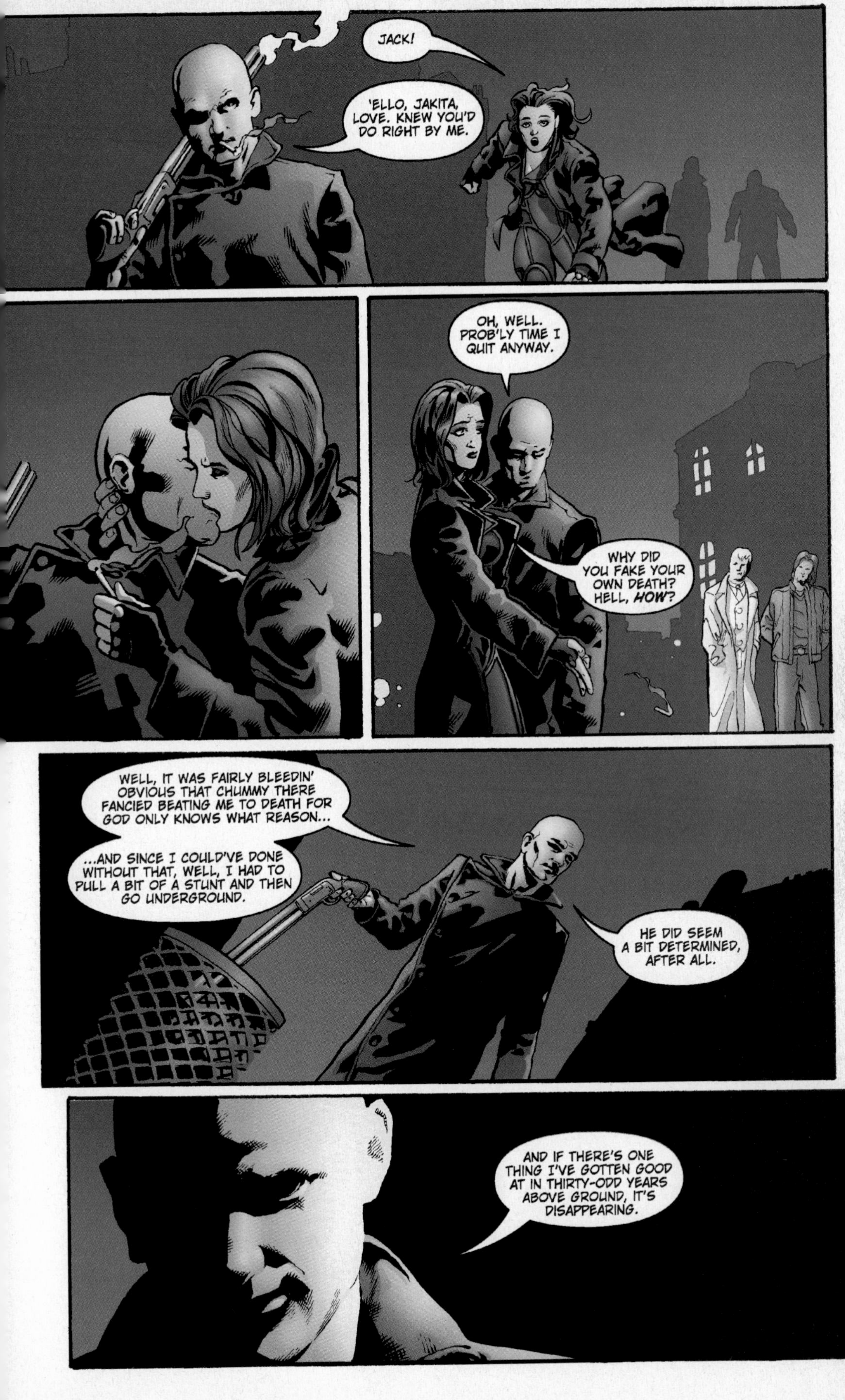
JACK!
'ELLO, JAKITA, LOVE. KNEW YOU'D DO RIGHT BY ME.
OH, WELL. PROB'LY TIME I QUIT ANYWAY.
WHY DID YOU FAKE YOUR OWN DEATH? HELL, *HOW*?
WELL, IT WAS FAIRLY BLEEDIN' OBVIOUS THAT CHUMMY THERE FANCIED BEATING ME TO DEATH FOR GOD ONLY KNOWS WHAT REASON...
...AND SINCE I COULD'VE DONE WITHOUT THAT, WELL, I HAD TO PULL A BIT OF A STUNT AND THEN GO UNDERGROUND.
HE DID SEEM A BIT DETERMINED, AFTER ALL.
AND IF THERE'S ONE THING I'VE GOTTEN GOOD AT IN THIRTY-ODD YEARS ABOVE GROUND, IT'S DISAPPEARING.

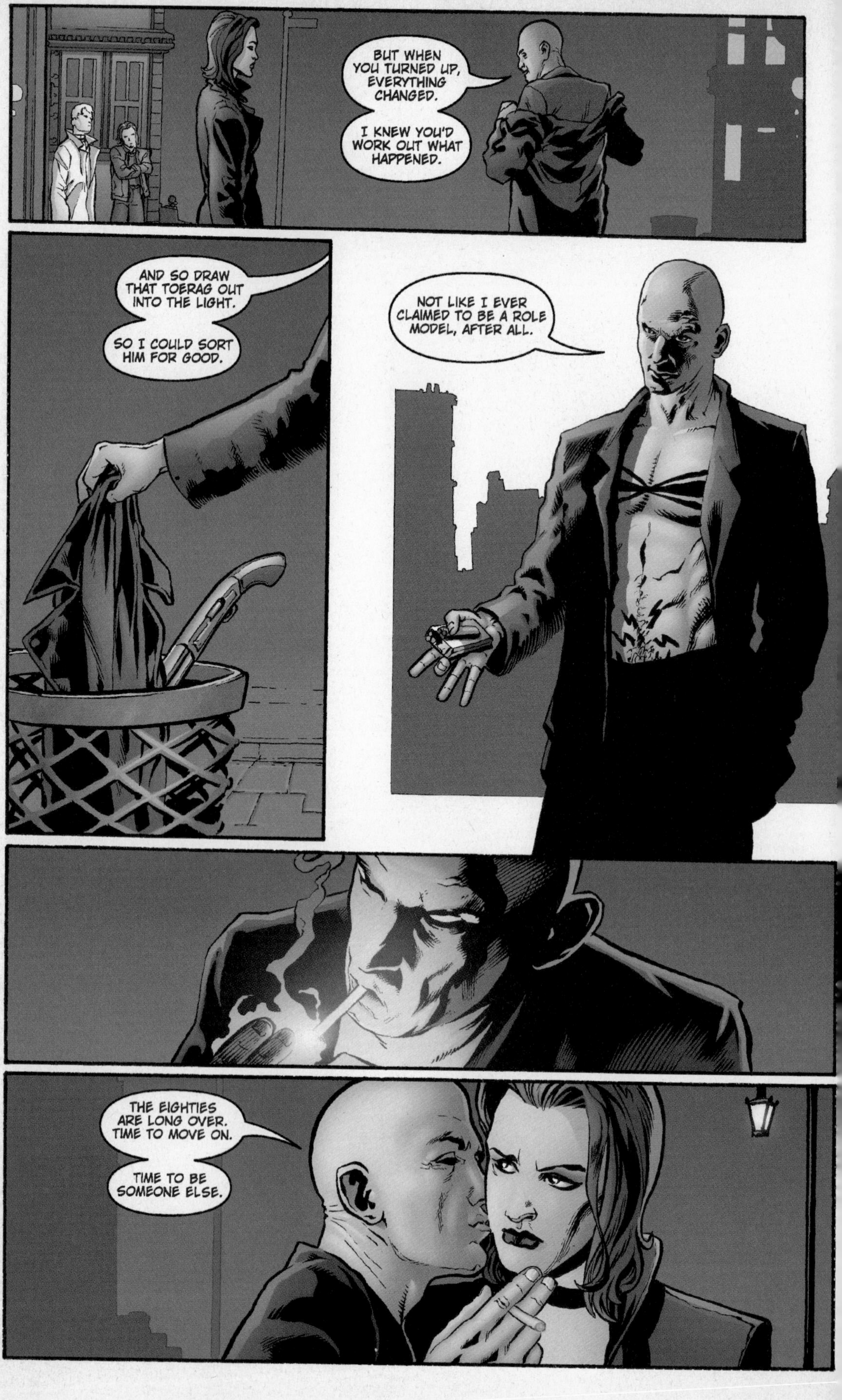
BUT WHEN YOU TURNED UP, EVERYTHING CHANGED.
I KNEW YOU'D WORK OUT WHAT HAPPENED.
AND SO DRAW THAT TOERAG OUT INTO THE LIGHT.
SO I COULD SORT HIM FOR GOOD.
NOT LIKE I EVER CLAIMED TO BE A ROLE MODEL, AFTER ALL.
THE EIGHTIES ARE LONG OVER. TIME TO MOVE ON.
TIME TO BE SOMEONE ELSE.

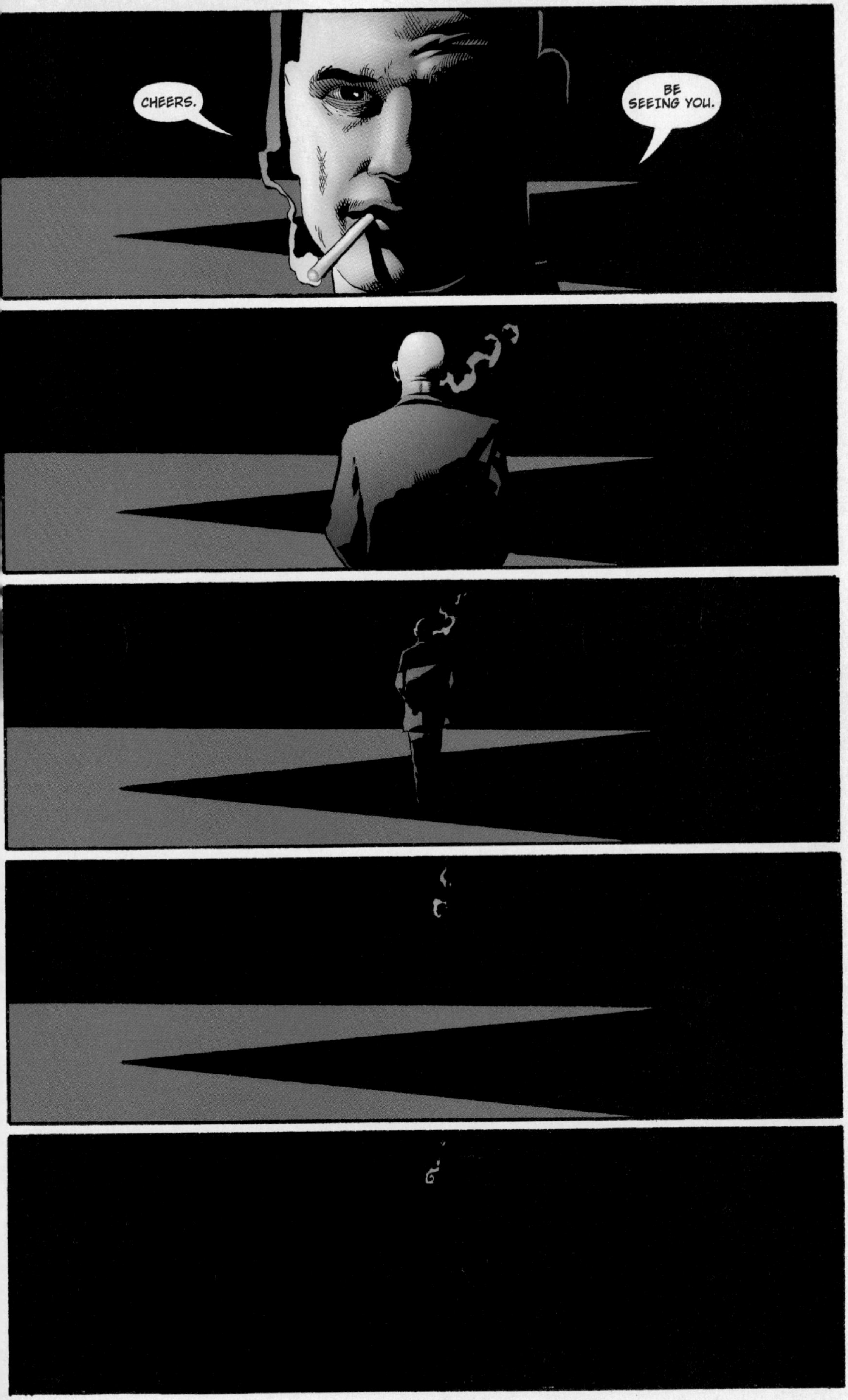
CHEERS.
BE SEEING YOU.

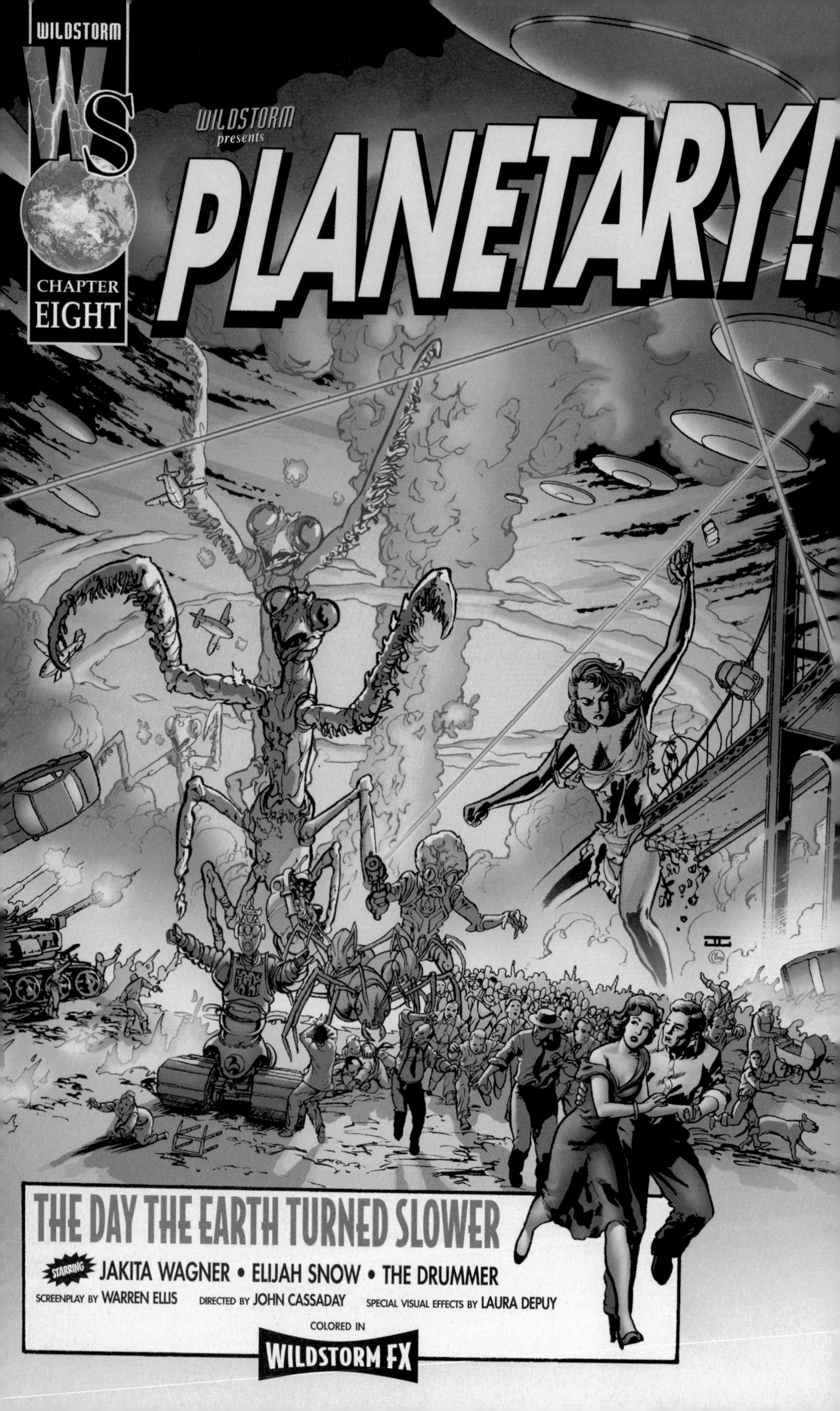
WILDSTORM
WS
CHAPTER
EIGHT
WILDSTORM presents
PLANETARY!
THE DAY THE EARTH TURNED SLOWER
STARRING JAKITA WAGNER • ELIJAH SNOW • THE DRUMMER
SCREENPLAY BY WARREN ELLIS DIRECTED BY JOHN CASSADAY SPECIAL VISUAL EFFECTS BY LAURA DEPUY
COLORED IN
WILDSTORM FX

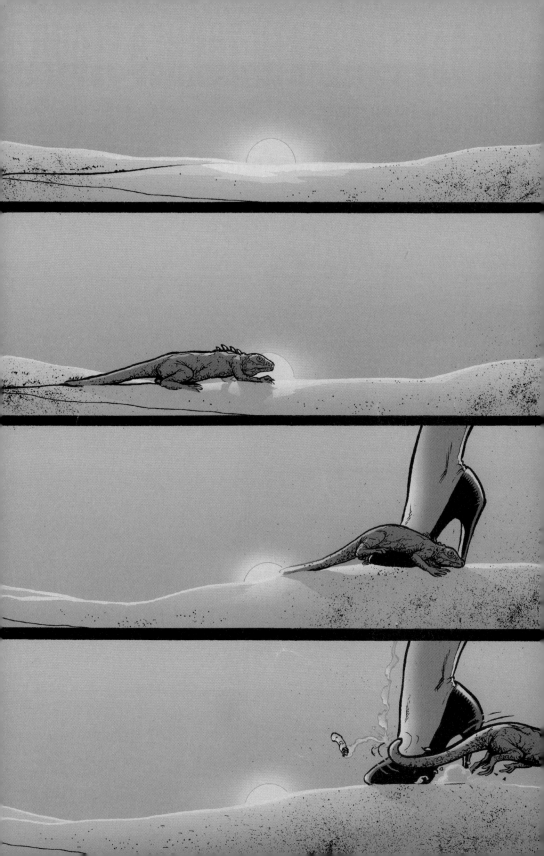

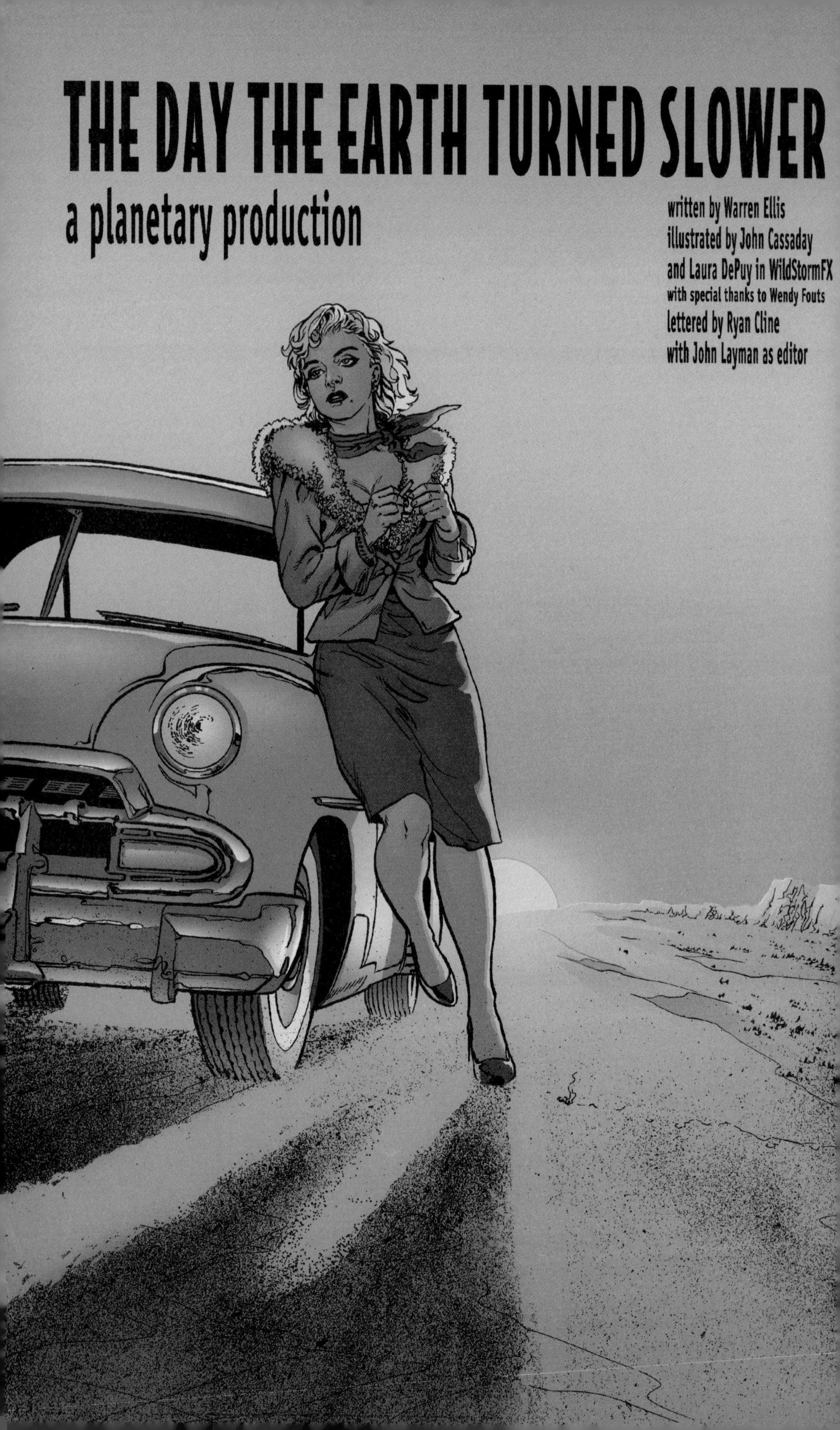
THE DAY THE EARTH TURNED SLOWER
a planetary production
written by Warren Ellis
illustrated by John Cassaday
and Laura DePuy in WildStormFX
with special thanks to Wendy Fouts
lettered by Ryan Cline
with John Layman as editor

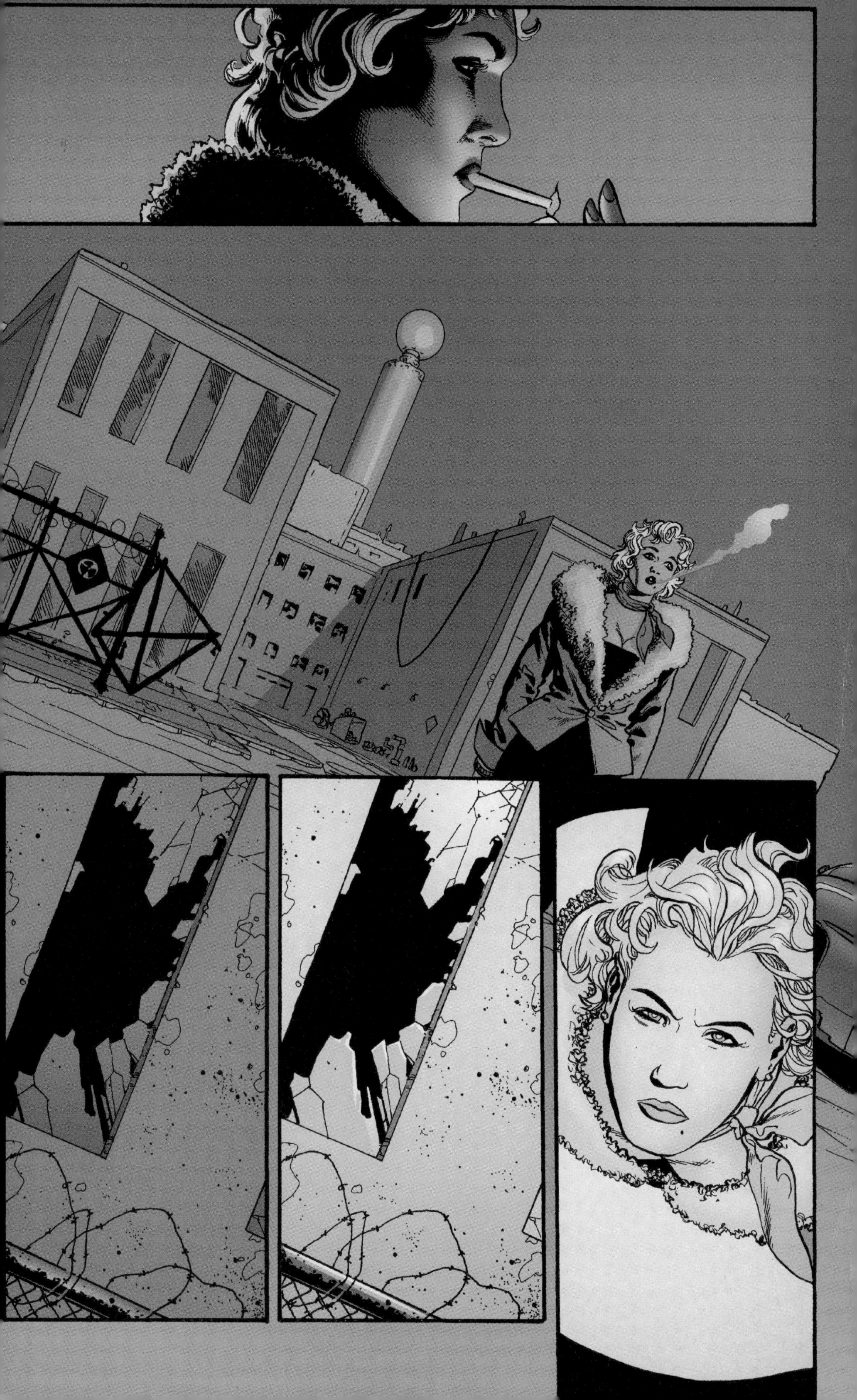

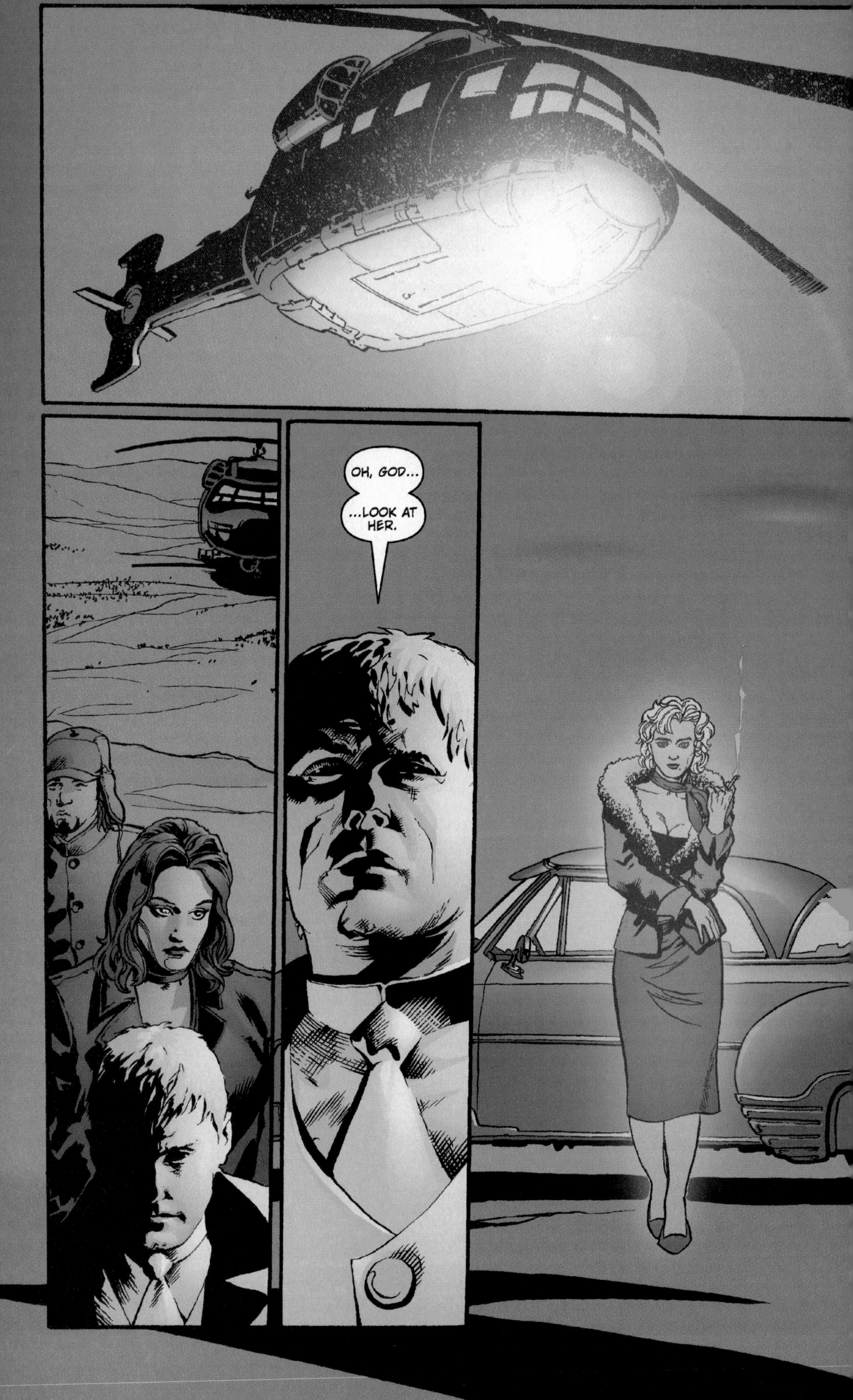
OH, GOD...
...LOOK AT HER.

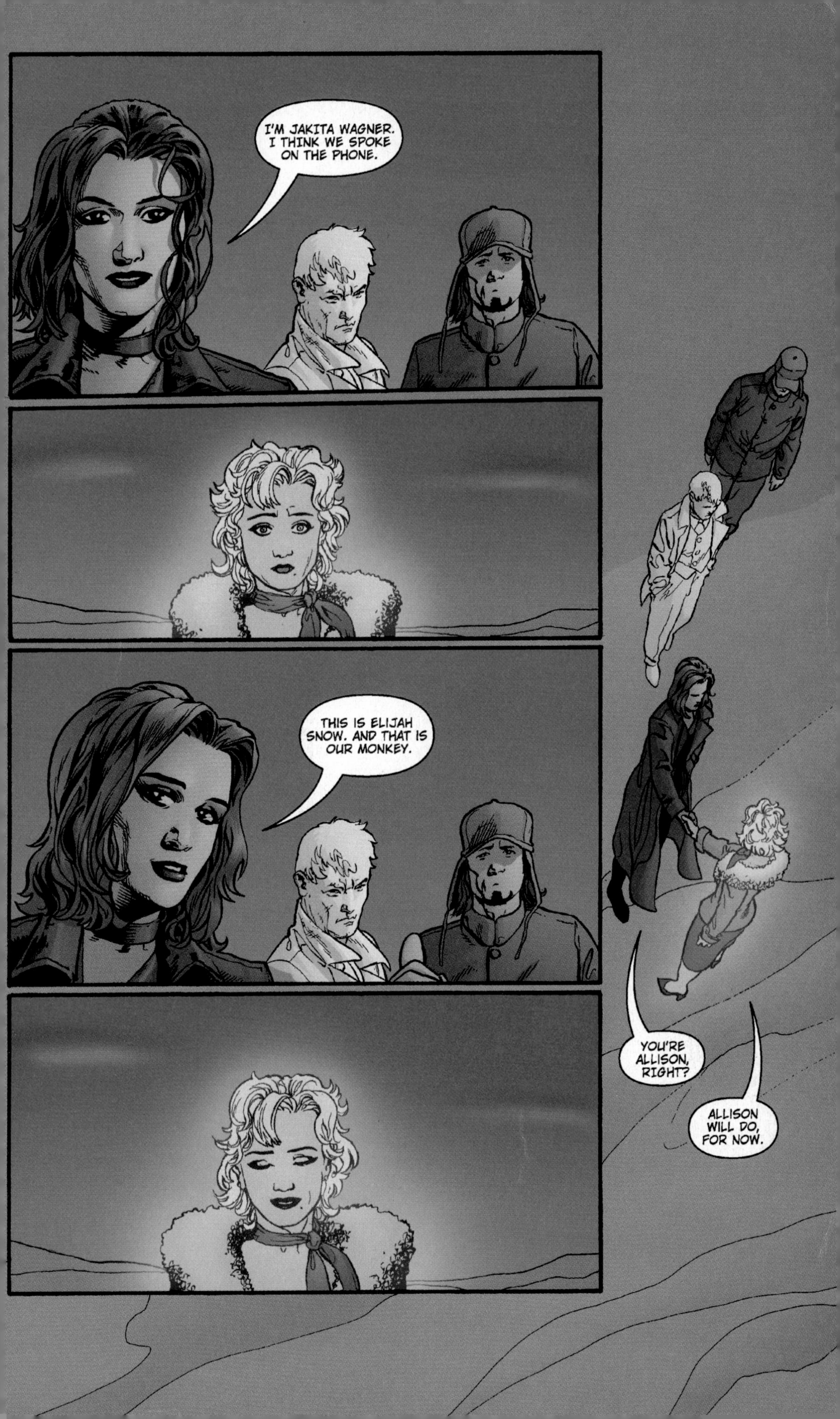
I'M JAKITA WAGNER. I THINK WE SPOKE ON THE PHONE.
THIS IS ELIJAH SNOW. AND THAT IS OUR MONKEY.
YOU'RE ALLISON, RIGHT?
ALLISON WILL DO, FOR NOW.

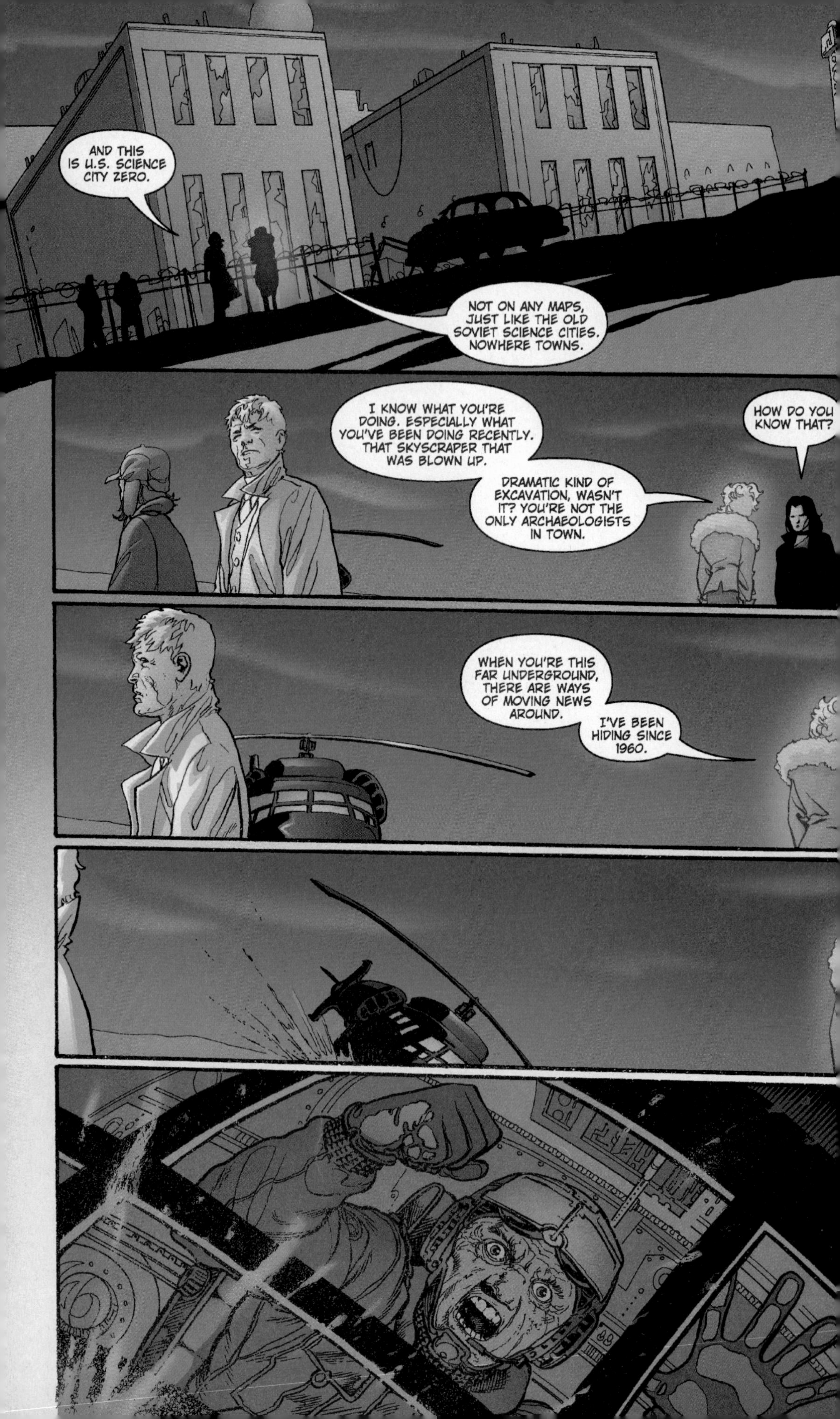
AND THIS IS U.S. SCIENCE CITY ZERO.
NOT ON ANY MAPS, JUST LIKE THE OLD SOVIET SCIENCE CITIES. NOWHERE TOWNS.
I KNOW WHAT YOU'RE DOING. ESPECIALLY WHAT YOU'VE BEEN DOING RECENTLY. THAT SKYSCRAPER THAT WAS BLOWN UP.
DRAMATIC KIND OF EXCAVATION, WASN'T IT? YOU'RE NOT THE ONLY ARCHAEOLOGISTS IN TOWN.
HOW DO YOU KNOW THAT?
WHEN YOU'RE THIS FAR UNDERGROUND, THERE ARE WAYS OF MOVING NEWS AROUND.
I'VE BEEN HIDING SINCE 1960.

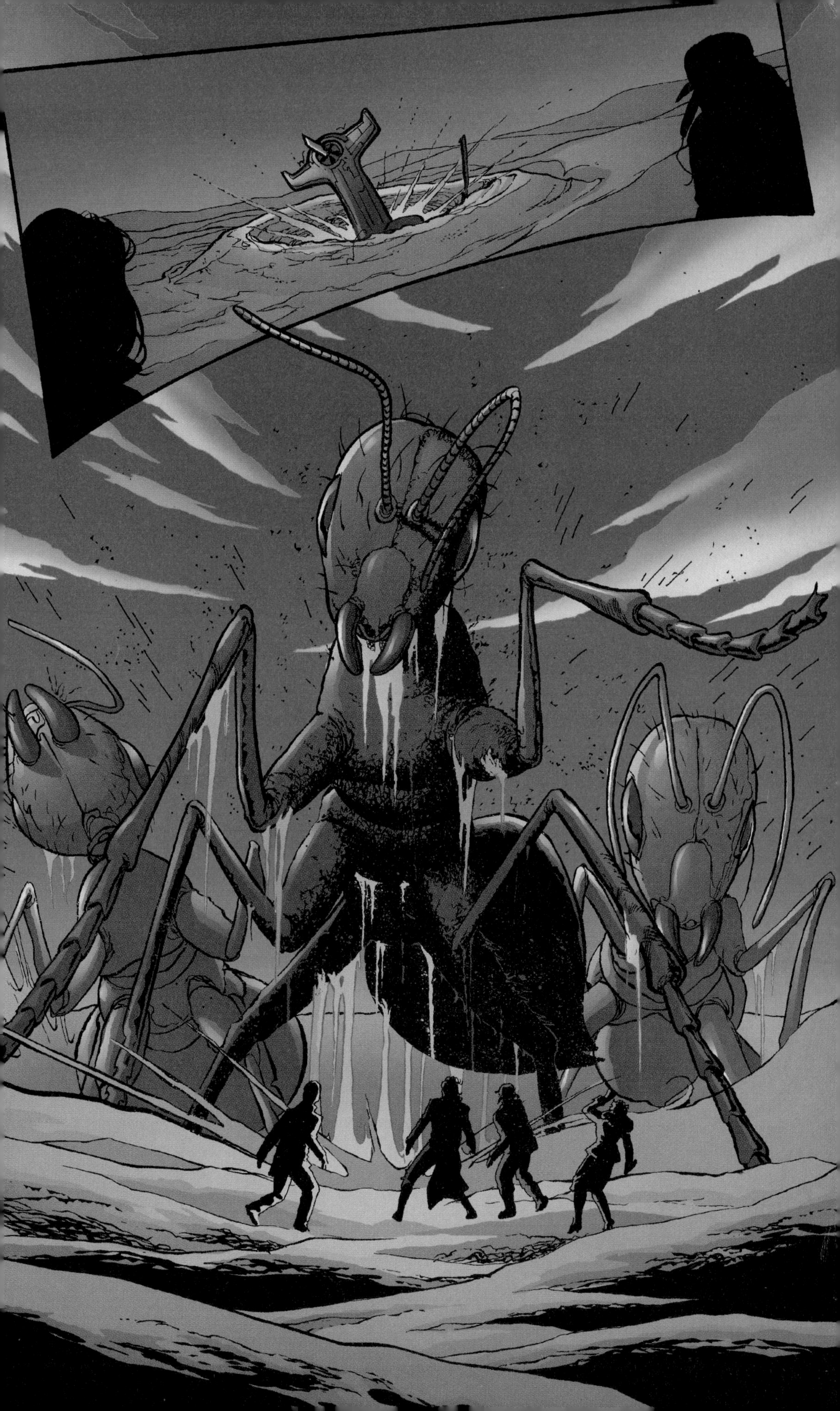

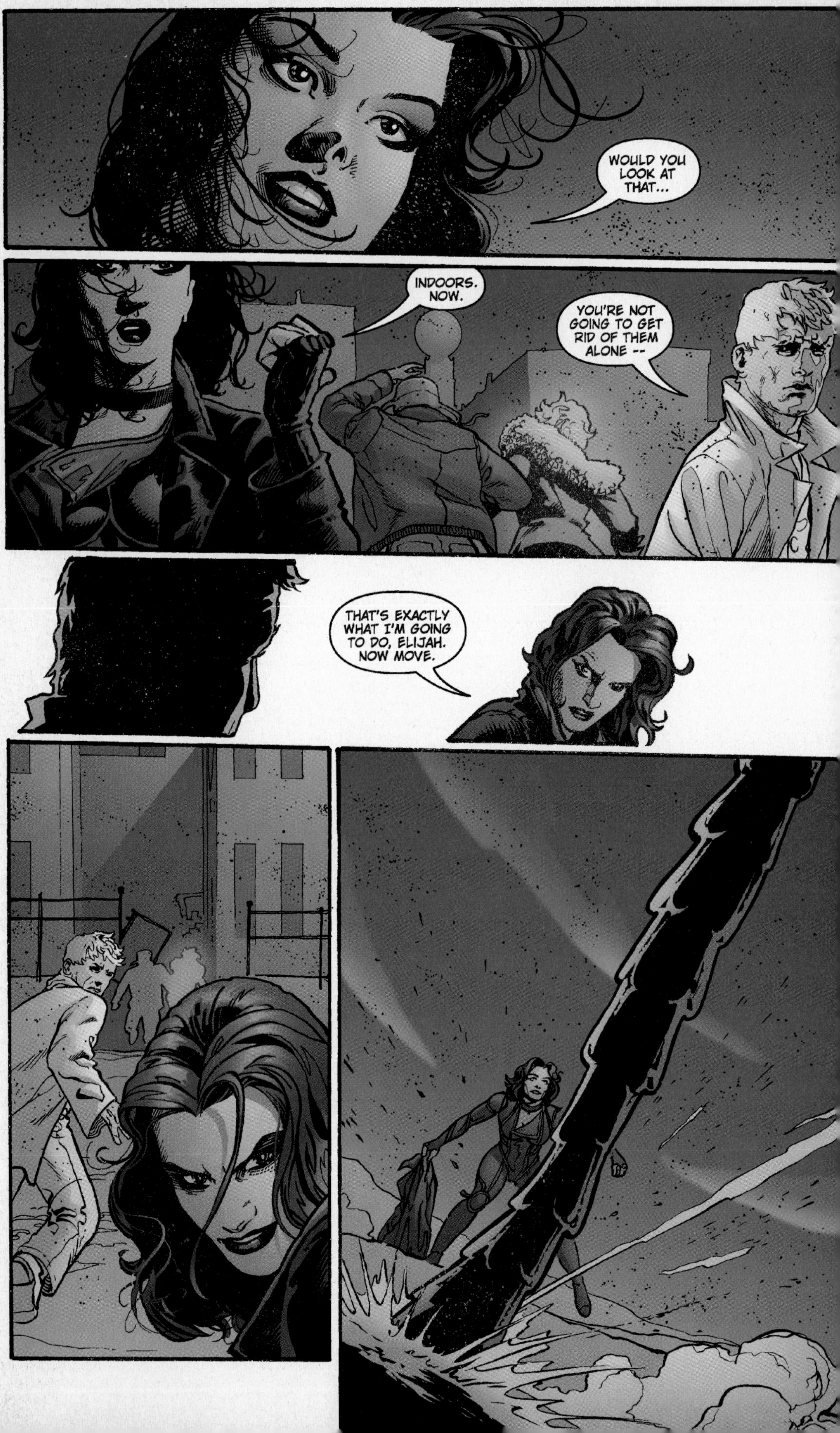
WOULD YOU LOOK AT THAT...
INDOORS. NOW.
YOU'RE NOT GOING TO GET RID OF THEM ALONE --
THAT'S EXACTLY WHAT I'M GOING TO DO, ELIJAH. NOW MOVE.

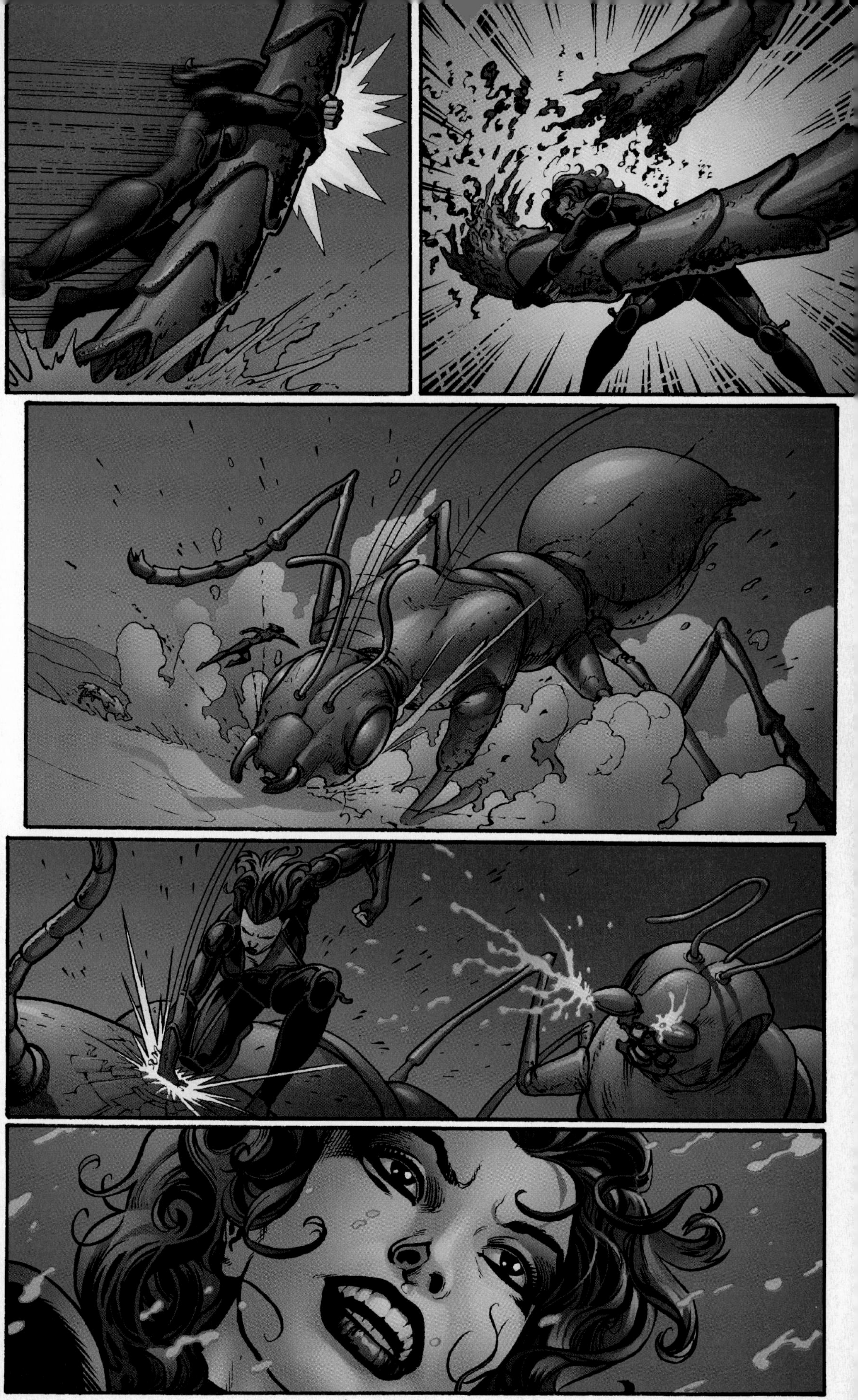

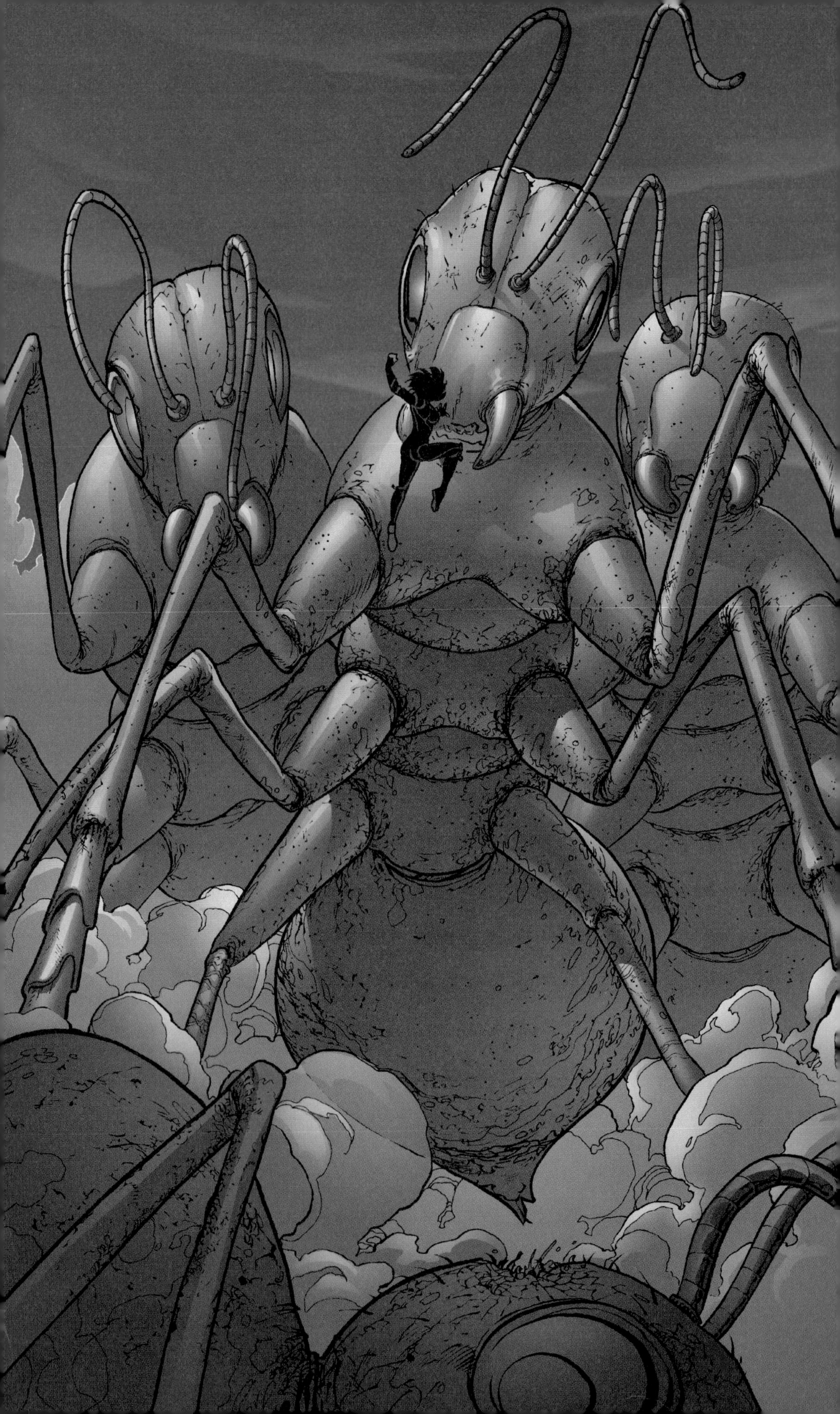

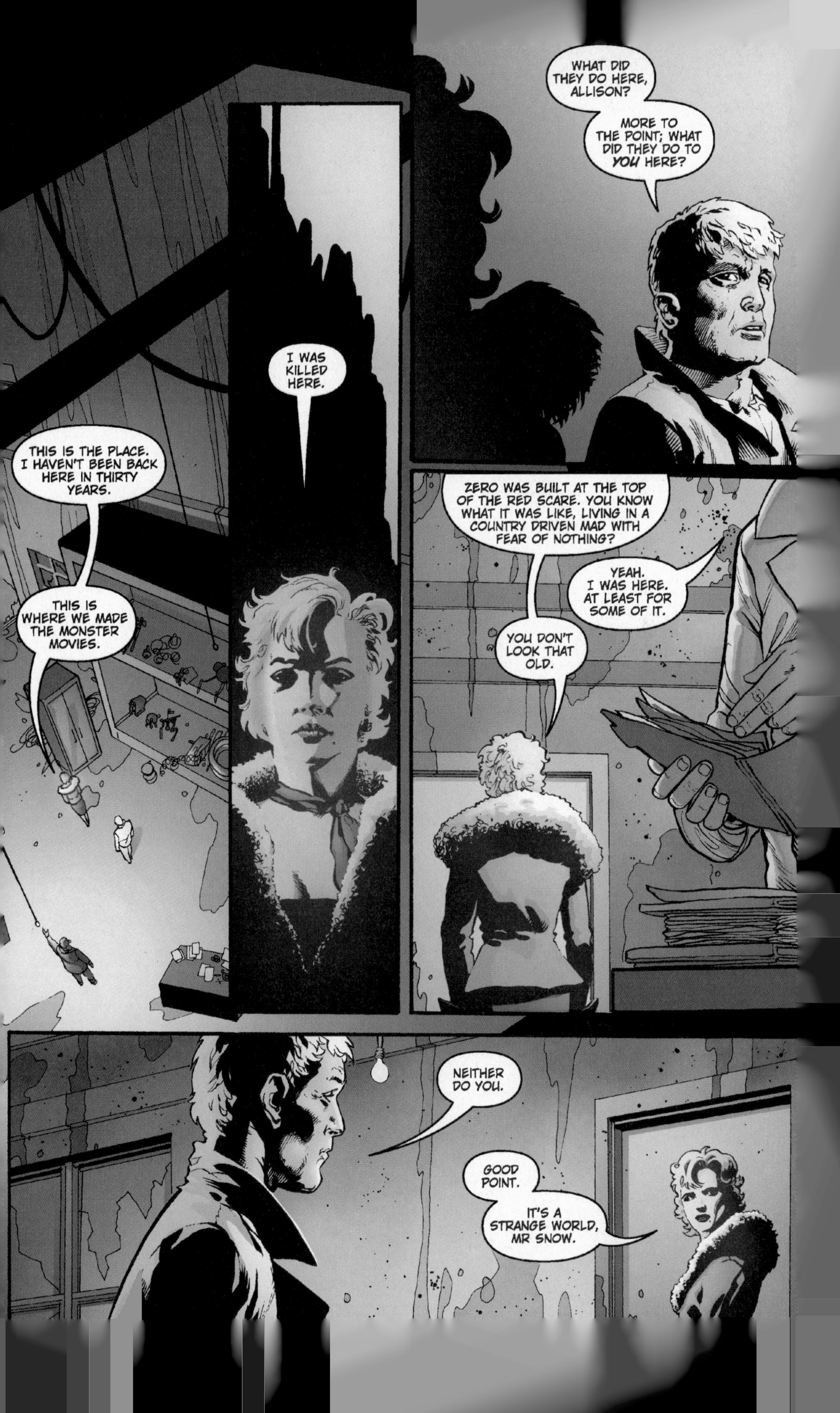

THIS IS THE PLACE. I HAVEN'T BEEN BACK HERE IN THIRTY YEARS.
THIS IS WHERE WE MADE THE MONSTER MOVIES.
I WAS KILLED HERE.
WHAT DID THEY DO HERE, ALLISON?
MORE TO THE POINT; WHAT DID THEY DO TO *YOU* HERE?
ZERO WAS BUILT AT THE TOP OF THE RED SCARE. YOU KNOW WHAT IT WAS LIKE, LIVING IN A COUNTRY DRIVEN MAD WITH FEAR OF NOTHING?
YEAH. I WAS HERE. AT LEAST FOR SOME OF IT.
YOU DON'T LOOK THAT OLD.
NEITHER DO YOU.
GOOD POINT.
IT'S A STRANGE WORLD, MR SNOW.

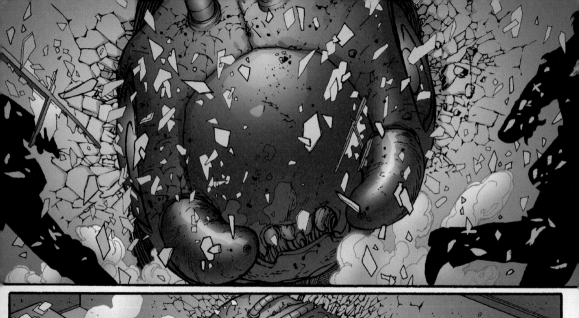

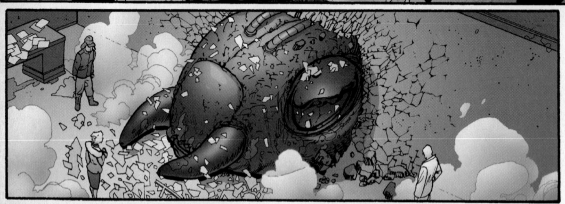

SORRY ABOUT THAT.

I KICKED IT A LITTLE TOO HARD.

HAVE FUN?

HELL, YES.

GOT OUR PILOT OUT TOO.

HOW'RE WE DOING, ALLISON?

I NEVER EXPECTED TO BE BACK HERE. I MEAN, I USED TO HAVE NIGHTMARES ABOUT ENDING UP HERE.

DO YOU HAVE ANY IDEA OF WHAT HAPPENED HERE?

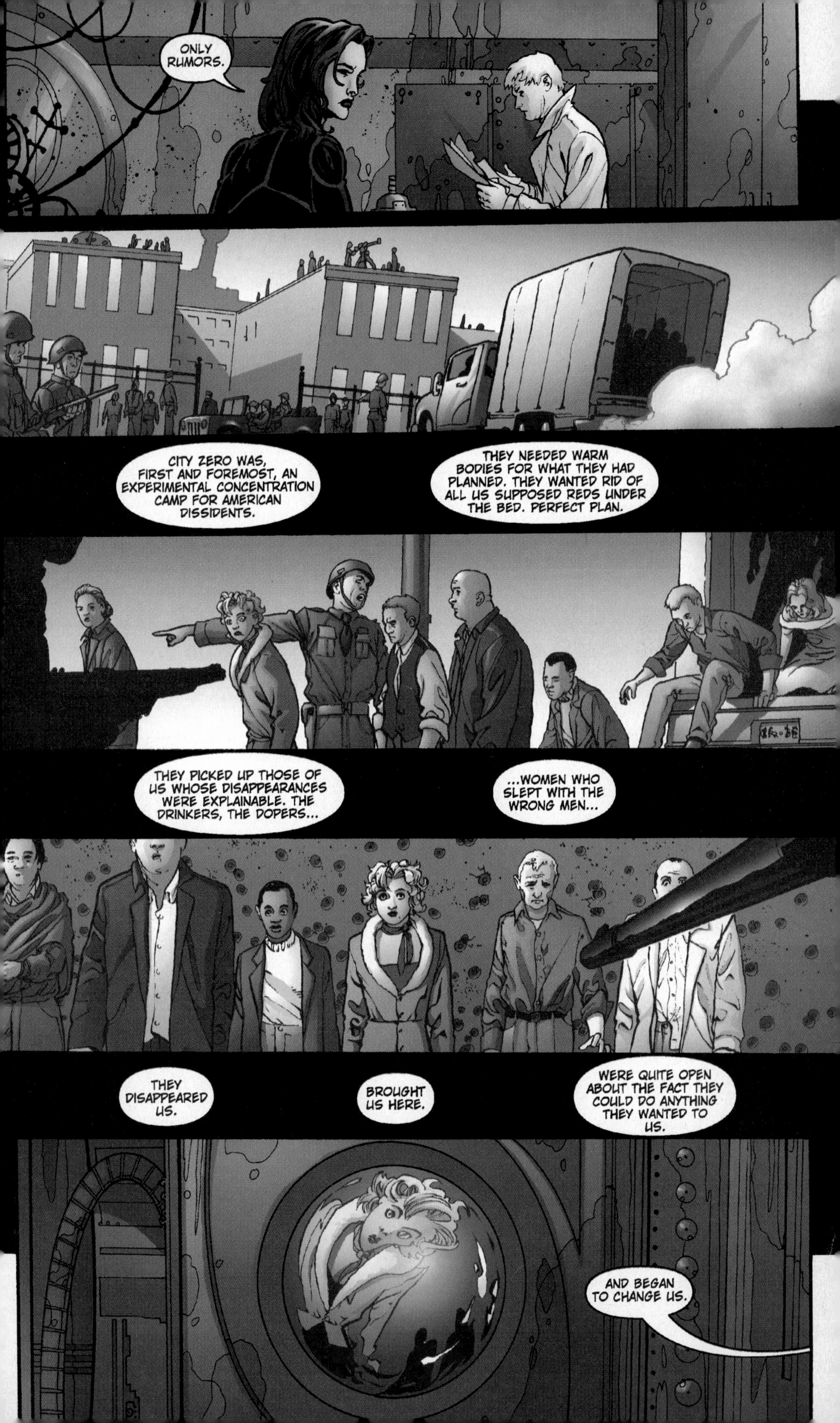
ONLY RUMORS.
CITY ZERO WAS, FIRST AND FOREMOST, AN EXPERIMENTAL CONCENTRATION CAMP FOR AMERICAN DISSIDENTS.
THEY NEEDED WARM BODIES FOR WHAT THEY HAD PLANNED. THEY WANTED RID OF ALL US SUPPOSED REDS UNDER THE BED. PERFECT PLAN.
THEY PICKED UP THOSE OF US WHOSE DISAPPEARANCES WERE EXPLAINABLE. THE DRINKERS, THE DOPERS...
...WOMEN WHO SLEPT WITH THE WRONG MEN...
THEY DISAPPEARED US.
BROUGHT US HERE.
WERE QUITE OPEN ABOUT THE FACT THEY COULD DO ANYTHING THEY WANTED TO US.
AND BEGAN TO CHANGE US.

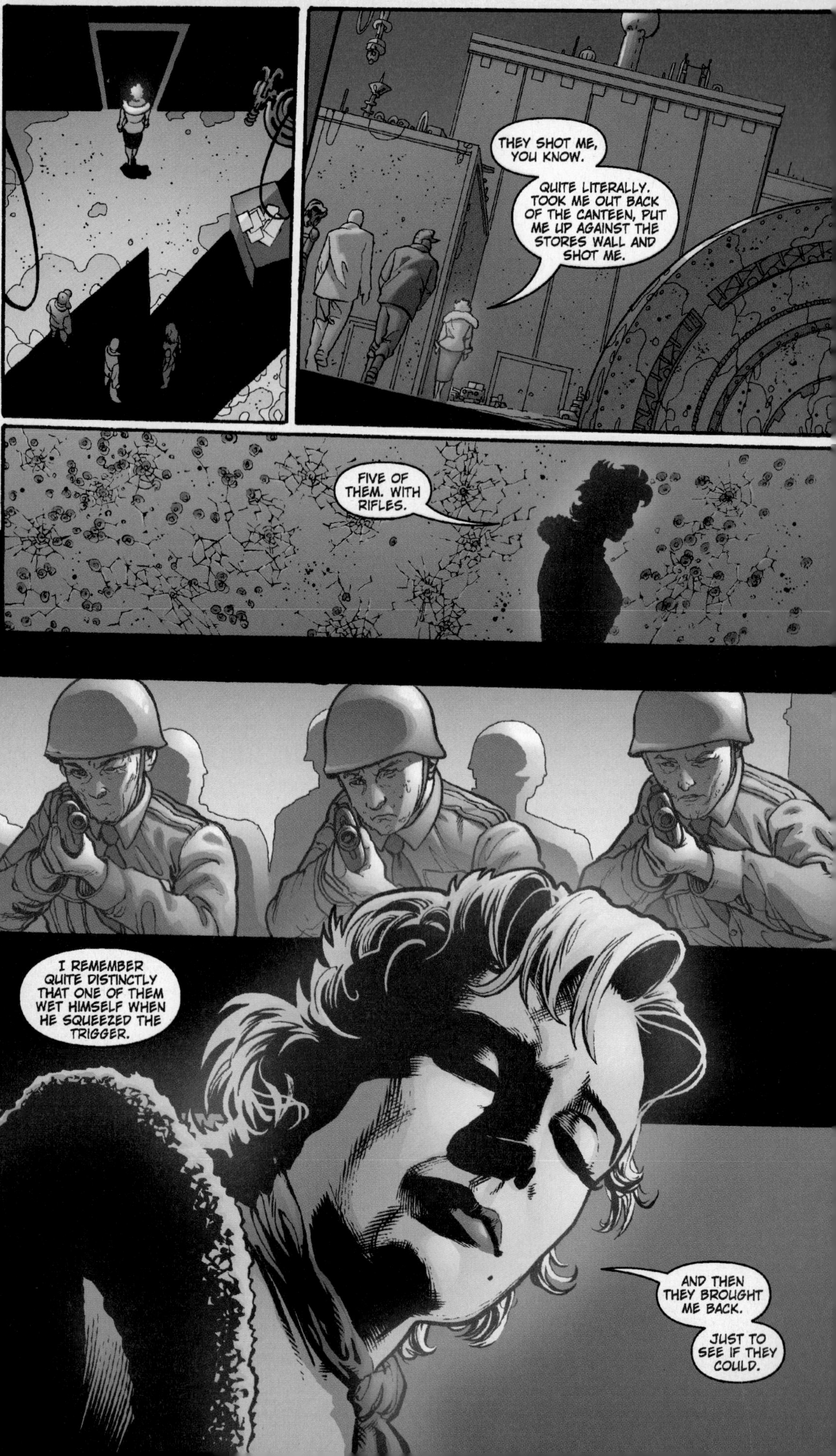
THEY SHOT ME, YOU KNOW.
QUITE LITERALLY. TOOK ME OUT BACK OF THE CANTEEN, PUT ME UP AGAINST THE STORES WALL AND SHOT ME.
FIVE OF THEM. WITH RIFLES.
I REMEMBER QUITE DISTINCTLY THAT ONE OF THEM WET HIMSELF WHEN HE SQUEEZED THE TRIGGER.
AND THEN THEY BROUGHT ME BACK.
JUST TO SEE IF THEY COULD.

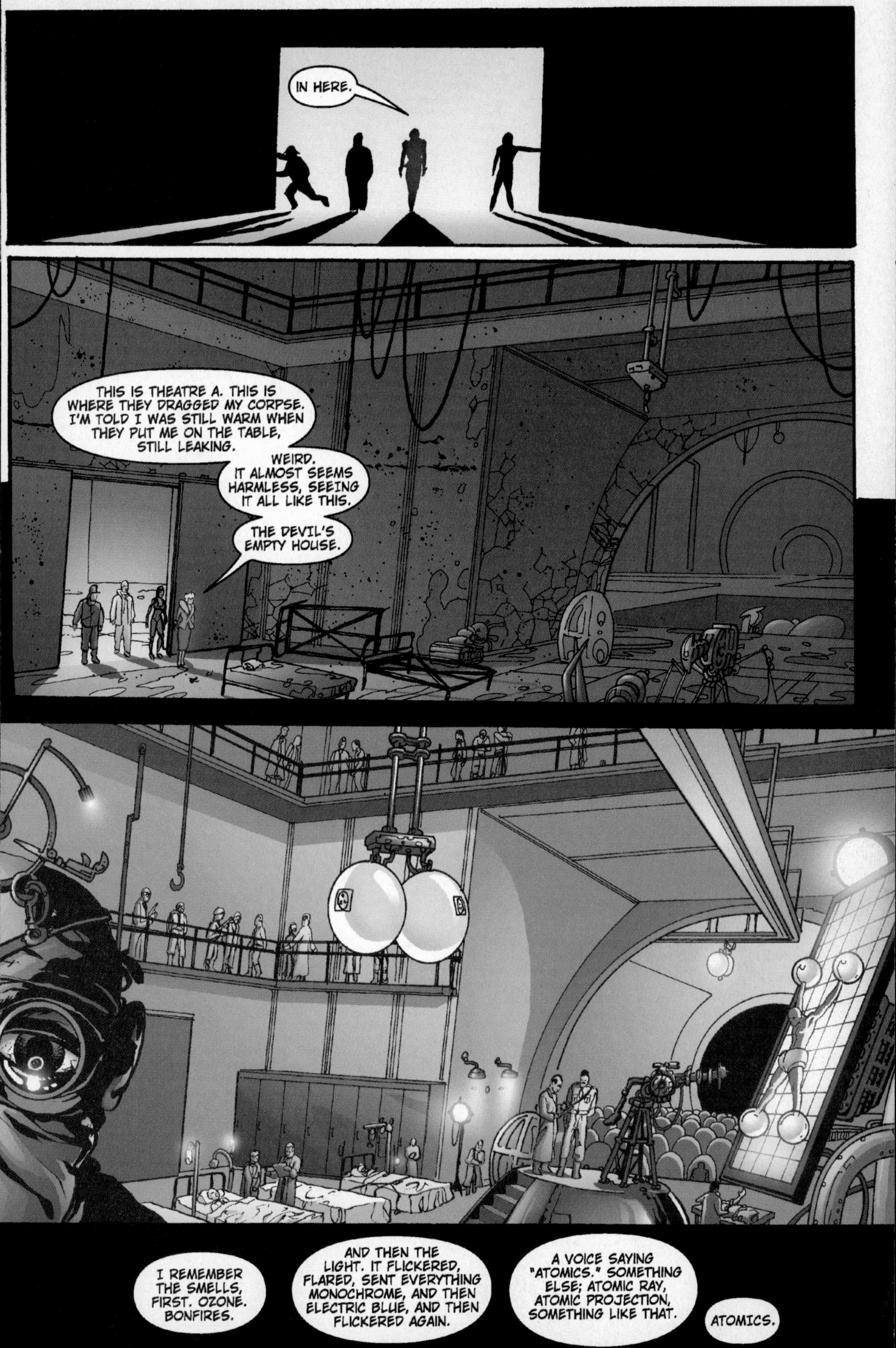
IN HERE.
THIS IS THEATRE A. THIS IS WHERE THEY DRAGGED MY CORPSE. I'M TOLD I WAS STILL WARM WHEN THEY PUT ME ON THE TABLE, STILL LEAKING.
WEIRD. IT ALMOST SEEMS HARMLESS, SEEING IT ALL LIKE THIS.
THE DEVIL'S EMPTY HOUSE.
I REMEMBER THE SMELLS, FIRST. OZONE. BONFIRES.
AND THEN THE LIGHT. IT FLICKERED, FLARED, SENT EVERYTHING MONOCHROME, AND THEN ELECTRIC BLUE, AND THEN FLICKERED AGAIN.
A VOICE SAYING "ATOMICS." SOMETHING ELSE; ATOMIC RAY, ATOMIC PROJECTION, SOMETHING LIKE THAT.
ATOMICS.

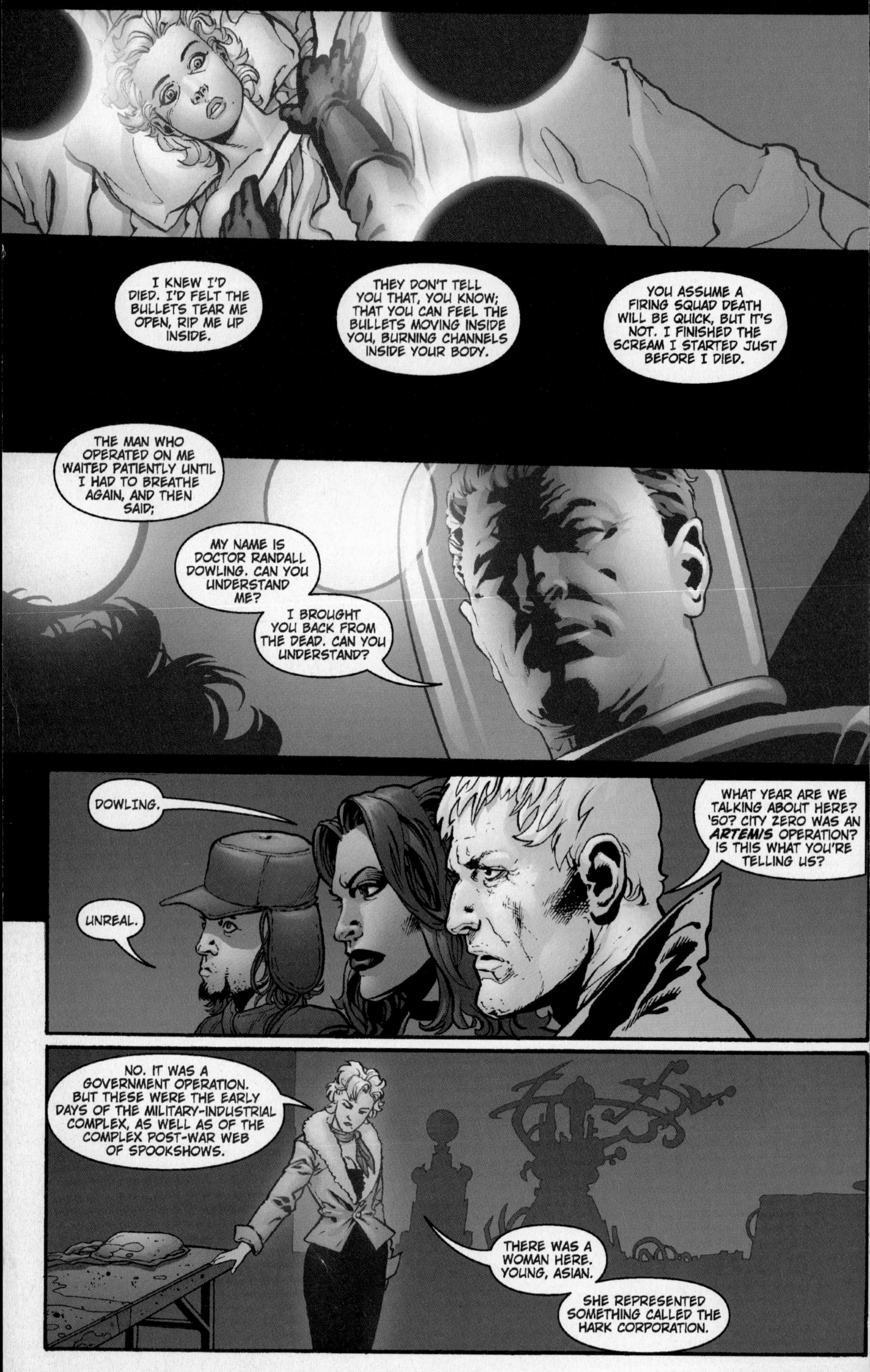

I KNEW I'D DIED. I'D FELT THE BULLETS TEAR ME OPEN, RIP ME UP INSIDE.
THEY DON'T TELL YOU THAT, YOU KNOW; THAT YOU CAN FEEL THE BULLETS MOVING INSIDE YOU, BURNING CHANNELS INSIDE YOUR BODY.
YOU ASSUME A FIRING SQUAD DEATH WILL BE QUICK, BUT IT'S NOT. I FINISHED THE SCREAM I STARTED JUST BEFORE I DIED.
THE MAN WHO OPERATED ON ME WAITED PATIENTLY UNTIL I HAD TO BREATHE AGAIN, AND THEN SAID;
MY NAME IS DOCTOR RANDALL DOWLING. CAN YOU UNDERSTAND ME?
I BROUGHT YOU BACK FROM THE DEAD. CAN YOU UNDERSTAND?
DOWLING.
UNREAL.
WHAT YEAR ARE WE TALKING ABOUT HERE? '50? CITY ZERO WAS AN *ARTEMIS* OPERATION? IS THIS WHAT YOU'RE TELLING US?
NO. IT WAS A GOVERNMENT OPERATION. BUT THESE WERE THE EARLY DAYS OF THE MILITARY-INDUSTRIAL COMPLEX, AS WELL AS OF THE COMPLEX POST-WAR WEB OF SPOOKSHOWS.
THERE WAS A WOMAN HERE. YOUNG, ASIAN.
SHE REPRESENTED SOMETHING CALLED THE HARK CORPORATION.

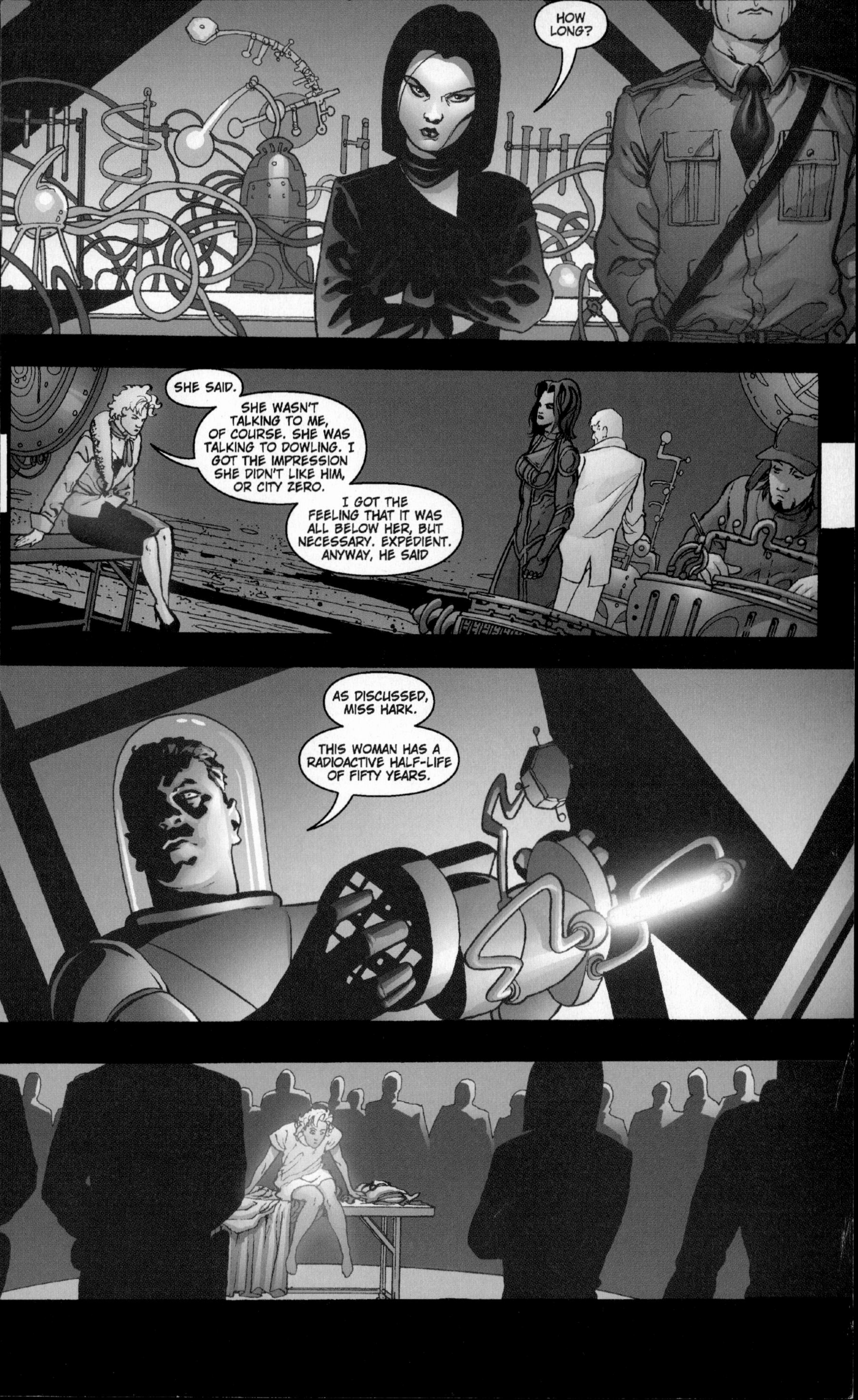
HOW LONG?
SHE SAID.
SHE WASN'T TALKING TO ME, OF COURSE. SHE WAS TALKING TO DOWLING. I GOT THE IMPRESSION SHE DIDN'T LIKE HIM, OR CITY ZERO.
I GOT THE FEELING THAT IT WAS ALL BELOW HER, BUT NECESSARY. EXPEDIENT. ANYWAY, HE SAID
AS DISCUSSED, MISS HARK.
THIS WOMAN HAS A RADIOACTIVE HALF-LIFE OF FIFTY YEARS.

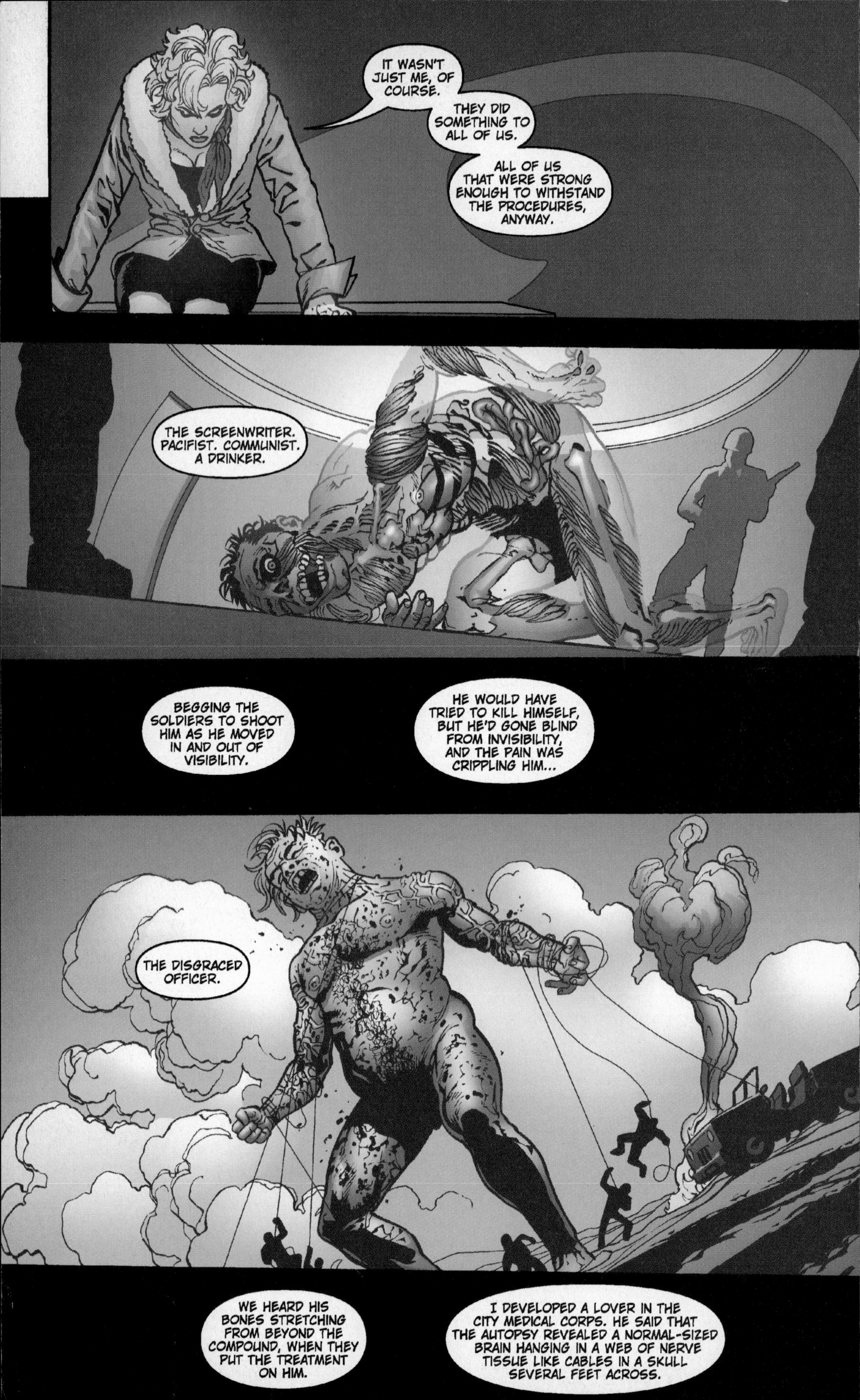
IT WASN'T JUST ME, OF COURSE.
THEY DID SOMETHING TO ALL OF US.
ALL OF US THAT WERE STRONG ENOUGH TO WITHSTAND THE PROCEDURES, ANYWAY.
THE SCREENWRITER. PACIFIST. COMMUNIST. A DRINKER.
BEGGING THE SOLDIERS TO SHOOT HIM AS HE MOVED IN AND OUT OF VISIBILITY.
HE WOULD HAVE TRIED TO KILL HIMSELF, BUT HE'D GONE BLIND FROM INVISIBILITY, AND THE PAIN WAS CRIPPLING HIM...
THE DISGRACED OFFICER.
WE HEARD HIS BONES STRETCHING FROM BEYOND THE COMPOUND, WHEN THEY PUT THE TREATMENT ON HIM.
I DEVELOPED A LOVER IN THE CITY MEDICAL CORPS. HE SAID THAT THE AUTOPSY REVEALED A NORMAL-SIZED BRAIN HANGING IN A WEB OF NERVE TISSUE LIKE CABLES IN A SKULL SEVERAL FEET ACROSS.

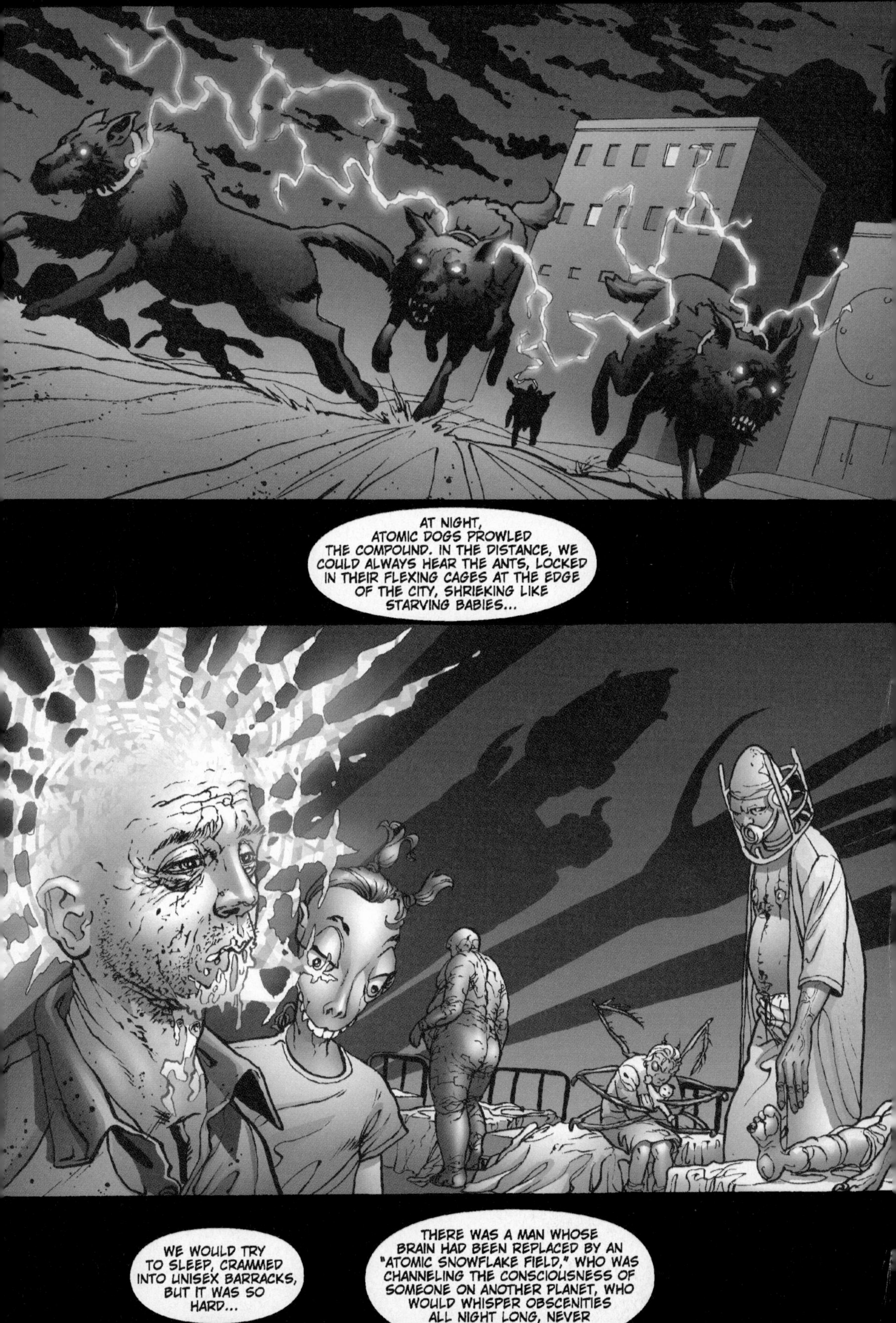
AT NIGHT, ATOMIC DOGS PROWLED THE COMPOUND. IN THE DISTANCE, WE COULD ALWAYS HEAR THE ANTS, LOCKED IN THEIR FLEXING CAGES AT THE EDGE OF THE CITY, SHRIEKING LIKE STARVING BABIES...
WE WOULD TRY TO SLEEP, CRAMMED INTO UNISEX BARRACKS, BUT IT WAS SO HARD...
THERE WAS A MAN WHOSE BRAIN HAD BEEN REPLACED BY AN "ATOMIC SNOWFLAKE FIELD," WHO WAS CHANNELING THE CONSCIOUSNESS OF SOMEONE ON ANOTHER PLANET, WHO WOULD WHISPER OBSCENITIES ALL NIGHT LONG, NEVER REPEATING HIMSELF...

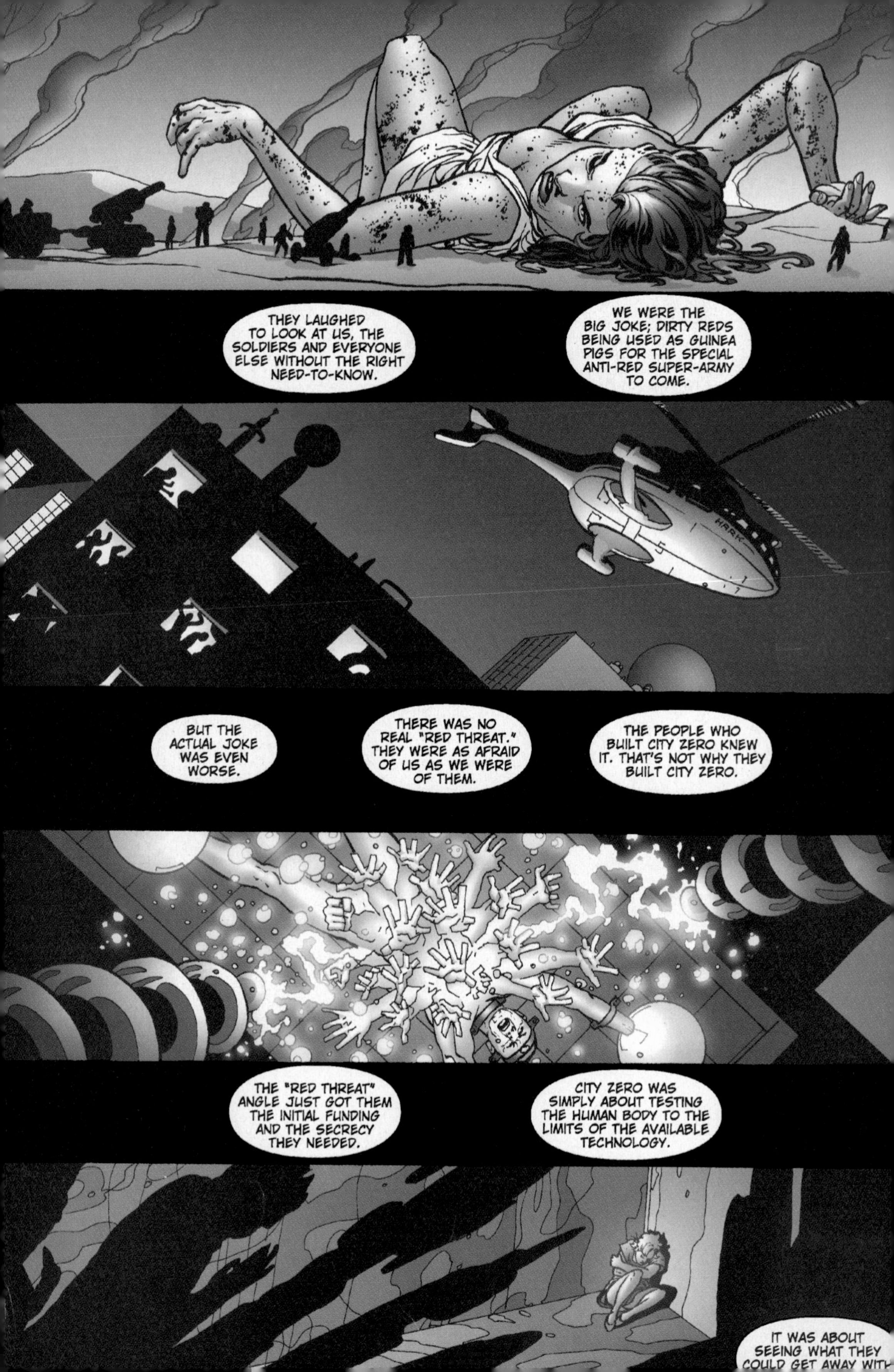
THEY LAUGHED TO LOOK AT US, THE SOLDIERS AND EVERYONE ELSE WITHOUT THE RIGHT NEED-TO-KNOW.
WE WERE THE BIG JOKE; DIRTY REDS BEING USED AS GUINEA PIGS FOR THE SPECIAL ANTI-RED SUPER-ARMY TO COME.
BUT THE ACTUAL JOKE WAS EVEN WORSE.
THERE WAS NO REAL "RED THREAT." THEY WERE AS AFRAID OF US AS WE WERE OF THEM.
THE PEOPLE WHO BUILT CITY ZERO KNEW IT. THAT'S NOT WHY THEY BUILT CITY ZERO.
THE "RED THREAT" ANGLE JUST GOT THEM THE INITIAL FUNDING AND THE SECRECY THEY NEEDED.
CITY ZERO WAS SIMPLY ABOUT TESTING THE HUMAN BODY TO THE LIMITS OF THE AVAILABLE TECHNOLOGY.
IT WAS ABOUT SEEING WHAT THEY COULD GET AWAY WITH

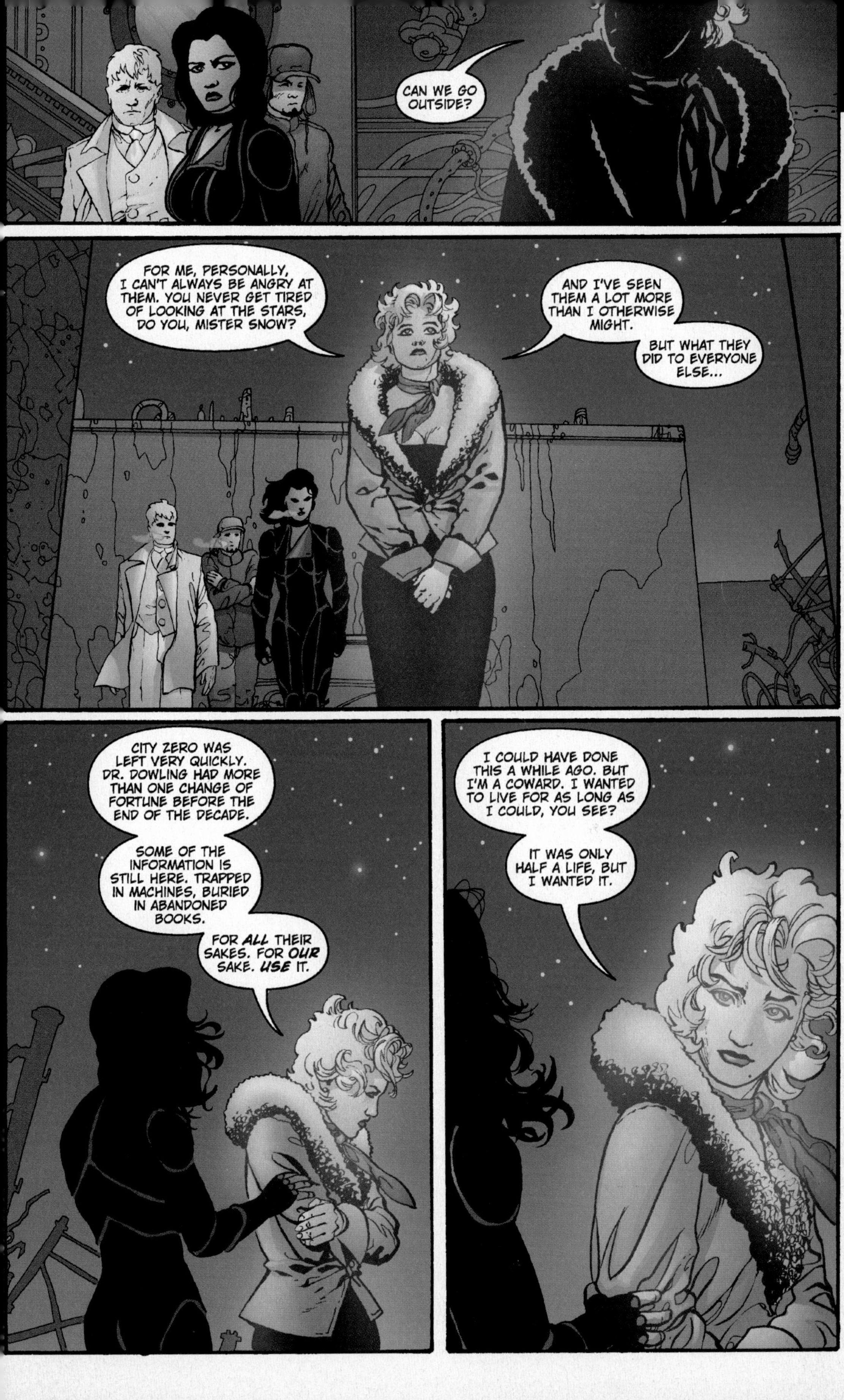
CAN WE GO OUTSIDE?
FOR ME, PERSONALLY, I CAN'T ALWAYS BE ANGRY AT THEM. YOU NEVER GET TIRED OF LOOKING AT THE STARS, DO YOU, MISTER SNOW?
AND I'VE SEEN THEM A LOT MORE THAN I OTHERWISE MIGHT.
BUT WHAT THEY DID TO EVERYONE ELSE...
CITY ZERO WAS LEFT VERY QUICKLY. DR. DOWLING HAD MORE THAN ONE CHANGE OF FORTUNE BEFORE THE END OF THE DECADE.
SOME OF THE INFORMATION IS STILL HERE. TRAPPED IN MACHINES, BURIED IN ABANDONED BOOKS.
FOR ALL THEIR SAKES. FOR OUR SAKE. USE IT.
I COULD HAVE DONE THIS A WHILE AGO. BUT I'M A COWARD. I WANTED TO LIVE FOR AS LONG AS I COULD, YOU SEE?
IT WAS ONLY HALF A LIFE, BUT I WANTED IT.

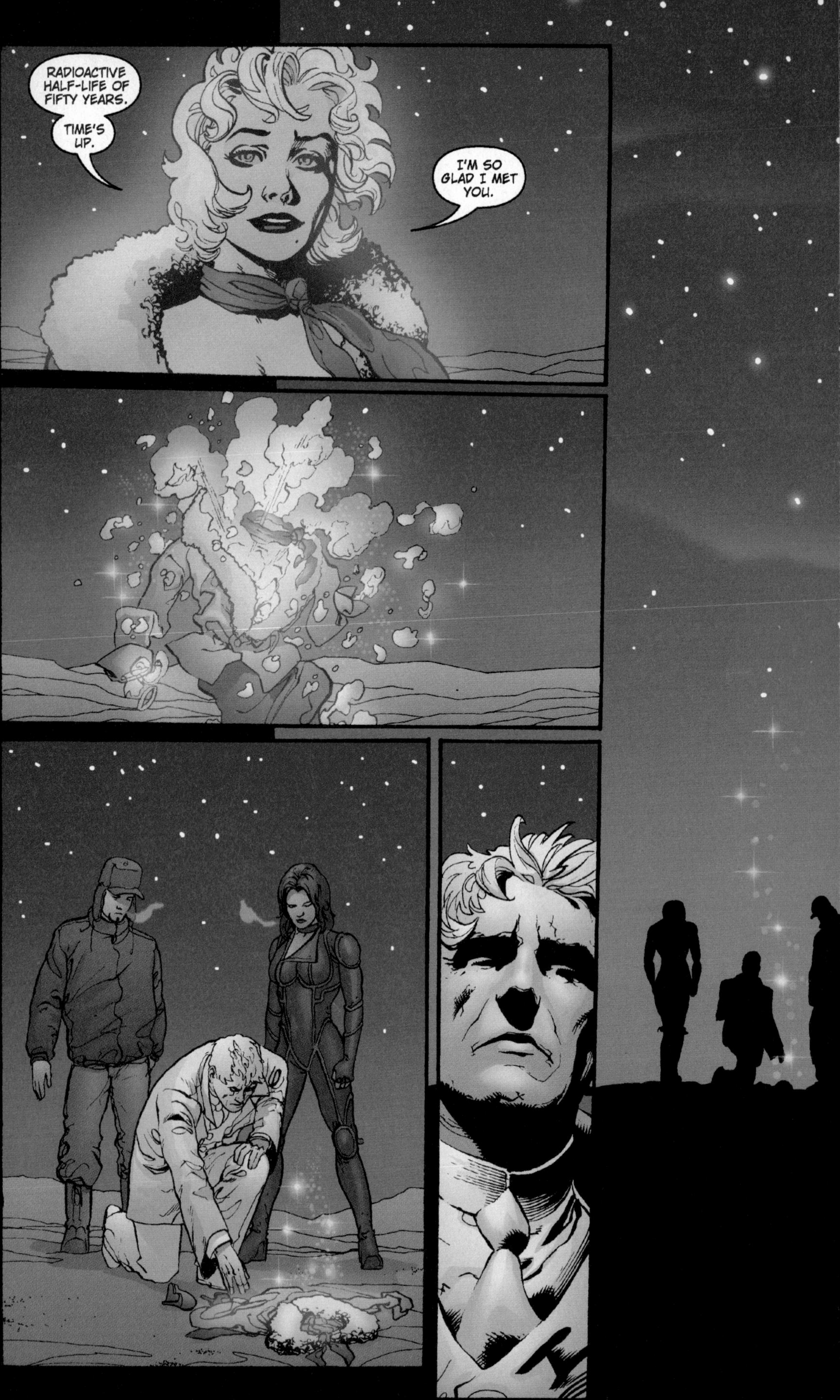
RADIOACTIVE HALF-LIFE OF FIFTY YEARS.
TIME'S UP.
I'M SO GLAD I MET YOU.

ILDSTORM
CHAPTER
NINE
number nine $2.50 u.s./$3.95 canada
PLANETARY
planet fiction • planet fiction • planet fiction
ellis • cassaday • baron • ellis • cassaday
$3.95 canada • number nine $

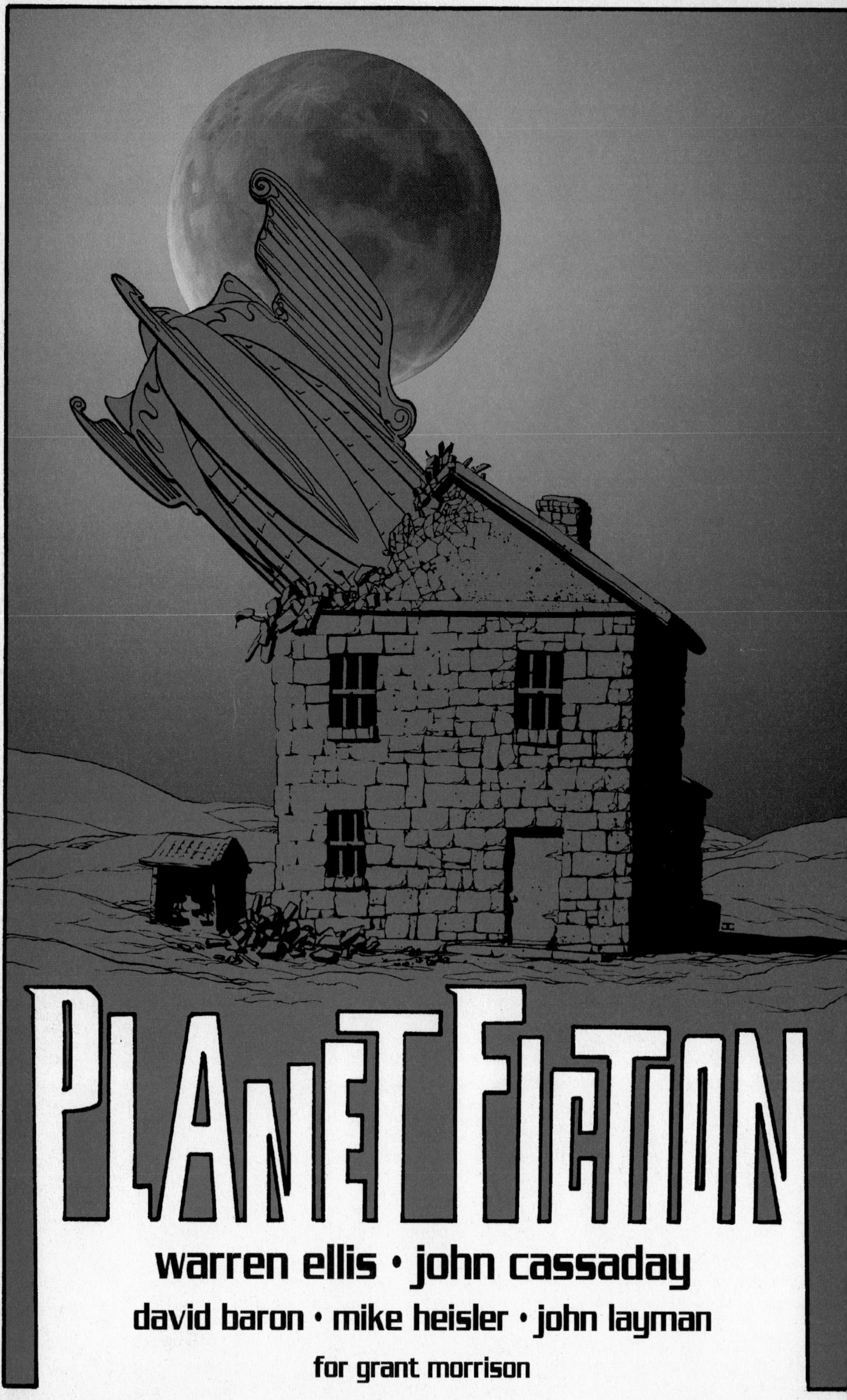

PLANET FICTION

warren ellis • john cassaday

david baron • mike heisler • john layman

for grant morrison

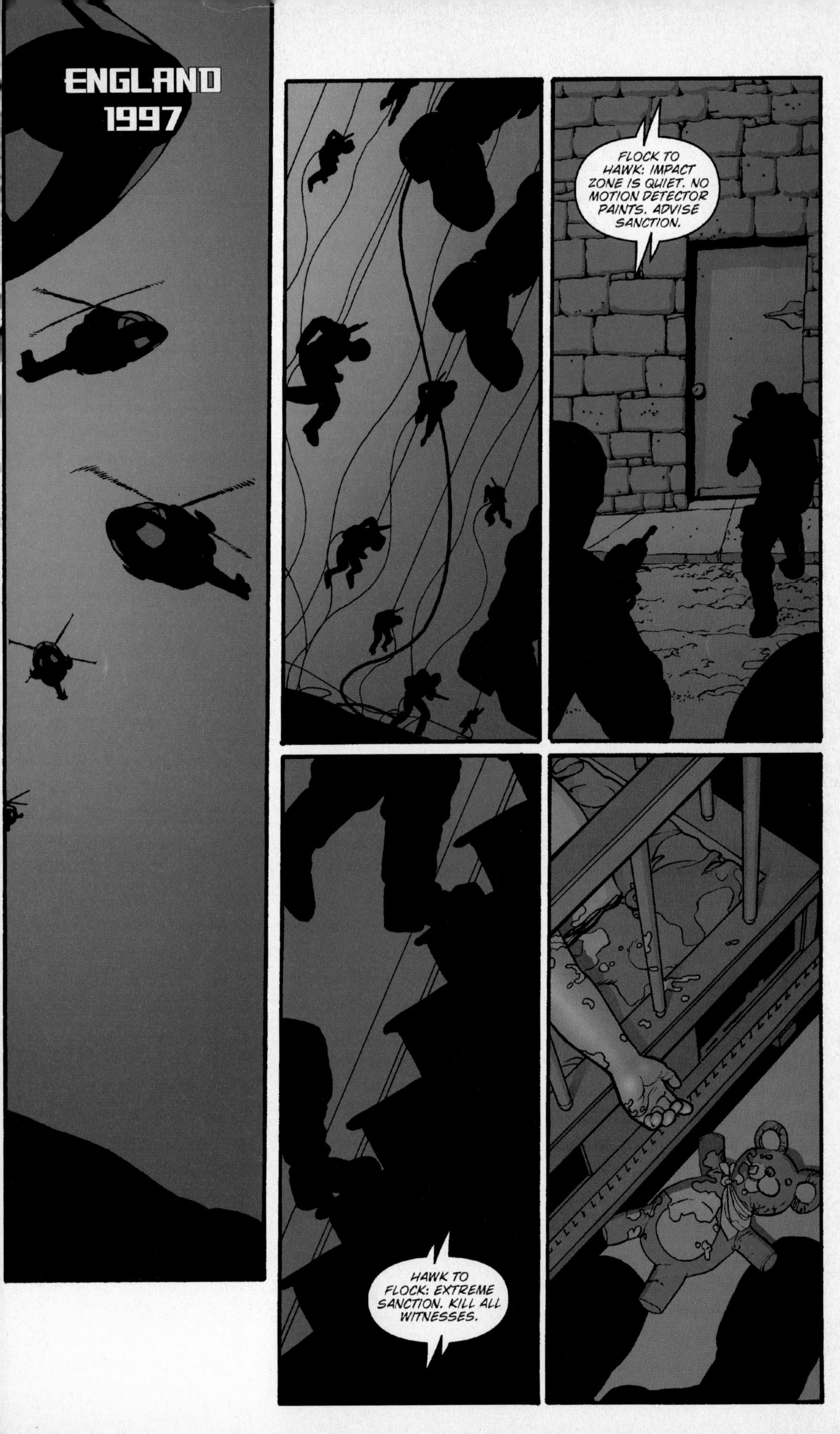
ENGLAND
1997
FLOCK TO HAWK: IMPACT ZONE IS QUIET. NO MOTION DETECTOR PAINTS. ADVISE SANCTION.
HAWK TO FLOCK: EXTREME SANCTION. KILL ALL WITNESSES.

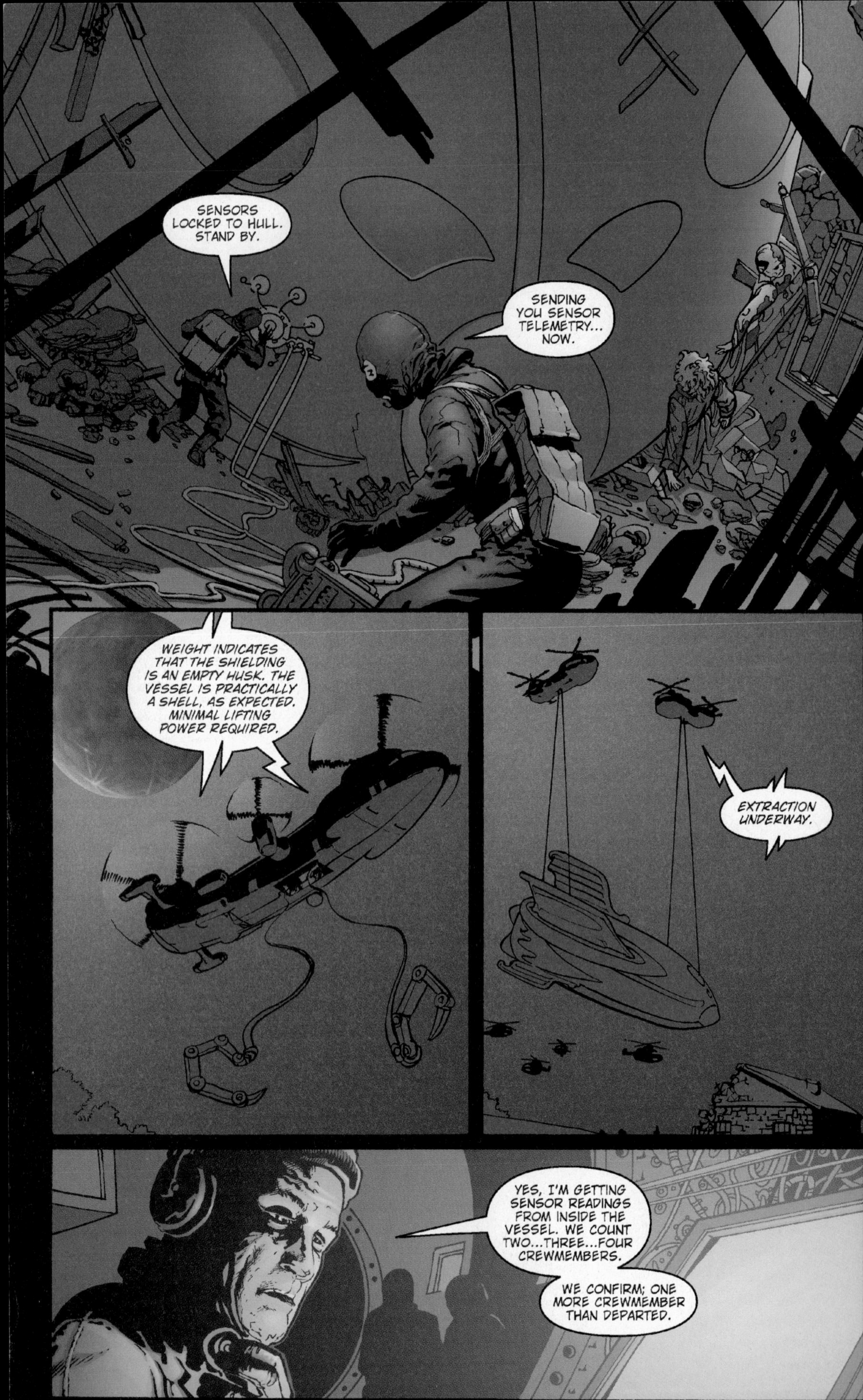
SENSORS LOCKED TO HULL. STAND BY.
SENDING YOU SENSOR TELEMETRY... NOW.
WEIGHT INDICATES THAT THE SHIELDING IS AN EMPTY HUSK. THE VESSEL IS PRACTICALLY A SHELL, AS EXPECTED. MINIMAL LIFTING POWER REQUIRED.
EXTRACTION UNDERWAY.
YES, I'M GETTING SENSOR READINGS FROM INSIDE THE VESSEL. WE COUNT TWO...THREE...FOUR CREWMEMBERS.
WE CONFIRM; ONE MORE CREWMEMBER THAN DEPARTED.

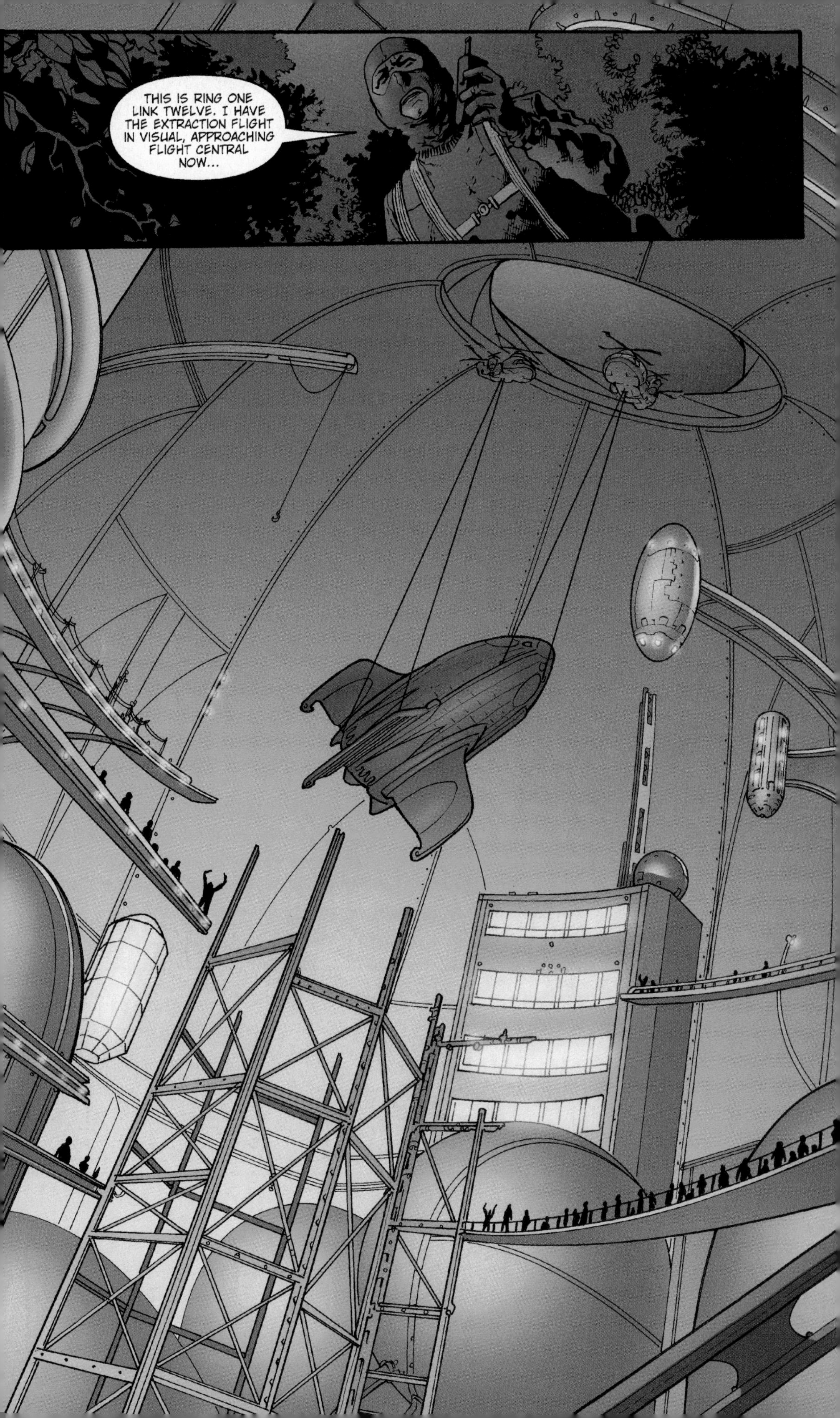
THIS IS RING ONE LINK TWELVE. I HAVE THE EXTRACTION FLIGHT IN VISUAL, APPROACHING FLIGHT CENTRAL NOW...

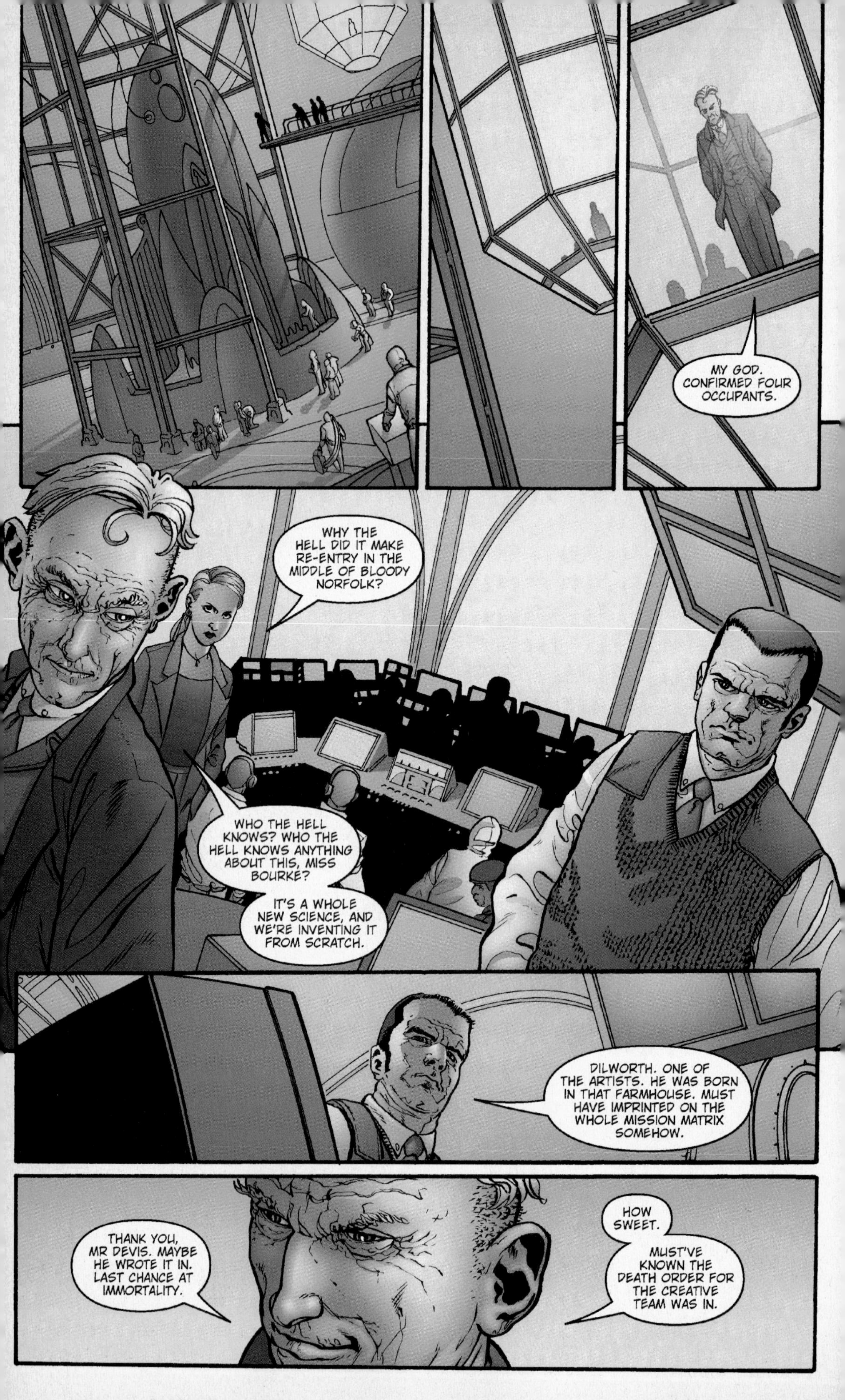
MY GOD. CONFIRMED FOUR OCCUPANTS.
WHY THE HELL DID IT MAKE RE-ENTRY IN THE MIDDLE OF BLOODY NORFOLK?
WHO THE HELL KNOWS? WHO THE HELL KNOWS ANYTHING ABOUT THIS, MISS BOURKE?
IT'S A WHOLE NEW SCIENCE, AND WE'RE INVENTING IT FROM SCRATCH.
DILWORTH. ONE OF THE ARTISTS. HE WAS BORN IN THAT FARMHOUSE. MUST HAVE IMPRINTED ON THE WHOLE MISSION MATRIX SOMEHOW.
HOW SWEET.
MUST'VE KNOWN THE DEATH ORDER FOR THE CREATIVE TEAM WAS IN.
THANK YOU, MR DEVIS. MAYBE HE WROTE IT IN. LAST CHANCE AT IMMORTALITY.

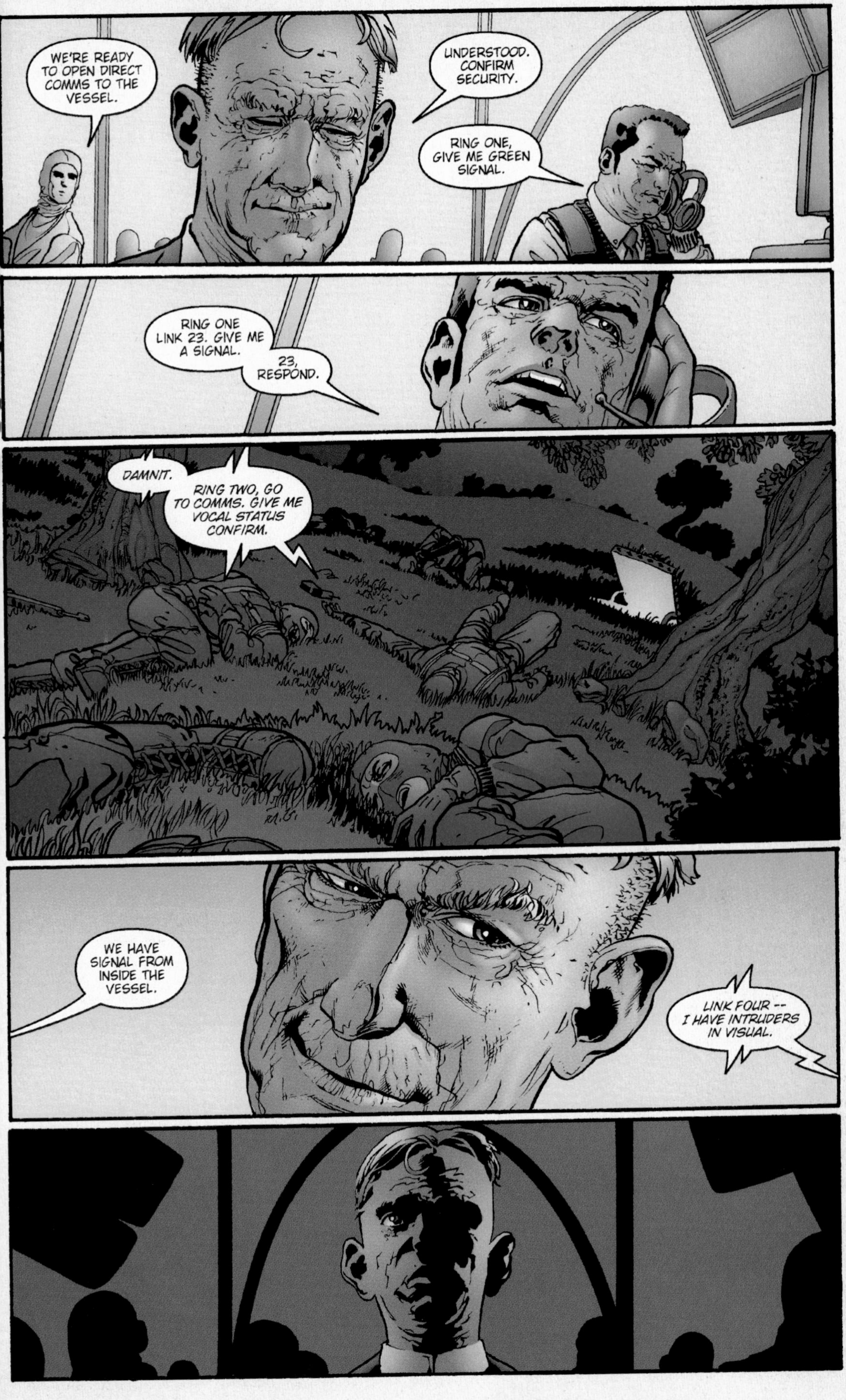
WE'RE READY TO OPEN DIRECT COMMS TO THE VESSEL.
UNDERSTOOD. CONFIRM SECURITY.
RING ONE, GIVE ME GREEN SIGNAL.
RING ONE LINK 23. GIVE ME A SIGNAL.
23, RESPOND.
DAMNIT.
RING TWO, GO TO COMMS. GIVE ME VOCAL STATUS CONFIRM.
WE HAVE SIGNAL FROM INSIDE THE VESSEL.
LINK FOUR -- I HAVE INTRUDERS IN VISUAL.

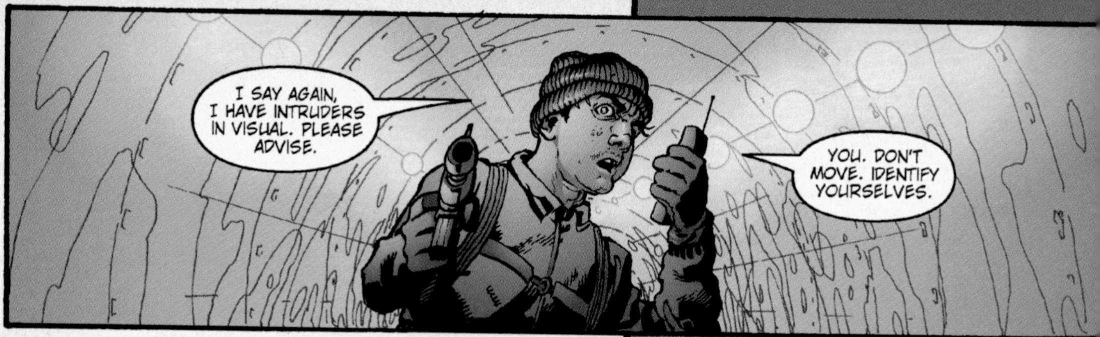
I SAY AGAIN, I HAVE INTRUDERS IN VISUAL. PLEASE ADVISE.
YOU. DON'T MOVE. IDENTIFY YOURSELVES.

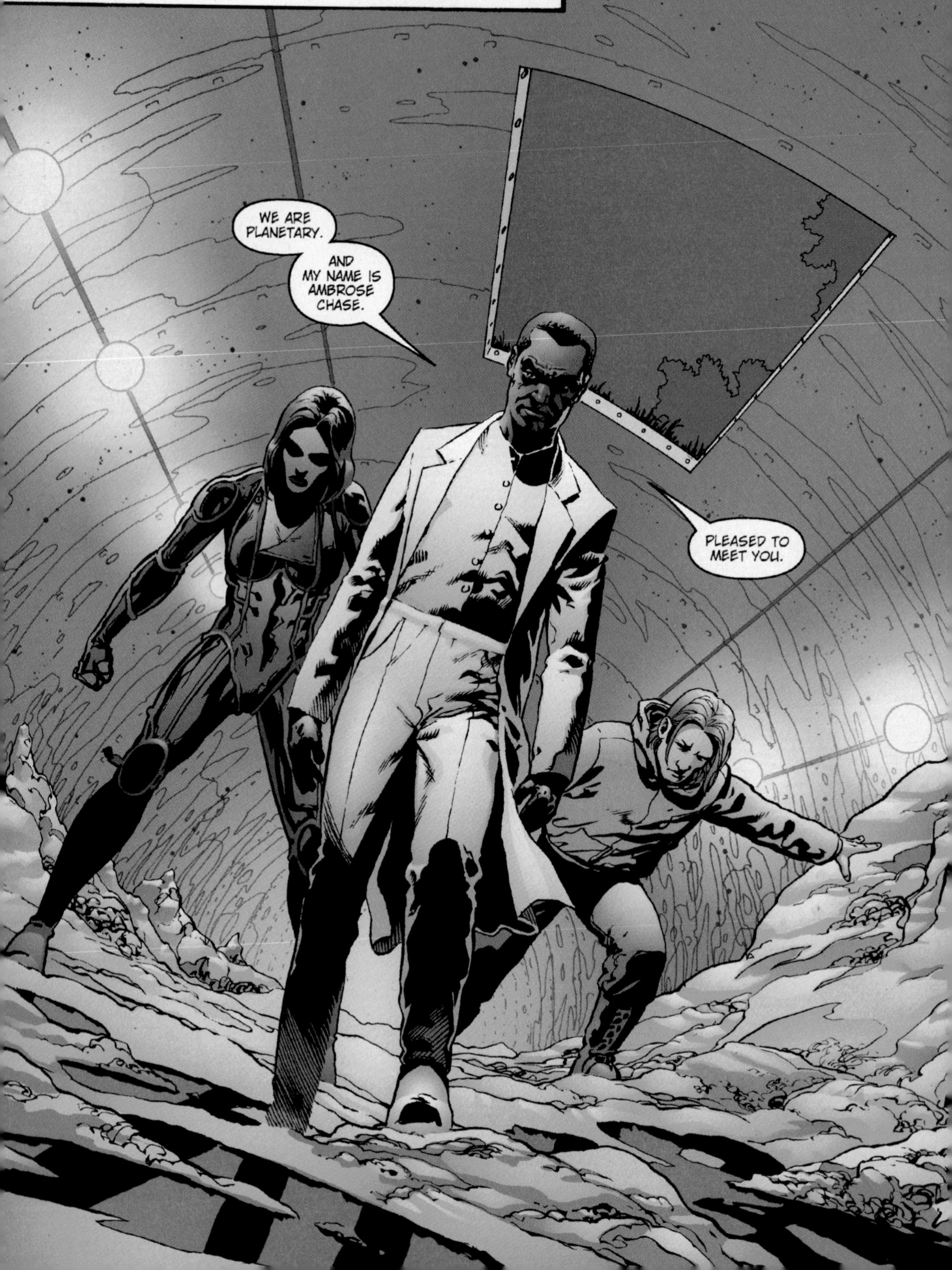
WE ARE PLANETARY.
AND MY NAME IS AMBROSE CHASE.
PLEASED TO MEET YOU.

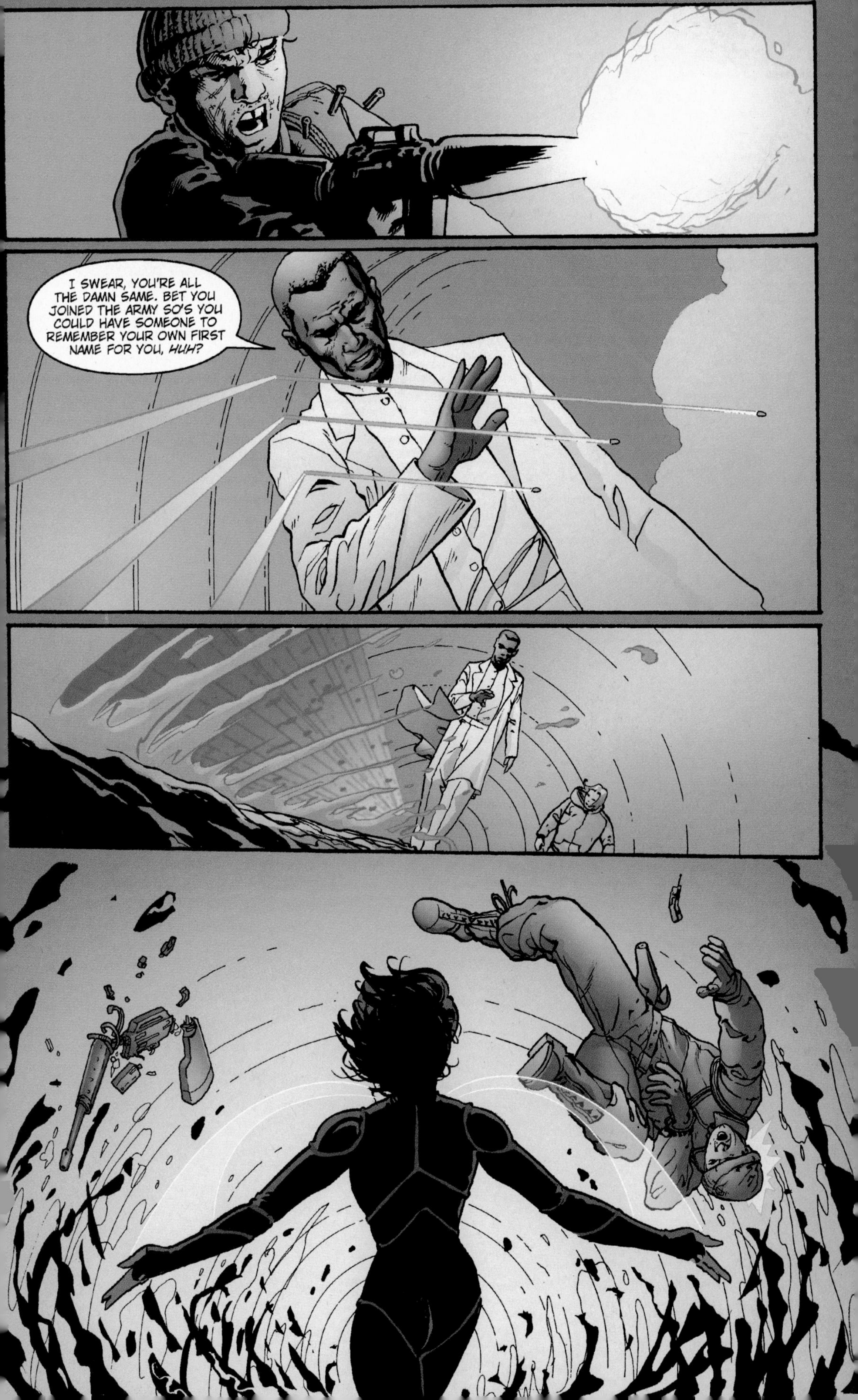
I SWEAR, YOU'RE ALL THE DAMN SAME. BET YOU JOINED THE ARMY SO'S YOU COULD HAVE SOMEONE TO REMEMBER YOUR OWN FIRST NAME FOR YOU, *HUH?*

TOO EASY. WE'RE GOOD, BUT NOT THIS GOOD. WE KNOW THERE'S A STRENGTH OF TWO THOUSAND ON THIS SITE. DRUMS, TALK TO ME.

DATA FLOW'S GETTING SLUGGISH IN HERE. LOOKS LIKE THEY'VE GOT A PARTIAL POWER OUTAGE IN THE SITE'S CENTRAL SECTIONS.

AMBROSE?

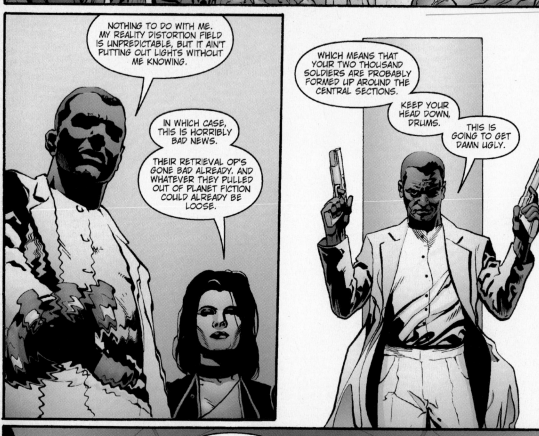

NOTHING TO DO WITH ME. MY REALITY DISTORTION FIELD IS UNPREDICTABLE, BUT IT AIN'T PUTTING OUT LIGHTS WITHOUT ME KNOWING.

IN WHICH CASE, THIS IS HORRIBLY BAD NEWS.

THEIR RETRIEVAL OP'S GONE BAD ALREADY. AND WHATEVER THEY PULLED OUT OF PLANET FICTION COULD ALREADY BE LOOSE.

WHICH MEANS THAT YOUR TWO THOUSAND SOLDIERS ARE PROBABLY FORMED UP AROUND THE CENTRAL SECTIONS.

KEEP YOUR HEAD DOWN, DRUMS.

THIS IS GOING TO GET DAMN UGLY.

I KNEW IT WAS GOING TO GET UGLY WHEN I TAPPED THEIR COMMS.

FOUR CONFIRMED OCCUPANTS OF THE EXPLORATION VESSEL.

AND THEY ONLY SENT THREE PEOPLE IN.

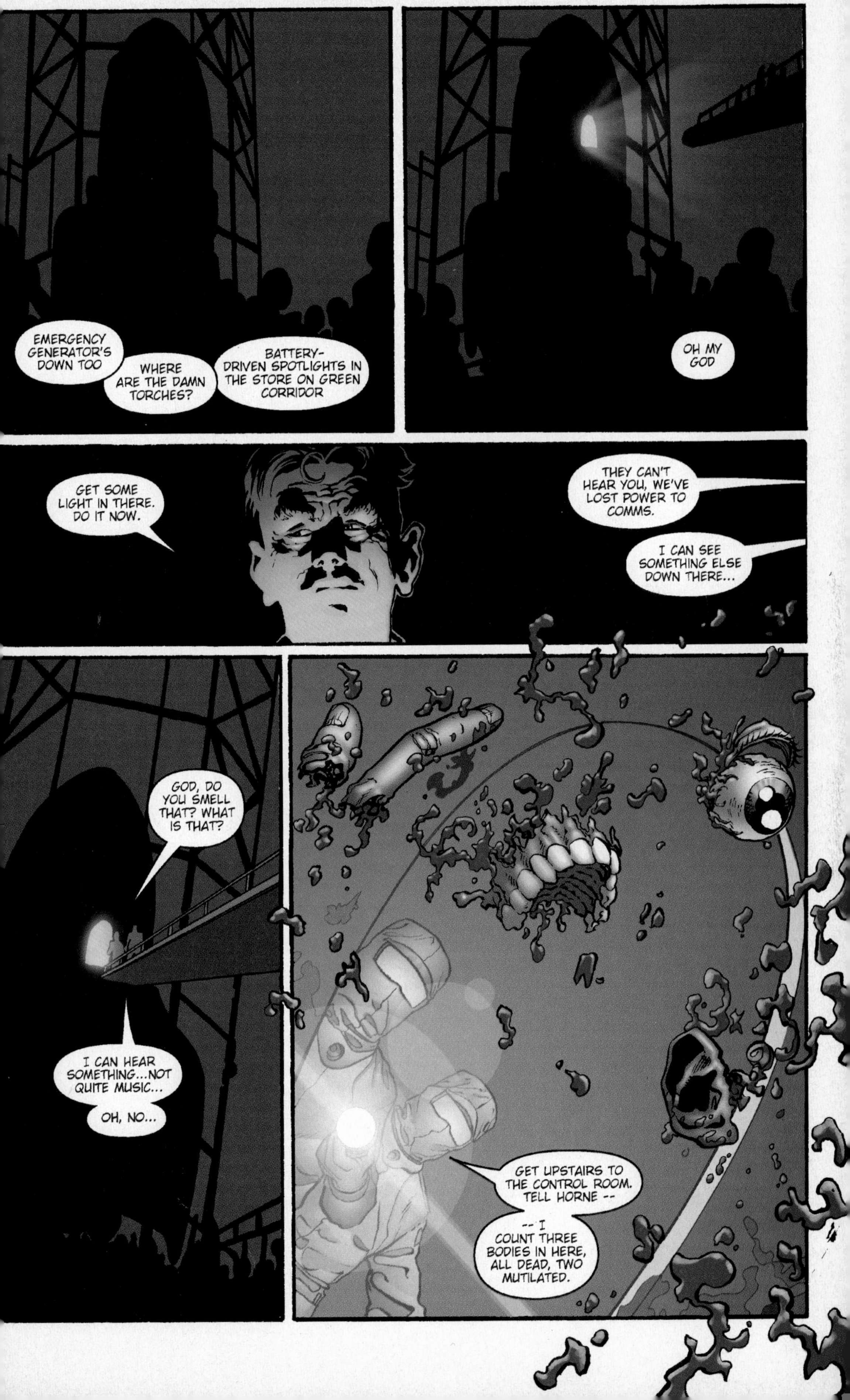
EMERGENCY GENERATOR'S DOWN TOO
WHERE ARE THE DAMN TORCHES?
BATTERY-DRIVEN SPOTLIGHTS IN THE STORE ON GREEN CORRIDOR
OH MY GOD
GET SOME LIGHT IN THERE. DO IT NOW.
THEY CAN'T HEAR YOU, WE'VE LOST POWER TO COMMS.
I CAN SEE SOMETHING ELSE DOWN THERE...
GOD, DO YOU SMELL THAT? WHAT IS THAT?
I CAN HEAR SOMETHING...NOT QUITE MUSIC...
OH, NO...
GET UPSTAIRS TO THE CONTROL ROOM. TELL HORNE --
-- I COUNT THREE BODIES IN HERE, ALL DEAD, TWO MUTILATED.

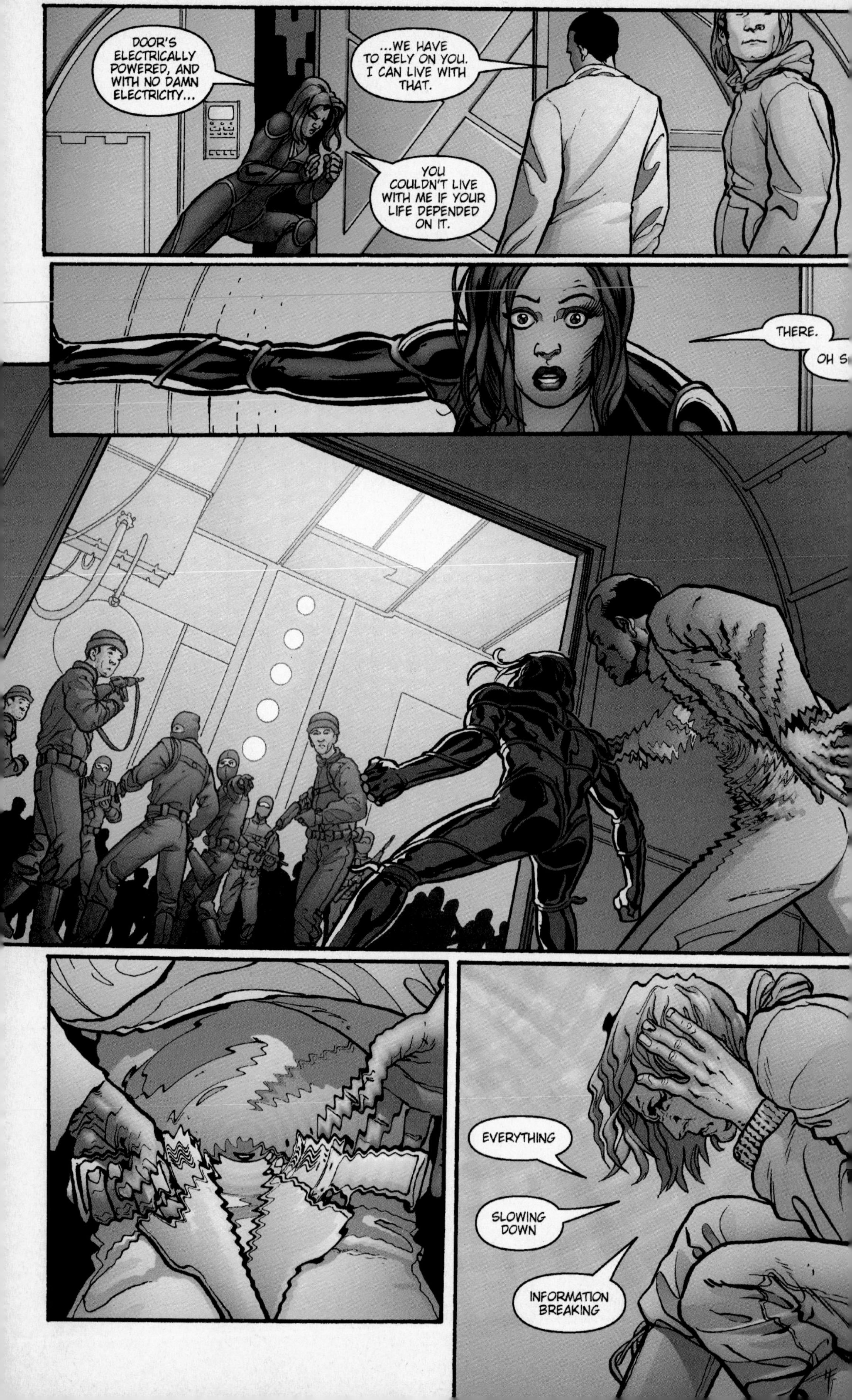
DOOR'S ELECTRICALLY POWERED, AND WITH NO DAMN ELECTRICITY...
...WE HAVE TO RELY ON YOU. I CAN LIVE WITH THAT.
YOU COULDN'T LIVE WITH ME IF YOUR LIFE DEPENDED ON IT.
THERE.
EVERYTHING
SLOWING DOWN
INFORMATION BREAKING

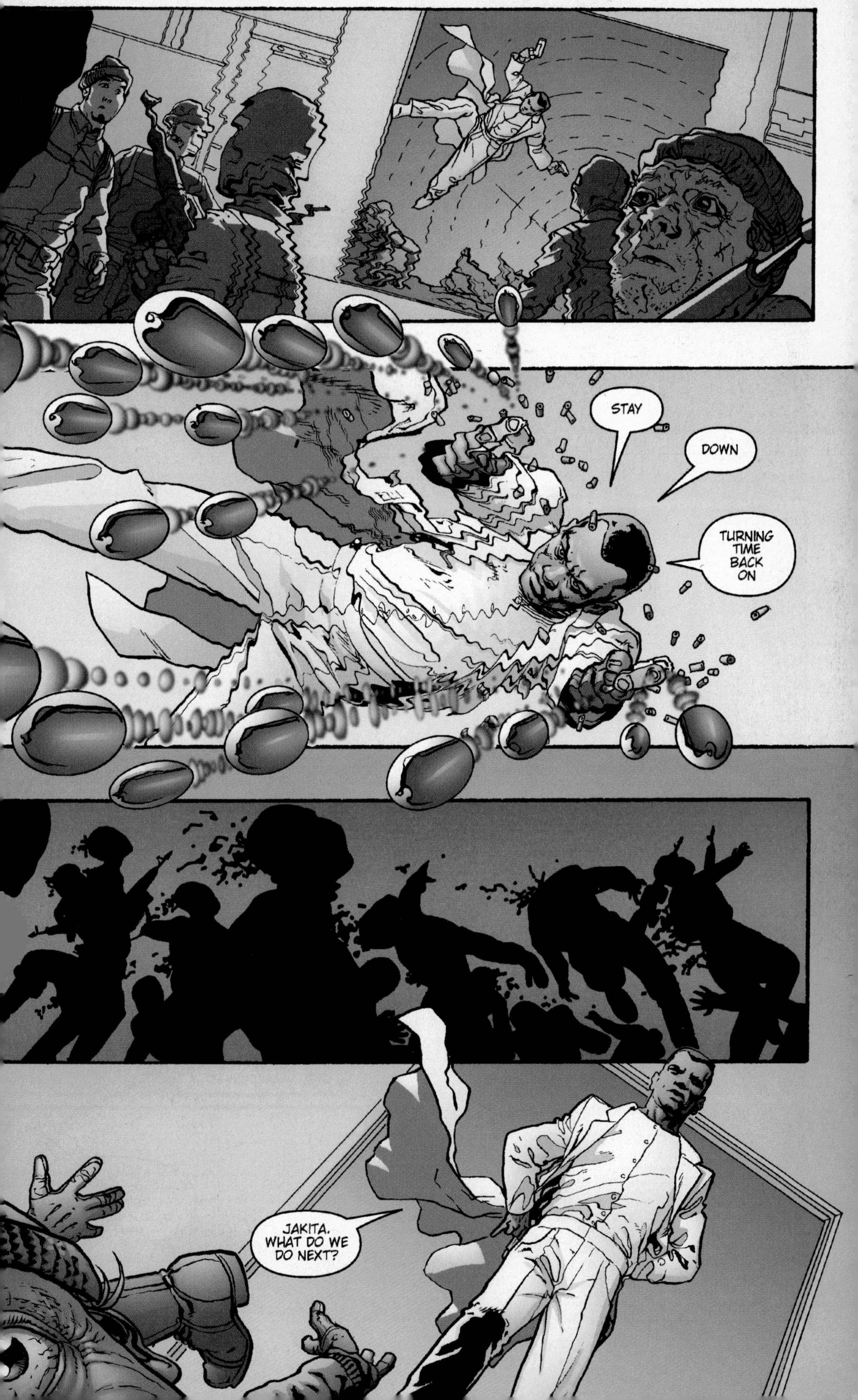
STAY
DOWN
TURNING TIME BACK ON
JAKITA. WHAT DO WE DO NEXT?

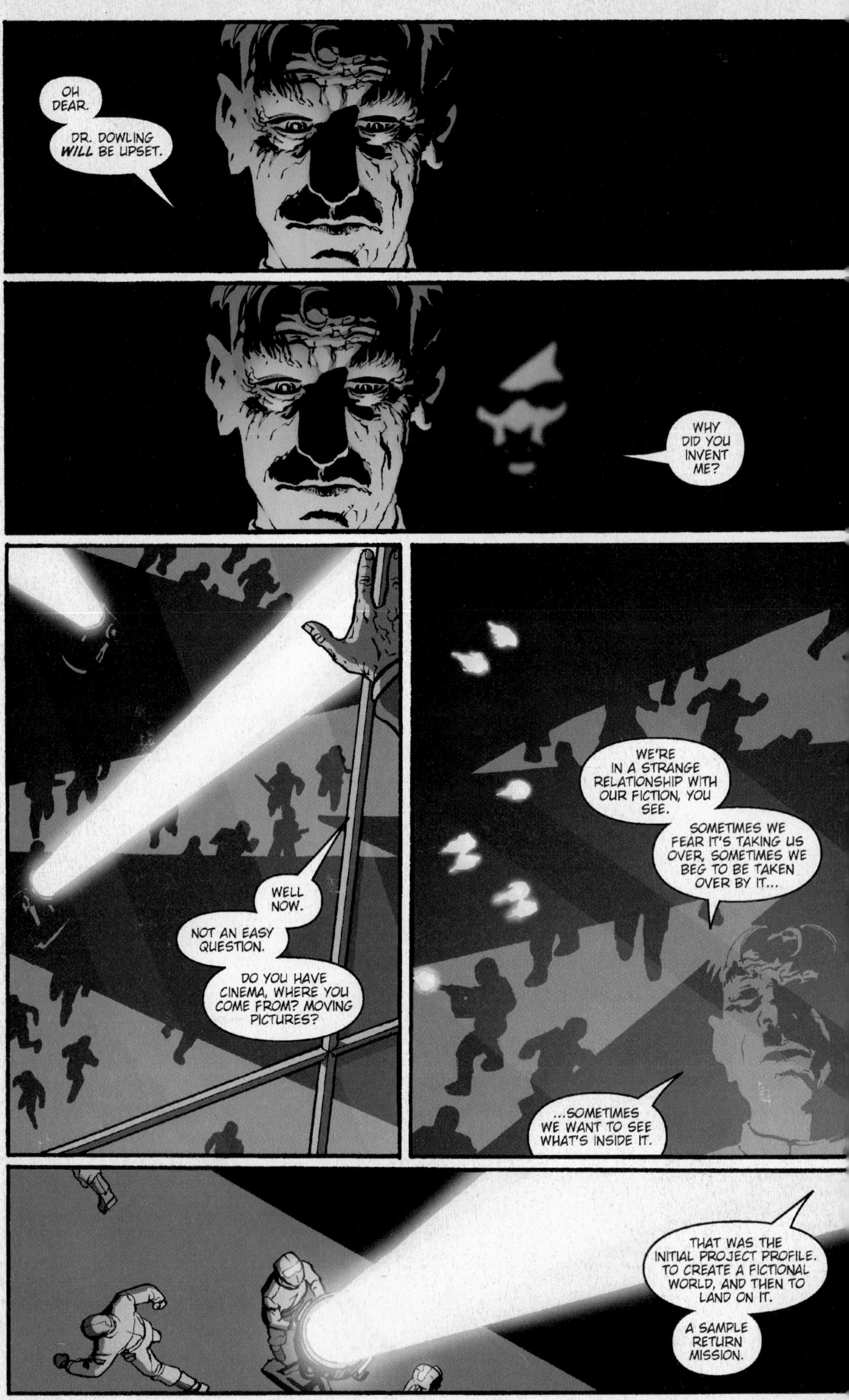
OH DEAR.
DR. DOWLING *WILL* BE UPSET.
WHY DID YOU INVENT ME?
WELL NOW.
NOT AN EASY QUESTION.
DO YOU HAVE CINEMA, WHERE YOU COME FROM? MOVING PICTURES?
WE'RE IN A STRANGE RELATIONSHIP WITH OUR FICTION, YOU SEE.
SOMETIMES WE FEAR IT'S TAKING US OVER, SOMETIMES WE BEG TO BE TAKEN OVER BY IT...
...SOMETIMES WE WANT TO SEE WHAT'S INSIDE IT.
THAT WAS THE INITIAL PROJECT PROFILE. TO CREATE A FICTIONAL WORLD, AND THEN TO LAND ON IT.
A SAMPLE RETURN MISSION.

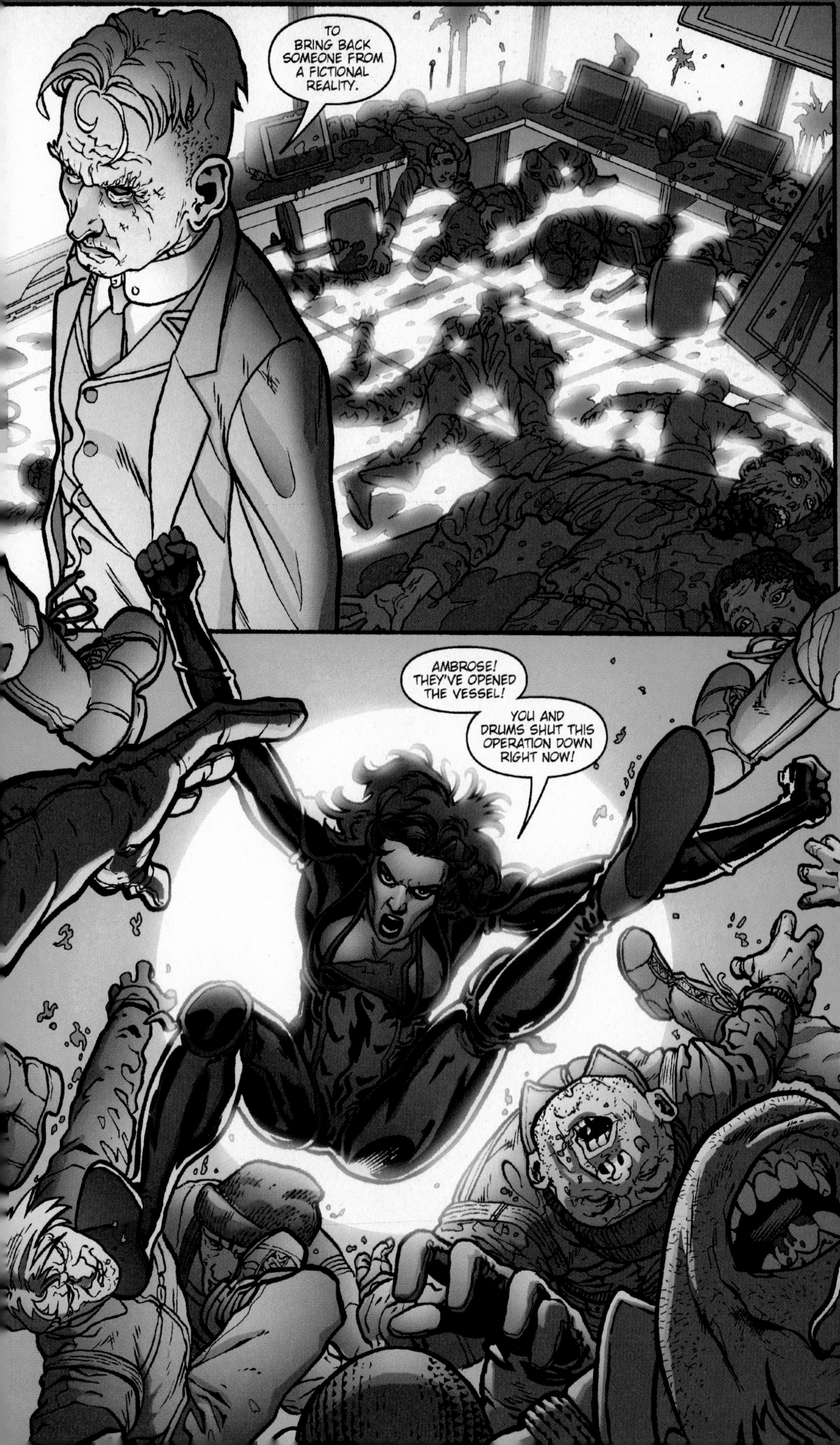
TO BRING BACK SOMEONE FROM A FICTIONAL REALITY.
AMBROSE! THEY'VE OPENED THE VESSEL!
YOU AND DRUMS SHUT THIS OPERATION DOWN RIGHT NOW!

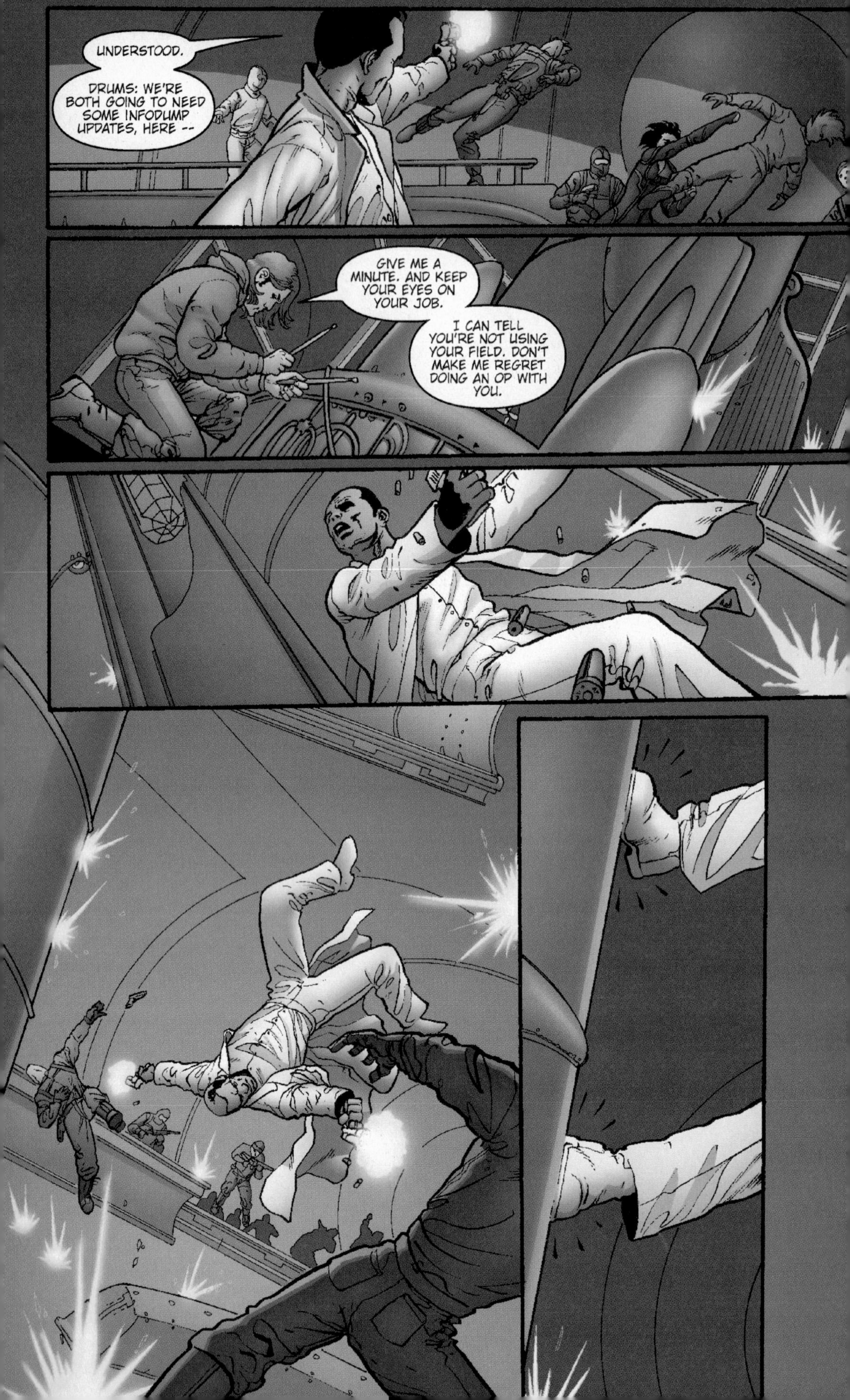
UNDERSTOOD.
DRUMS: WE'RE BOTH GOING TO NEED SOME INFODUMP UPDATES, HERE --
GIVE ME A MINUTE. AND KEEP YOUR EYES ON YOUR JOB.
I CAN TELL YOU'RE NOT USING YOUR FIELD. DON'T MAKE ME REGRET DOING AN OP WITH YOU.

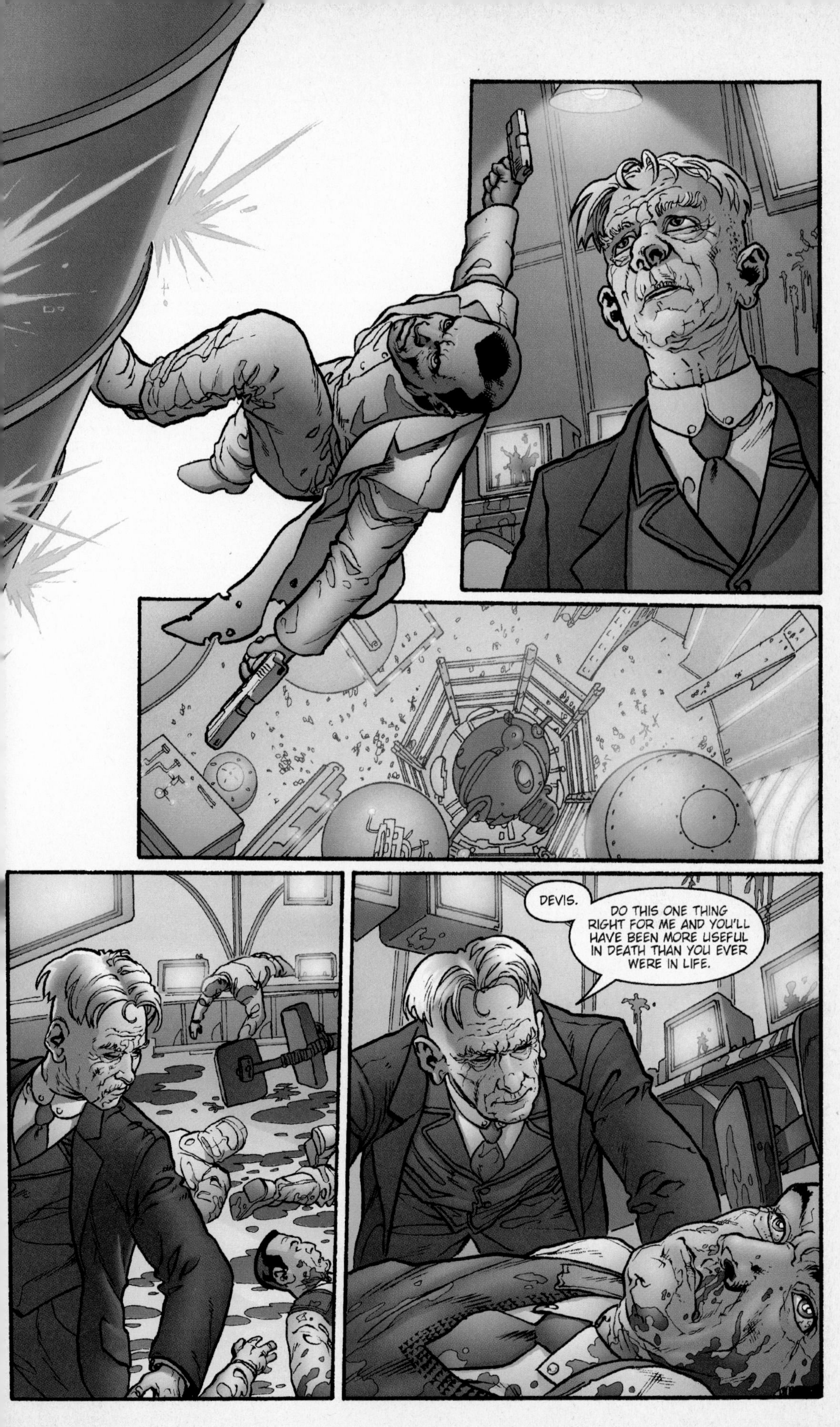
DEVIS.
DO THIS ONE THING RIGHT FOR ME AND YOU'LL HAVE BEEN MORE USEFUL IN DEATH THAN YOU EVER WERE IN LIFE.

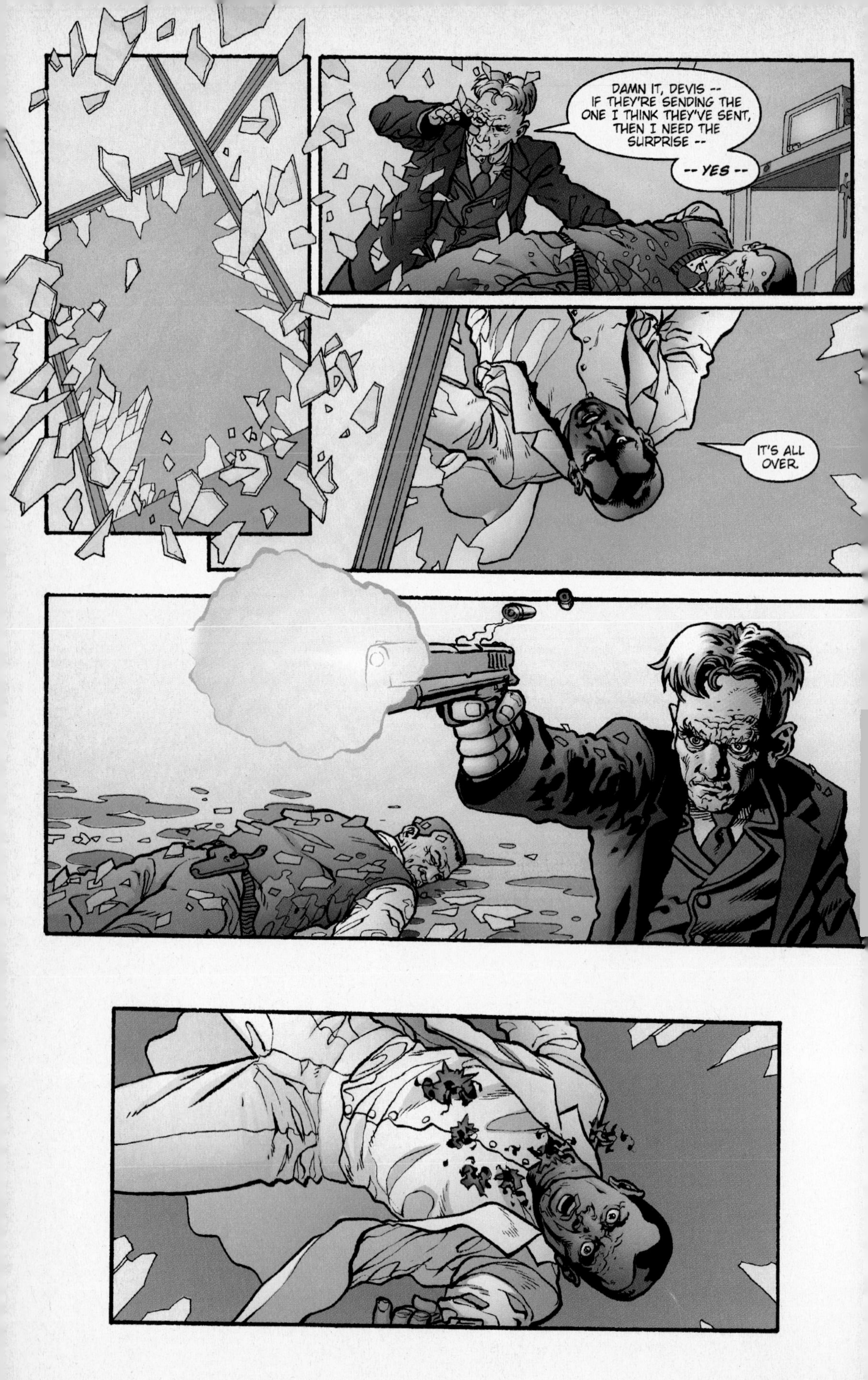
DAMN IT, DEVIS -- IF THEY'RE SENDING THE ONE I THINK THEY'VE SENT, THEN I NEED THE SURPRISE --
-- YES --
IT'S ALL OVER.

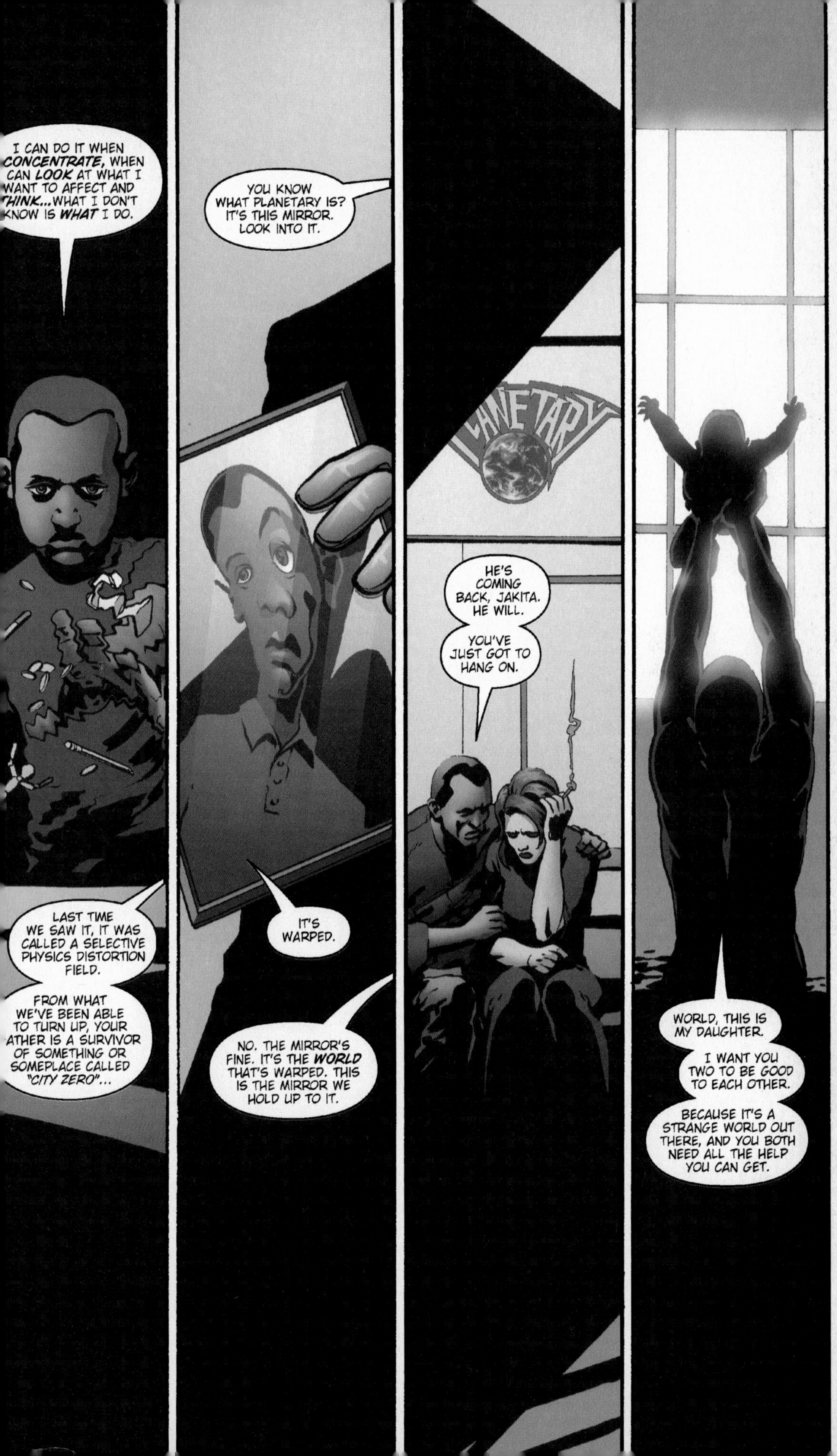
I CAN DO IT WHEN CONCENTRATE, WHEN CAN LOOK AT WHAT I WANT TO AFFECT AND THINK...WHAT I DON'T KNOW IS WHAT I DO.
LAST TIME WE SAW IT, IT WAS CALLED A SELECTIVE PHYSICS DISTORTION FIELD.
FROM WHAT WE'VE BEEN ABLE TO TURN UP, YOUR ATHER IS A SURVIVOR OF SOMETHING OR SOMEPLACE CALLED "CITY ZERO"...
YOU KNOW WHAT PLANETARY IS? IT'S THIS MIRROR. LOOK INTO IT.
IT'S WARPED.
NO. THE MIRROR'S FINE. IT'S THE WORLD THAT'S WARPED. THIS IS THE MIRROR WE HOLD UP TO IT.
LANETARY
HE'S COMING BACK, JAKITA. HE WILL.
YOU'VE JUST GOT TO HANG ON.
WORLD, THIS IS MY DAUGHTER.
I WANT YOU TWO TO BE GOOD TO EACH OTHER.
BECAUSE IT'S A STRANGE WORLD OUT THERE, AND YOU BOTH NEED ALL THE HELP YOU CAN GET.

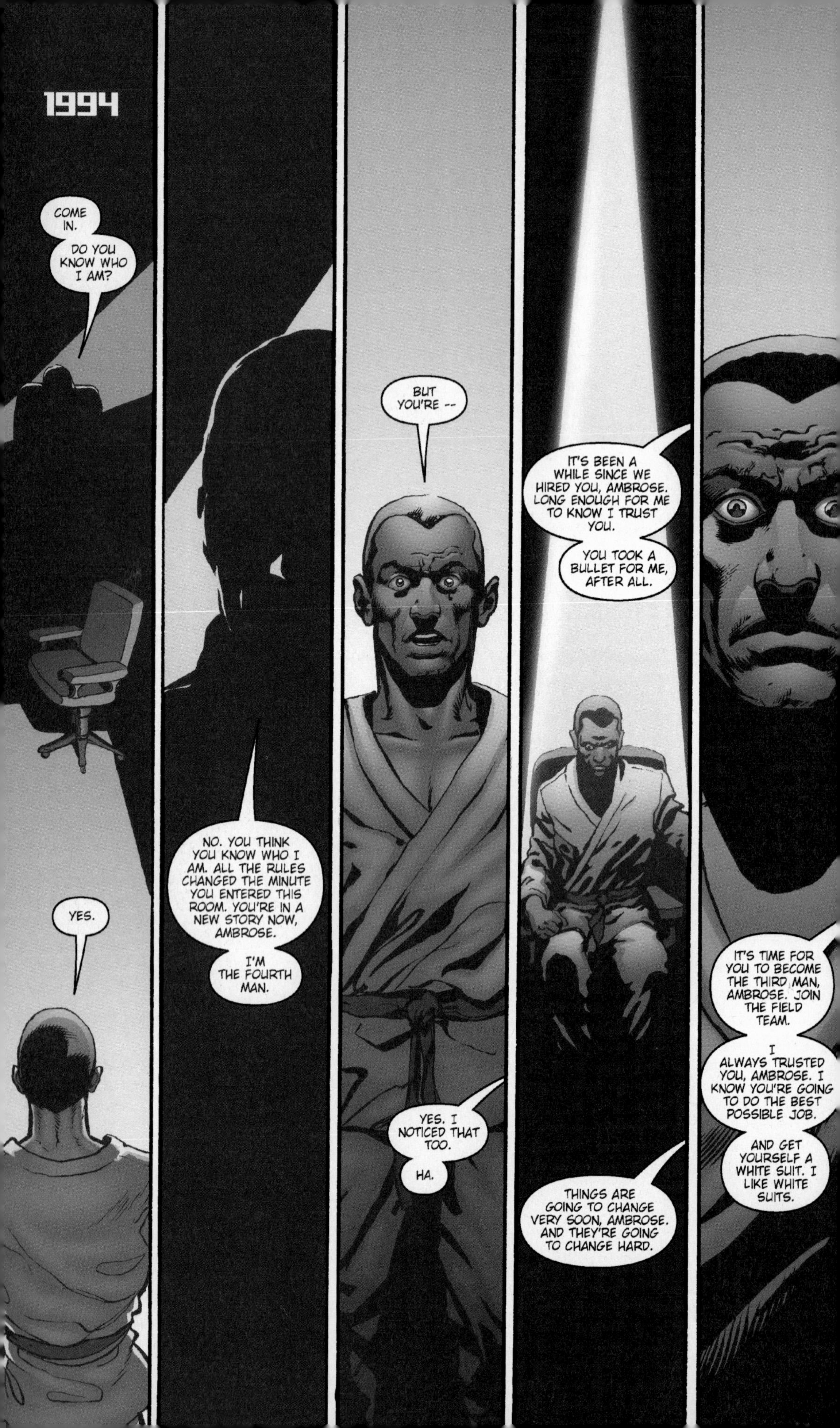
1994
COME IN.
DO YOU KNOW WHO I AM?
YES.
NO. YOU THINK YOU KNOW WHO I AM. ALL THE RULES CHANGED THE MINUTE YOU ENTERED THIS ROOM. YOU'RE IN A NEW STORY NOW, AMBROSE.
I'M THE FOURTH MAN.
BUT YOU'RE --
YES. I NOTICED THAT TOO.
HA.
IT'S BEEN A WHILE SINCE WE HIRED YOU, AMBROSE. LONG ENOUGH FOR ME TO KNOW I TRUST YOU.
YOU TOOK A BULLET FOR ME, AFTER ALL.
THINGS ARE GOING TO CHANGE VERY SOON, AMBROSE. AND THEY'RE GOING TO CHANGE HARD.
IT'S TIME FOR YOU TO BECOME THE THIRD MAN, AMBROSE. JOIN THE FIELD TEAM.
I ALWAYS TRUSTED YOU, AMBROSE. I KNOW YOU'RE GOING TO DO THE BEST POSSIBLE JOB.
AND GET YOURSELF A WHITE SUIT. I LIKE WHITE SUITS.

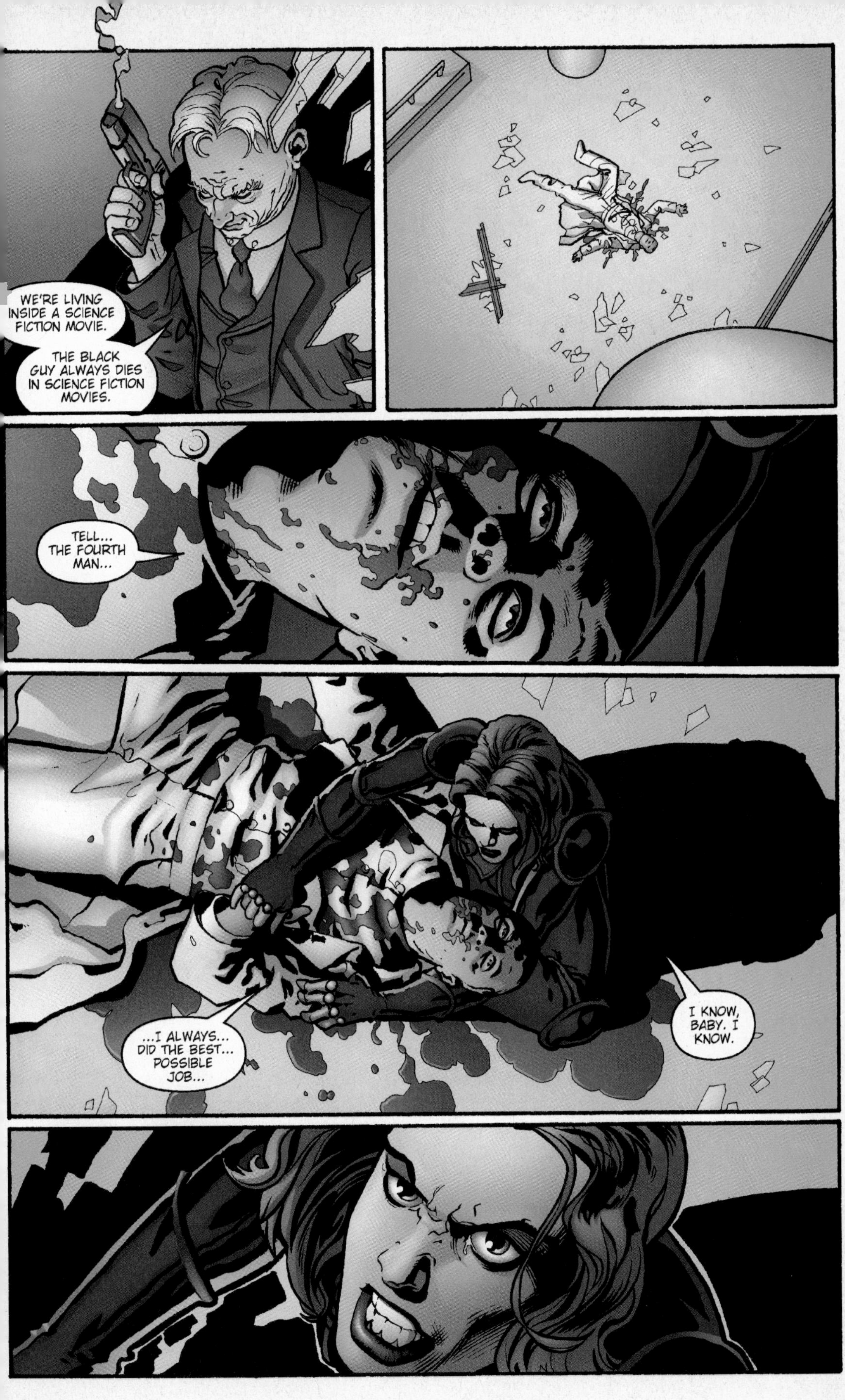
WE'RE LIVING INSIDE A SCIENCE FICTION MOVIE.
THE BLACK GUY ALWAYS DIES IN SCIENCE FICTION MOVIES.
TELL... THE FOURTH MAN...
...I ALWAYS... DID THE BEST... POSSIBLE JOB...
I KNOW, BABY. I KNOW.

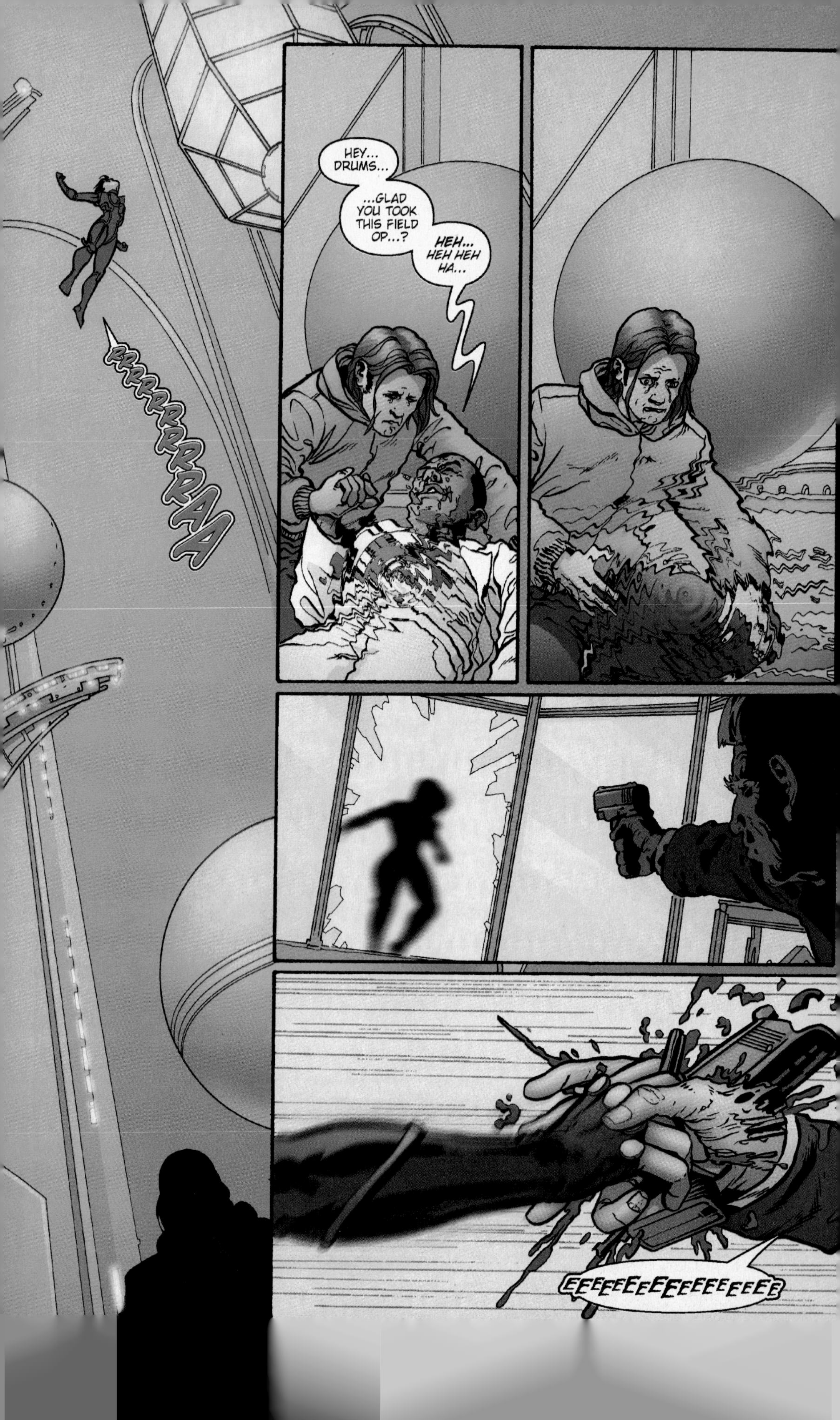
RRRRRRRRRAA
HEY... DRUMS...
...GLAD YOU TOOK THIS FIELD OP...?
HEH... HEH HEH HA...
EEEEEEEEEEEEEEEEE

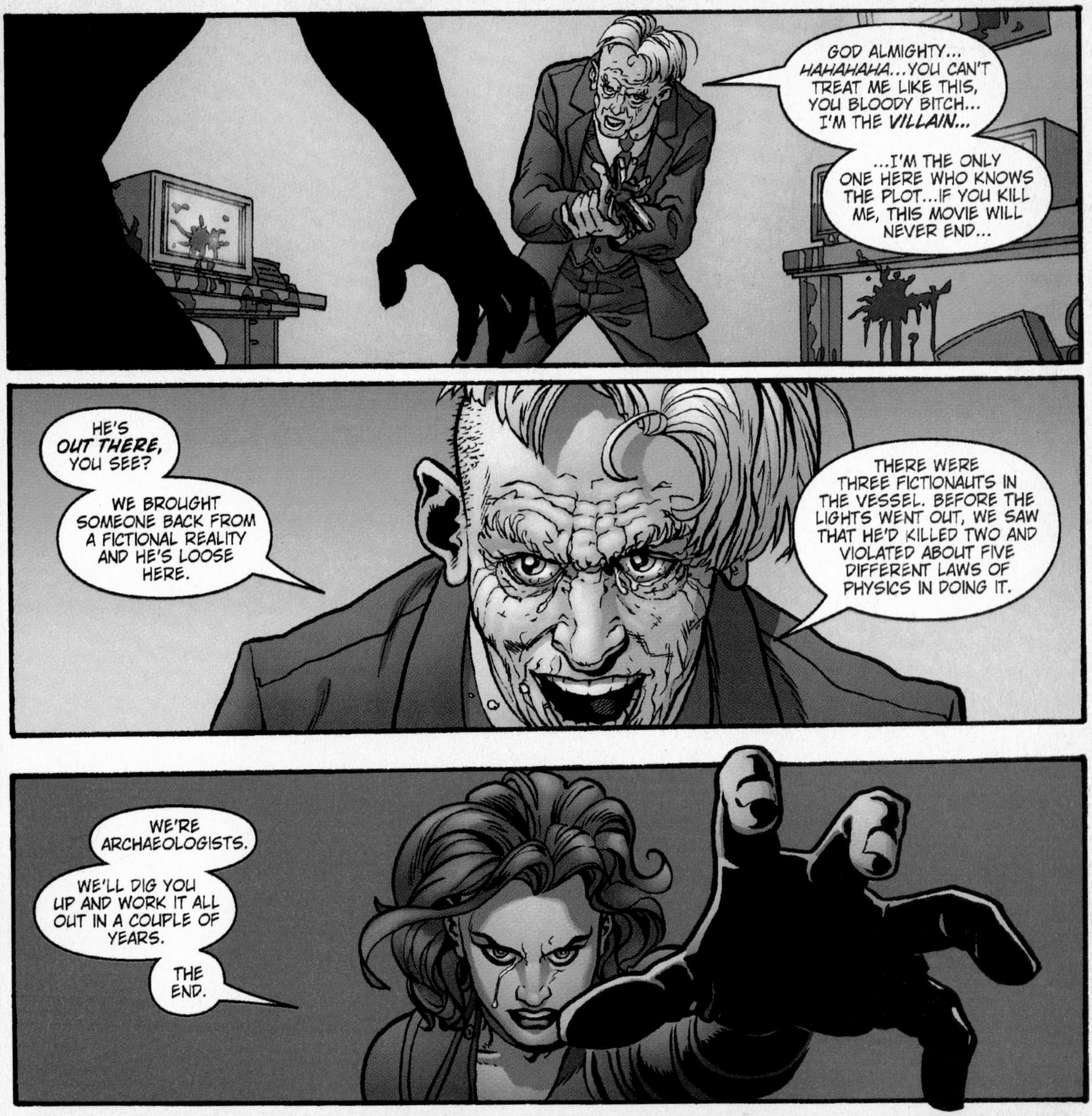
GOD ALMIGHTY... HAHAHAHA...YOU CAN'T TREAT ME LIKE THIS, YOU BLOODY BITCH... I'M THE VILLAIN...
...I'M THE ONLY ONE HERE WHO KNOWS THE PLOT...IF YOU KILL ME, THIS MOVIE WILL NEVER END...
HE'S OUT THERE, YOU SEE?
WE BROUGHT SOMEONE BACK FROM A FICTIONAL REALITY AND HE'S LOOSE HERE.
THERE WERE THREE FICTIONAUTS IN THE VESSEL. BEFORE THE LIGHTS WENT OUT, WE SAW THAT HE'D KILLED TWO AND VIOLATED ABOUT FIVE DIFFERENT LAWS OF PHYSICS IN DOING IT.
WE'RE ARCHAEOLOGISTS.
WE'LL DIG YOU UP AND WORK IT ALL OUT IN A COUPLE OF YEARS.
THE END.

IN 1997, THE FOURTH MAN WAS MISSING IN ACTION.

ELIJAH SNOW HAS NEVER HEARD OF AMBROSE CHASE.

JAKITA WAGNER WAS ALREADY A MEMBER OF PLANETARY WHEN AMBROSE CHASE BECAME THE THIRD MAN.

THE FOURTH INDIVIDUAL BROUGHT BACK FROM THE SAMPLE RETURN MISSION IS STILL AT LARGE.

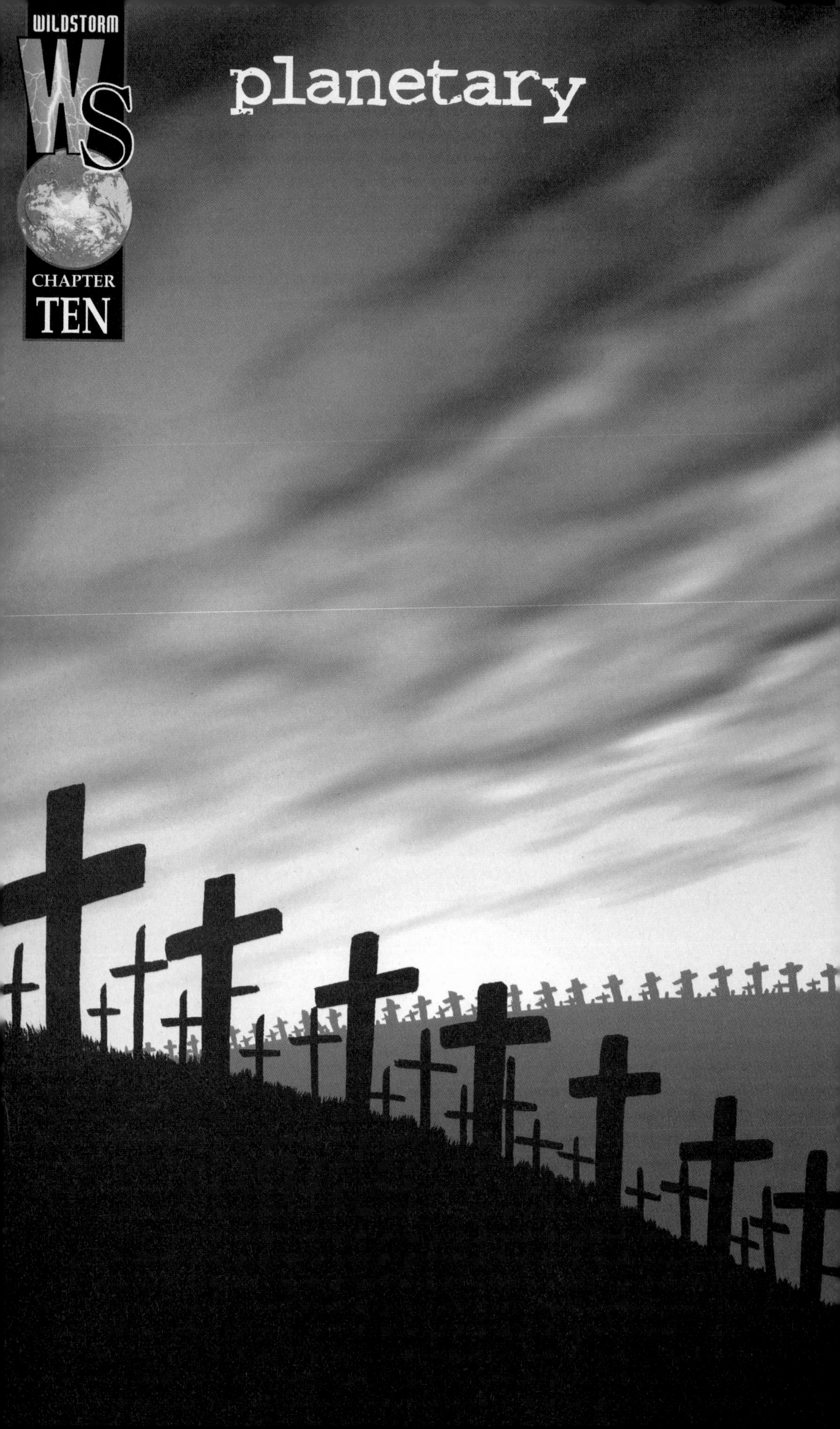
WILDSTORM
planetary
CHAPTER
TEN

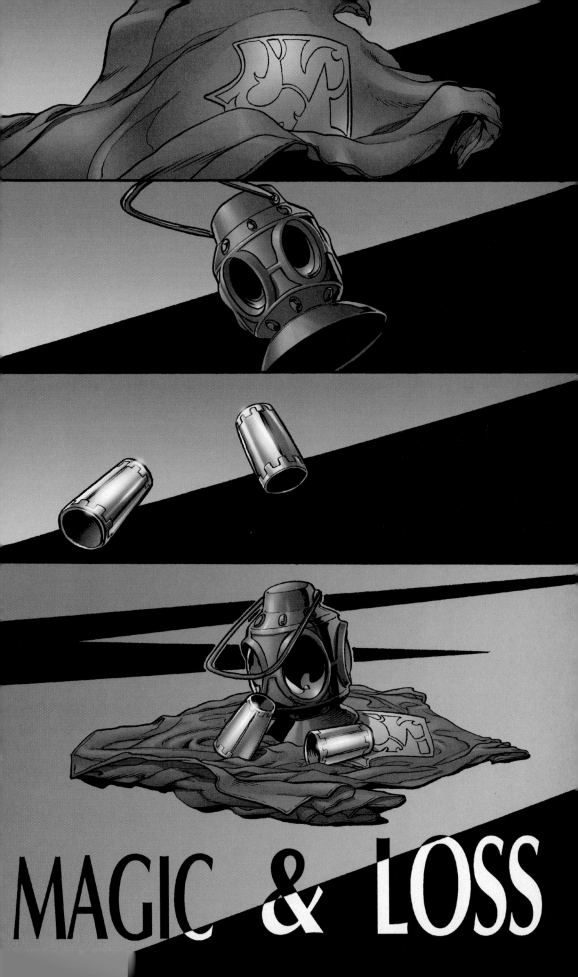

MAGIC & LOSS

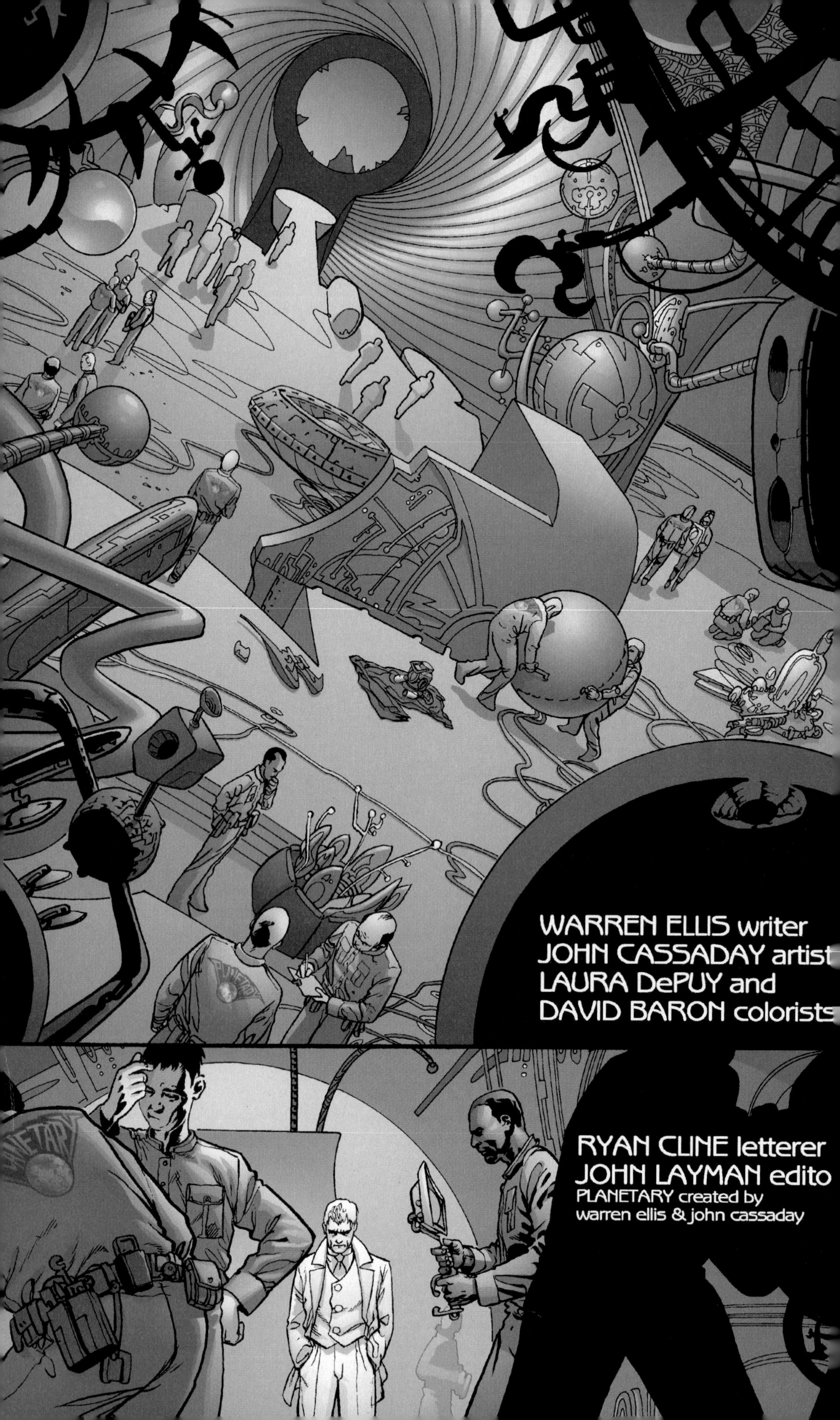
WARREN ELLIS writer
JOHN CASSADAY artist
LAURA DePUY and
DAVID BARON colorists
RYAN CLINE letterer
JOHN LAYMAN edito
PLANETARY created by
warren ellis & john cassaday

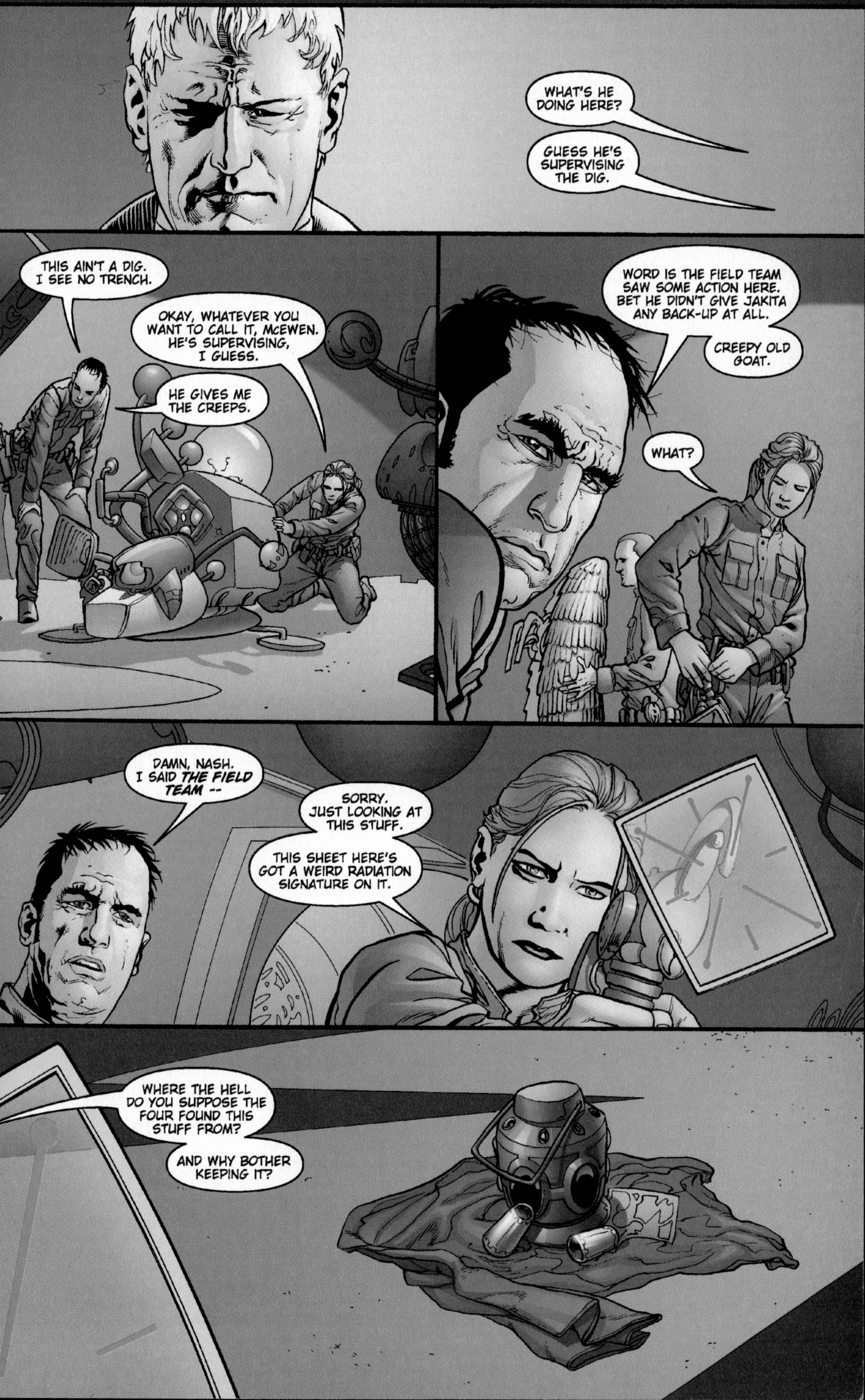
WHAT'S HE DOING HERE?
GUESS HE'S SUPERVISING THE DIG.
THIS AIN'T A DIG. I SEE NO TRENCH.
OKAY, WHATEVER YOU WANT TO CALL IT, McEWEN. HE'S SUPERVISING, I GUESS.
HE GIVES ME THE CREEPS.
WORD IS THE FIELD TEAM SAW SOME ACTION HERE. BET HE DIDN'T GIVE JAKITA ANY BACK-UP AT ALL.
CREEPY OLD GOAT.
WHAT?
DAMN, NASH. I SAID *THE FIELD TEAM* --
SORRY. JUST LOOKING AT THIS STUFF.
THIS SHEET HERE'S GOT A WEIRD RADIATION SIGNATURE ON IT.
WHERE THE HELL DO YOU SUPPOSE THE FOUR FOUND THIS STUFF FROM?
AND WHY BOTHER KEEPING IT?

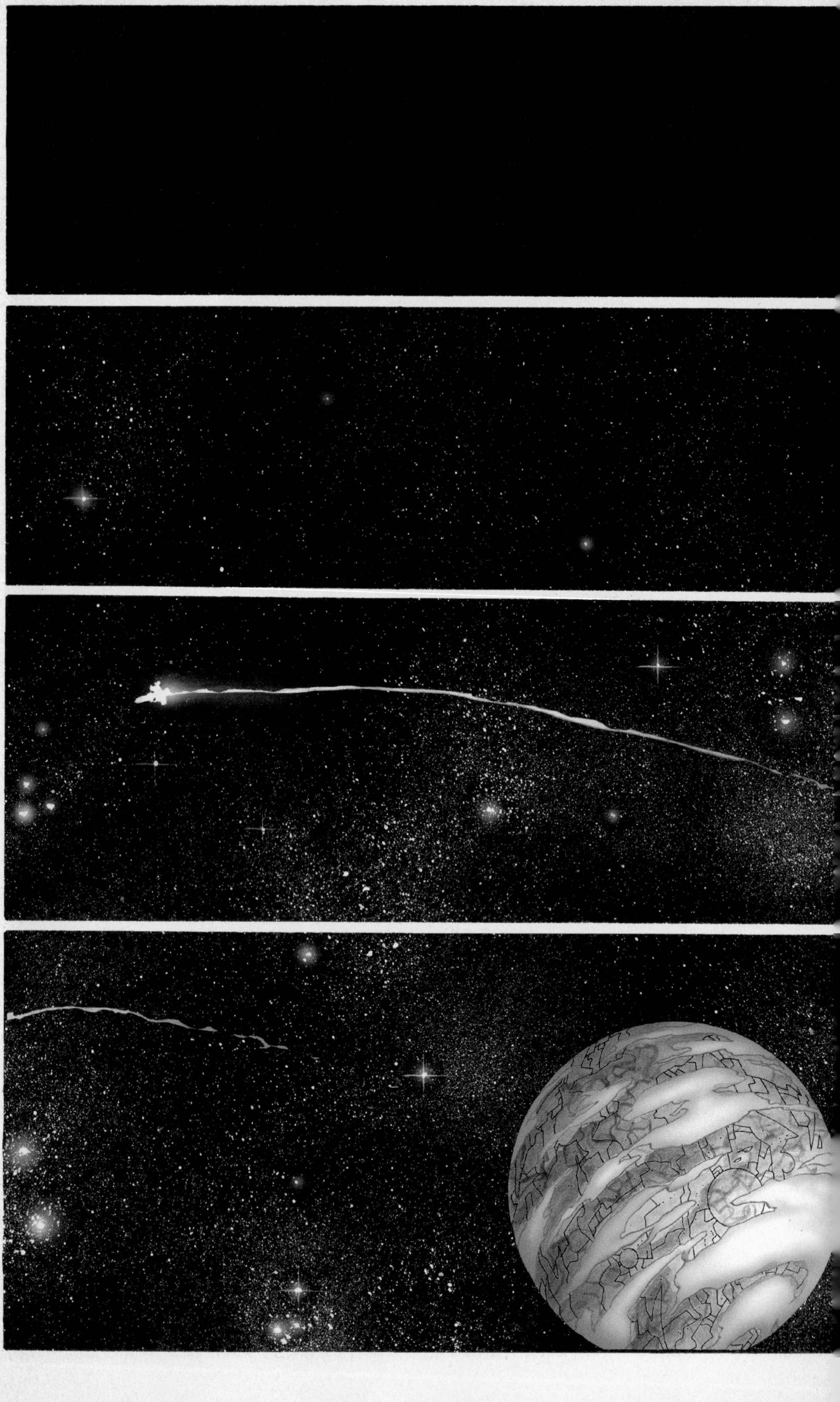

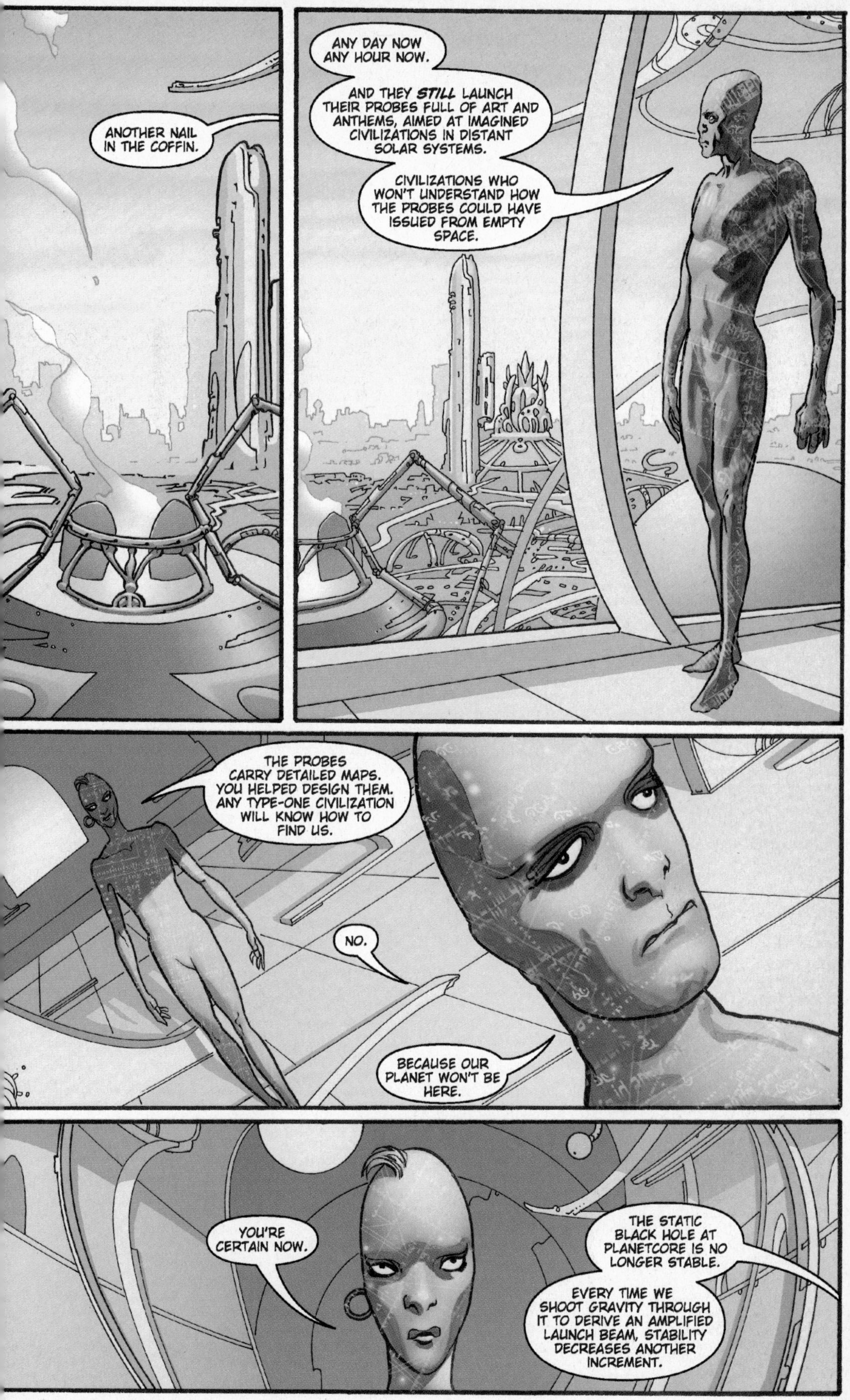
ANOTHER NAIL IN THE COFFIN.
ANY DAY NOW ANY HOUR NOW.
AND THEY STILL LAUNCH THEIR PROBES FULL OF ART AND ANTHEMS, AIMED AT IMAGINED CIVILIZATIONS IN DISTANT SOLAR SYSTEMS.
CIVILIZATIONS WHO WON'T UNDERSTAND HOW THE PROBES COULD HAVE ISSUED FROM EMPTY SPACE.
THE PROBES CARRY DETAILED MAPS. YOU HELPED DESIGN THEM. ANY TYPE-ONE CIVILIZATION WILL KNOW HOW TO FIND US.
NO.
BECAUSE OUR PLANET WON'T BE HERE.
YOU'RE CERTAIN NOW.
THE STATIC BLACK HOLE AT PLANETCORE IS NO LONGER STABLE.
EVERY TIME WE SHOOT GRAVITY THROUGH IT TO DERIVE AN AMPLIFIED LAUNCH BEAM, STABILITY DECREASES ANOTHER INCREMENT.

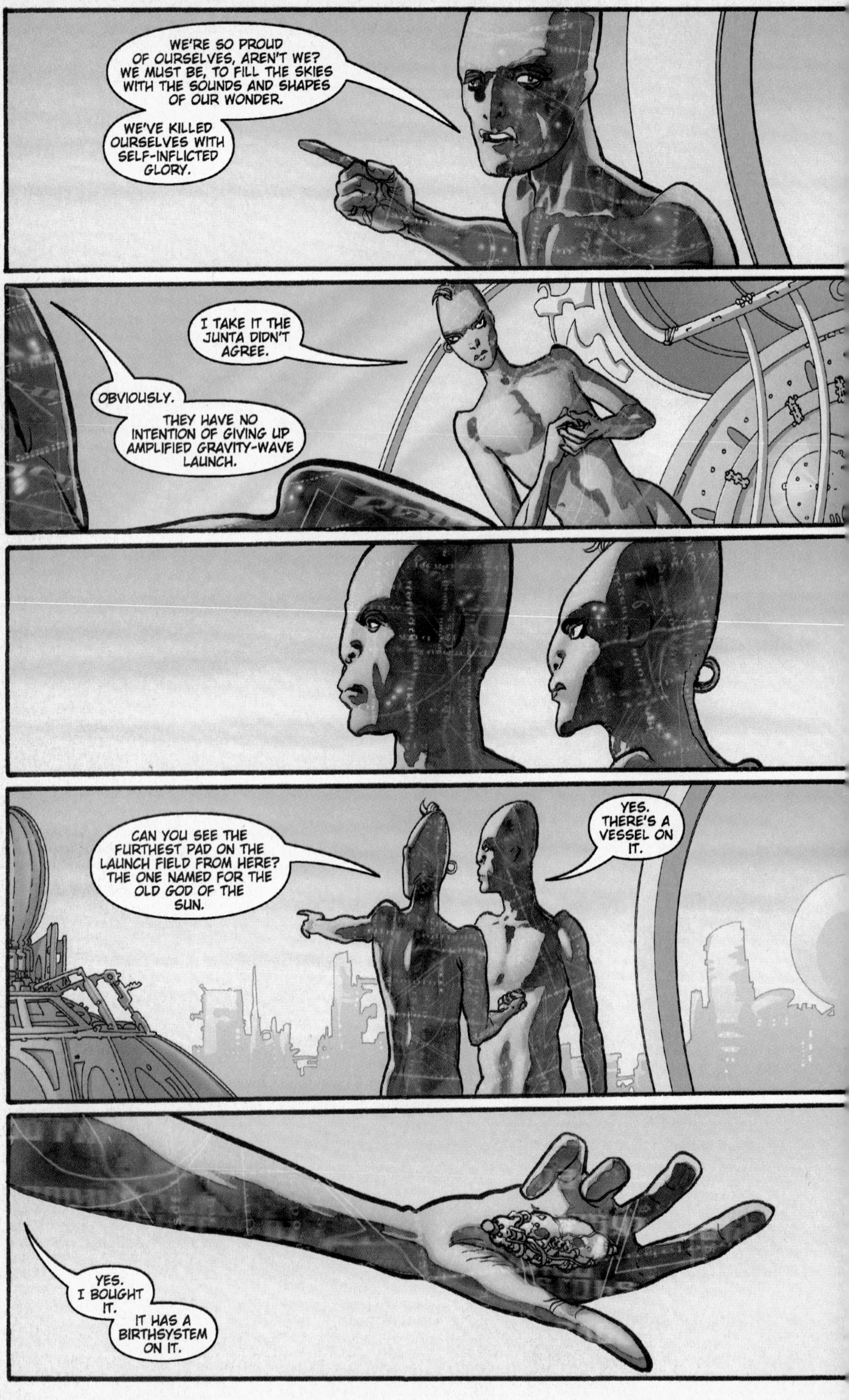
WE'RE SO PROUD OF OURSELVES, AREN'T WE? WE MUST BE, TO FILL THE SKIES WITH THE SOUNDS AND SHAPES OF OUR WONDER.
WE'VE KILLED OURSELVES WITH SELF-INFLICTED GLORY.
I TAKE IT THE JUNTA DIDN'T AGREE.
OBVIOUSLY.
THEY HAVE NO INTENTION OF GIVING UP AMPLIFIED GRAVITY-WAVE LAUNCH.
CAN YOU SEE THE FURTHEST PAD ON THE LAUNCH FIELD FROM HERE? THE ONE NAMED FOR THE OLD GOD OF THE SUN.
YES. THERE'S A VESSEL ON IT.
YES. I BOUGHT IT.
IT HAS A BIRTHSYSTEM ON IT.

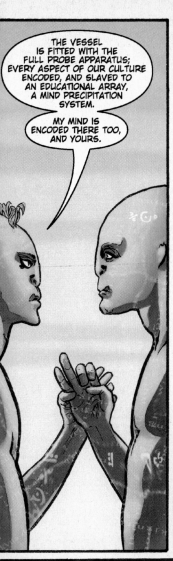

THE VESSEL IS FITTED WITH THE FULL PROBE APPARATUS; EVERY ASPECT OF OUR CULTURE ENCODED, AND SLAVED TO AN EDUCATIONAL ARRAY, A MIND PRECIPITATION SYSTEM.

MY MIND IS ENCODED THERE TOO, AND YOURS.

ACTUATE, AND THE PROBE IS LAUNCHED, THE BIRTHSYSTEM INITIATED.

THE CHILD WILL BE INCARNATE WHEN IT TOUCHES DOWN. THE PROBE IS AIMED AT A WORLD HIGH IN THE NORTH SPIRAL ARM WITH PERFECT ENVIRONMENT.

WE TALKED ABOUT INITIATING CHILDREN, BUT BUILDING NEW LIFE ON A DOOMED WORLD IS JUST A SICK JOKE.

ACTUATION

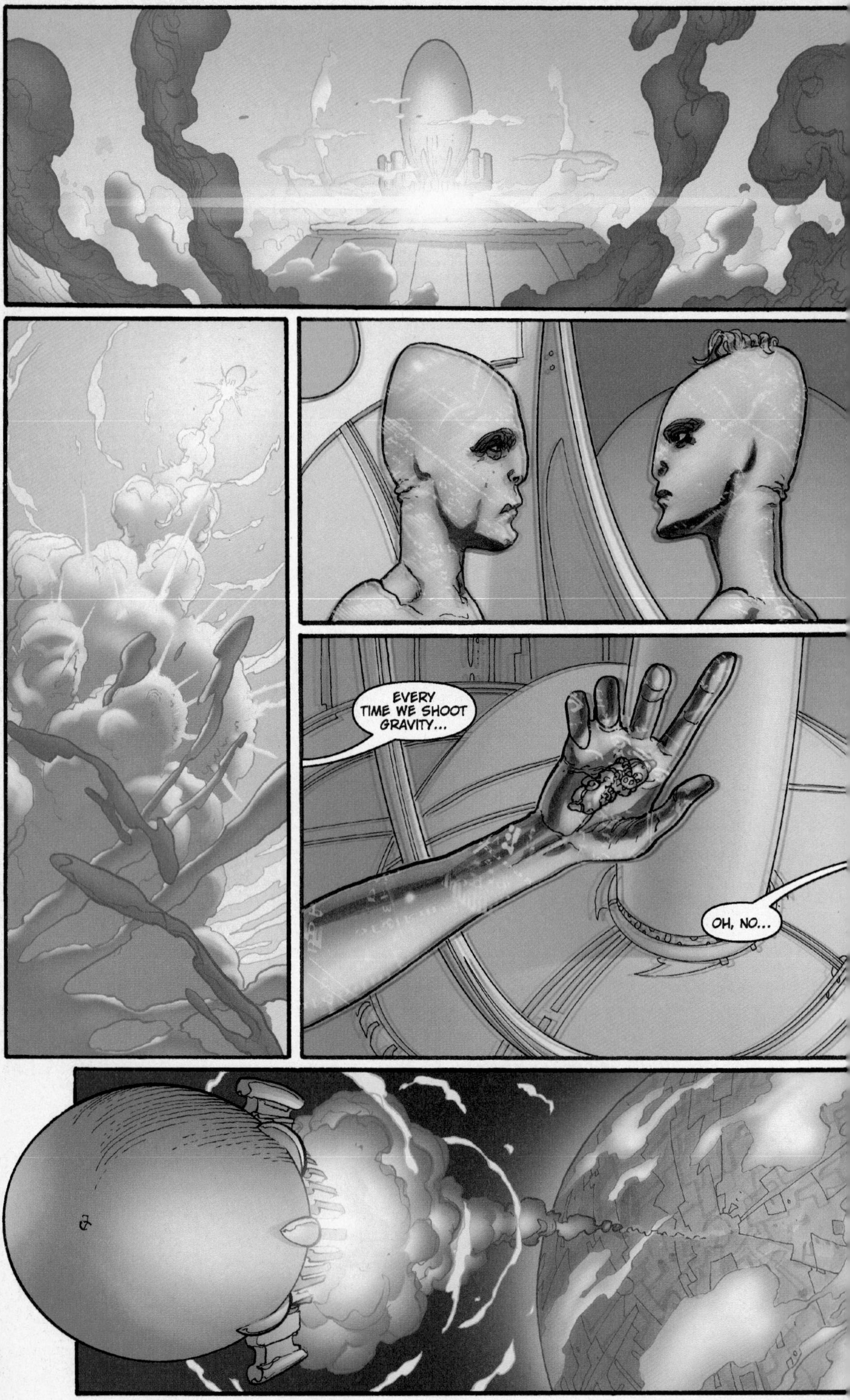
EVERY TIME WE SHOOT GRAVITY...
OH, NO...

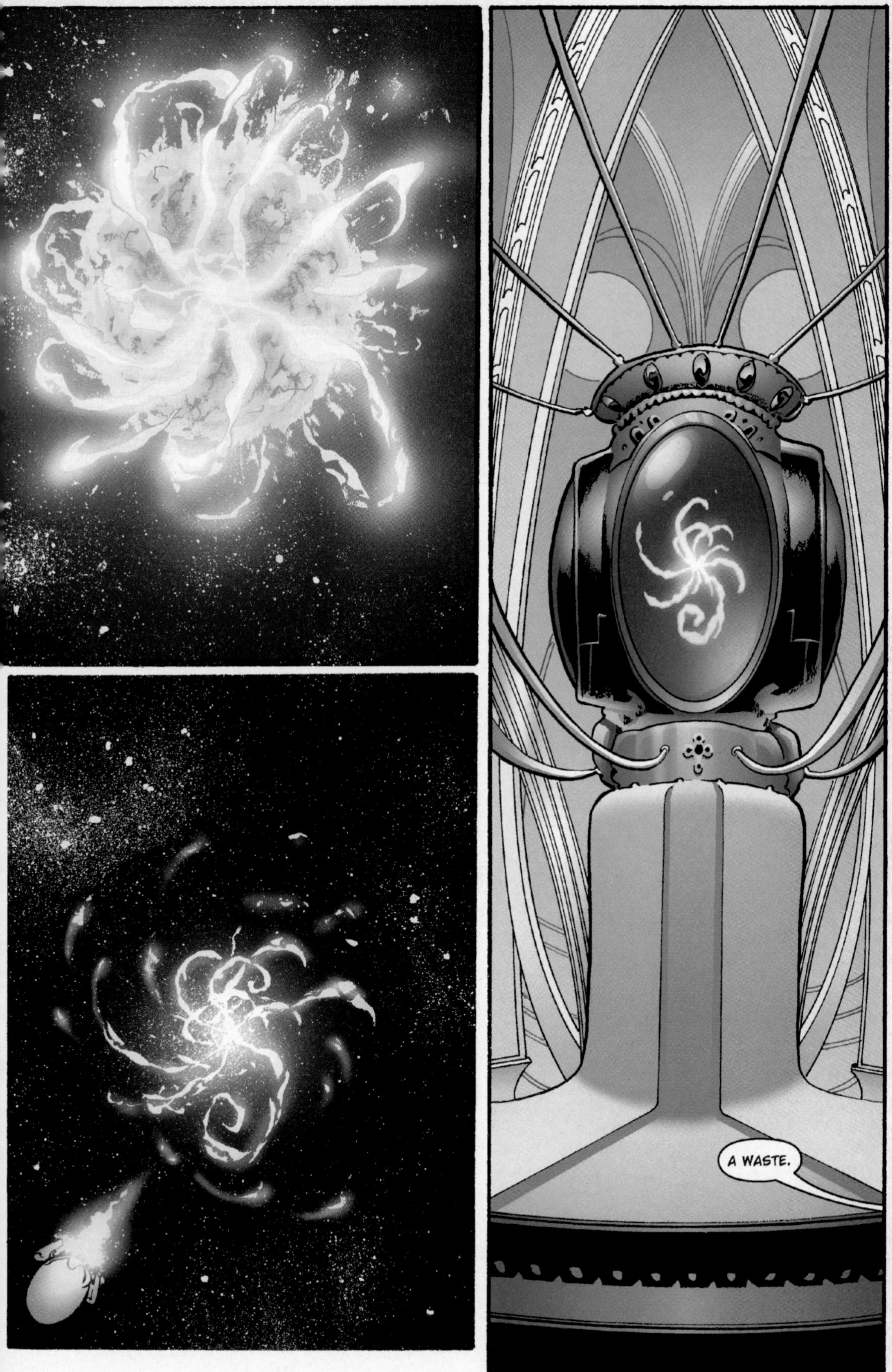
A WASTE.

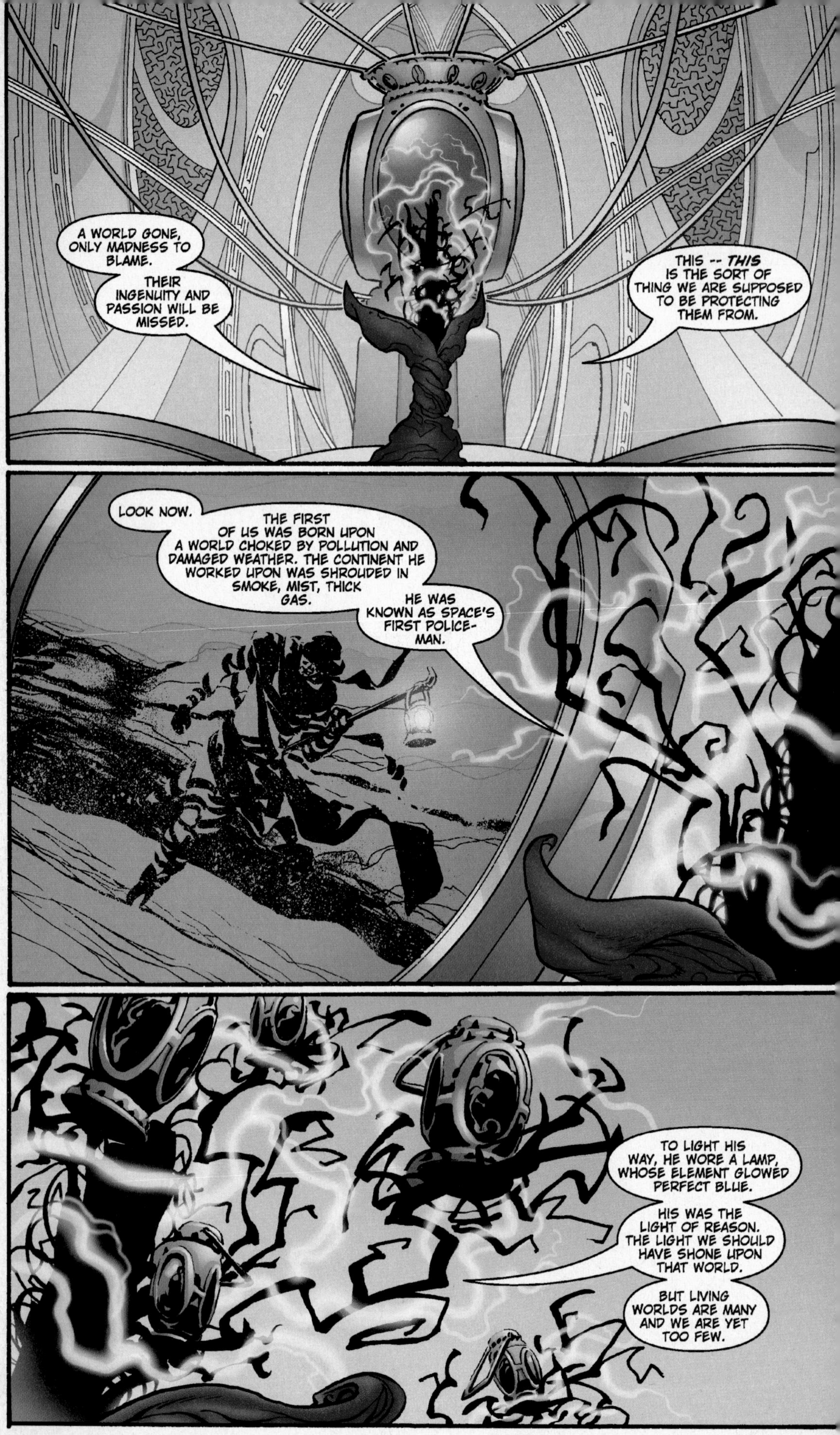
A WORLD GONE, ONLY MADNESS TO BLAME.
THEIR INGENUITY AND PASSION WILL BE MISSED.
THIS -- *THIS* IS THE SORT OF THING WE ARE SUPPOSED TO BE PROTECTING THEM FROM.
LOOK NOW.
THE FIRST OF US WAS BORN UPON A WORLD CHOKED BY POLLUTION AND DAMAGED WEATHER. THE CONTINENT HE WORKED UPON WAS SHROUDED IN SMOKE, MIST, THICK GAS.
HE WAS KNOWN AS SPACE'S FIRST POLICE-MAN.
TO LIGHT HIS WAY, HE WORE A LAMP, WHOSE ELEMENT GLOWED PERFECT BLUE.
HIS WAS THE LIGHT OF REASON. THE LIGHT WE SHOULD HAVE SHONE UPON THAT WORLD.
BUT LIVING WORLDS ARE MANY AND WE ARE YET TOO FEW.

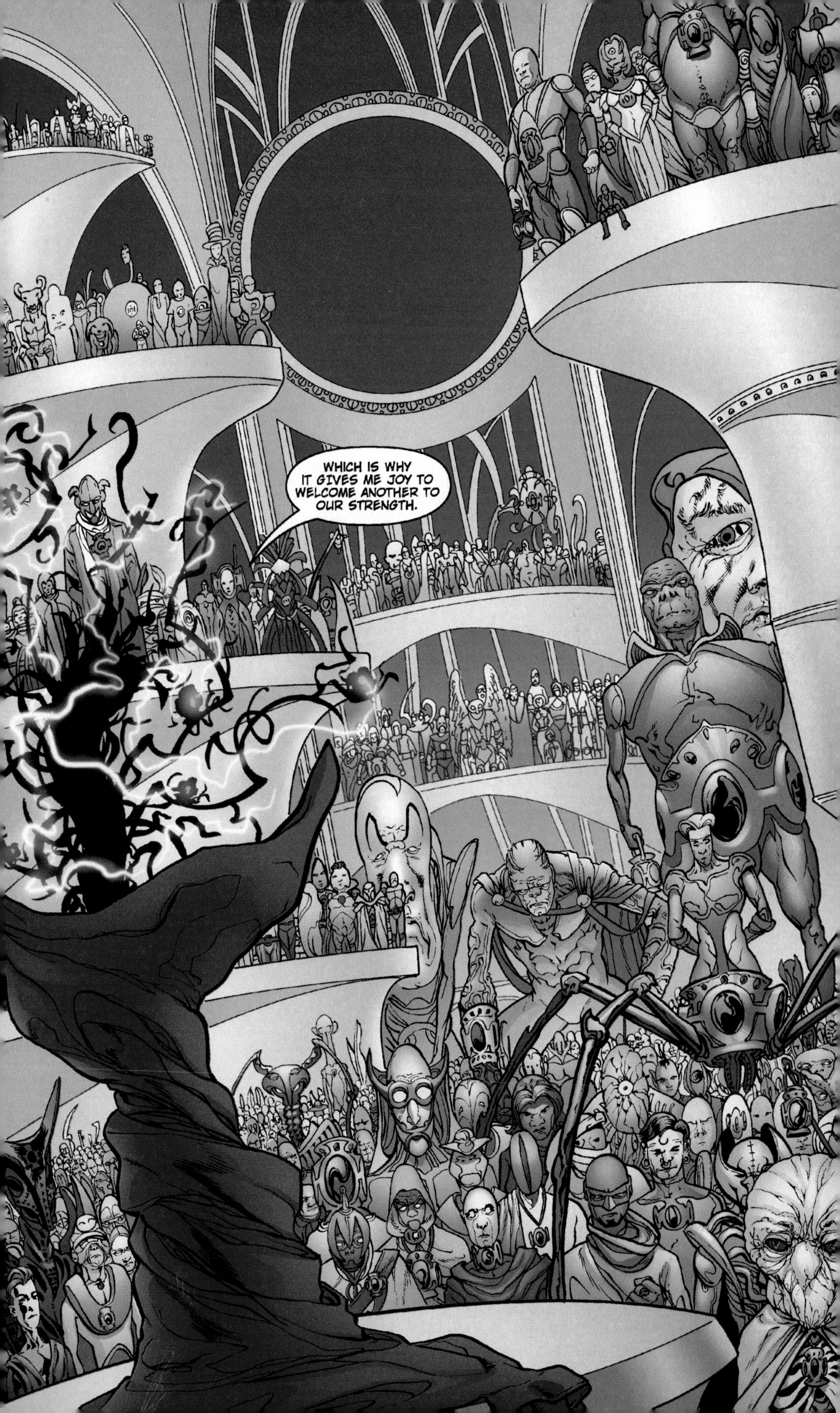
WHICH IS WHY IT GIVES ME JOY TO WELCOME ANOTHER TO OUR STRENGTH.

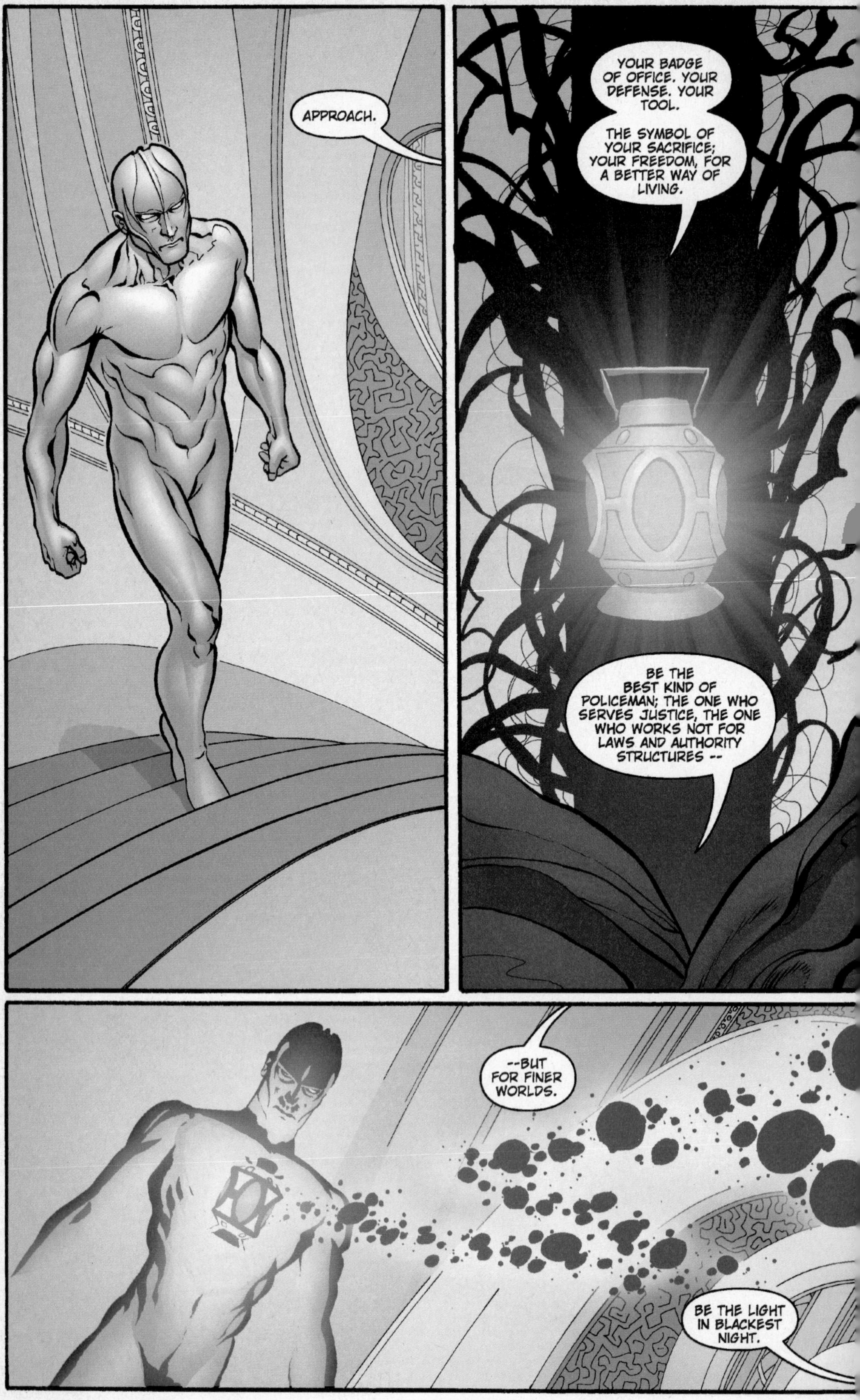

APPROACH.
YOUR BADGE OF OFFICE. YOUR DEFENSE. YOUR TOOL.
THE SYMBOL OF YOUR SACRIFICE; YOUR FREEDOM, FOR A BETTER WAY OF LIVING.
BE THE BEST KIND OF POLICEMAN; THE ONE WHO SERVES JUSTICE, THE ONE WHO WORKS NOT FOR LAWS AND AUTHORITY STRUCTURES --
--BUT FOR FINER WORLDS.
BE THE LIGHT IN BLACKEST NIGHT.

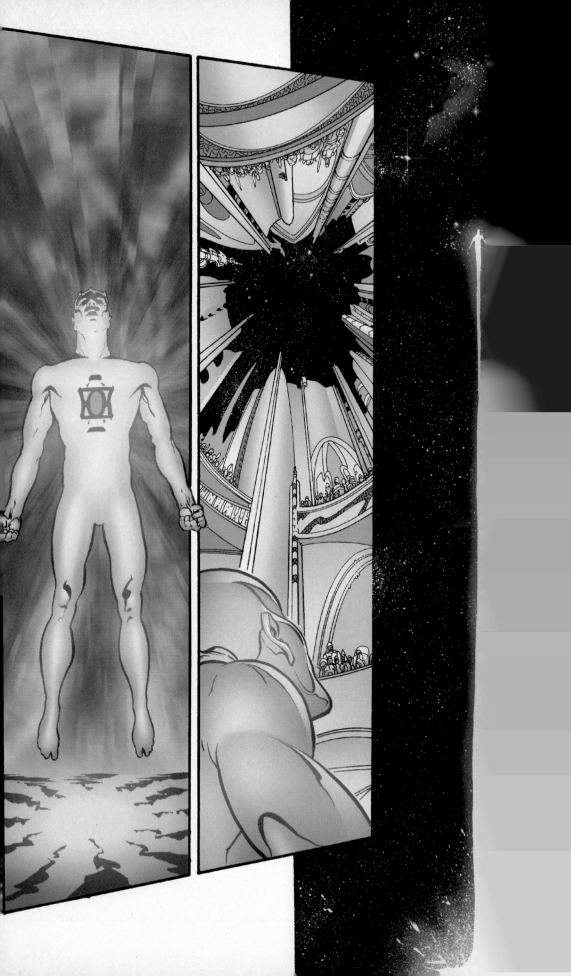

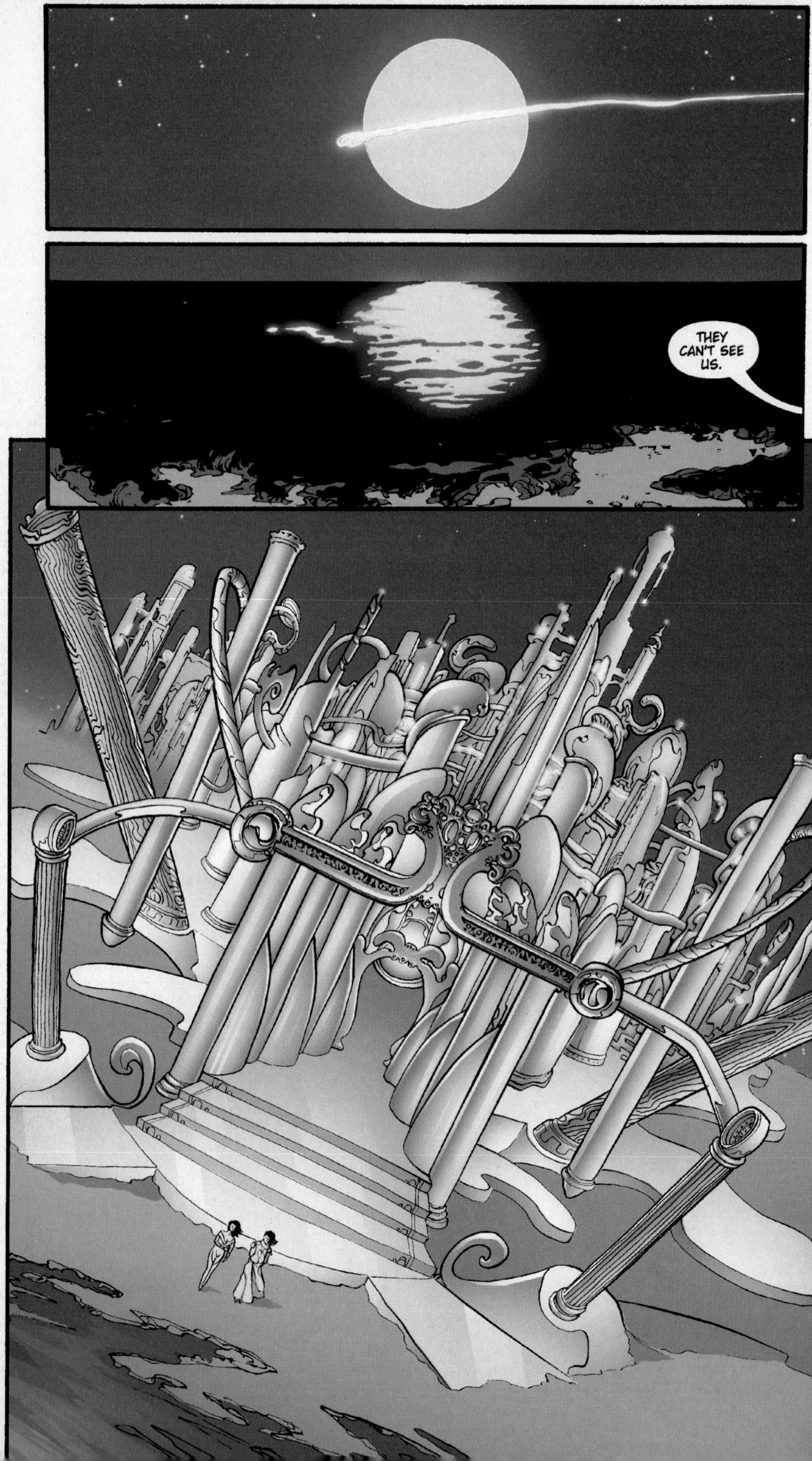
THEY CAN'T SEE US.

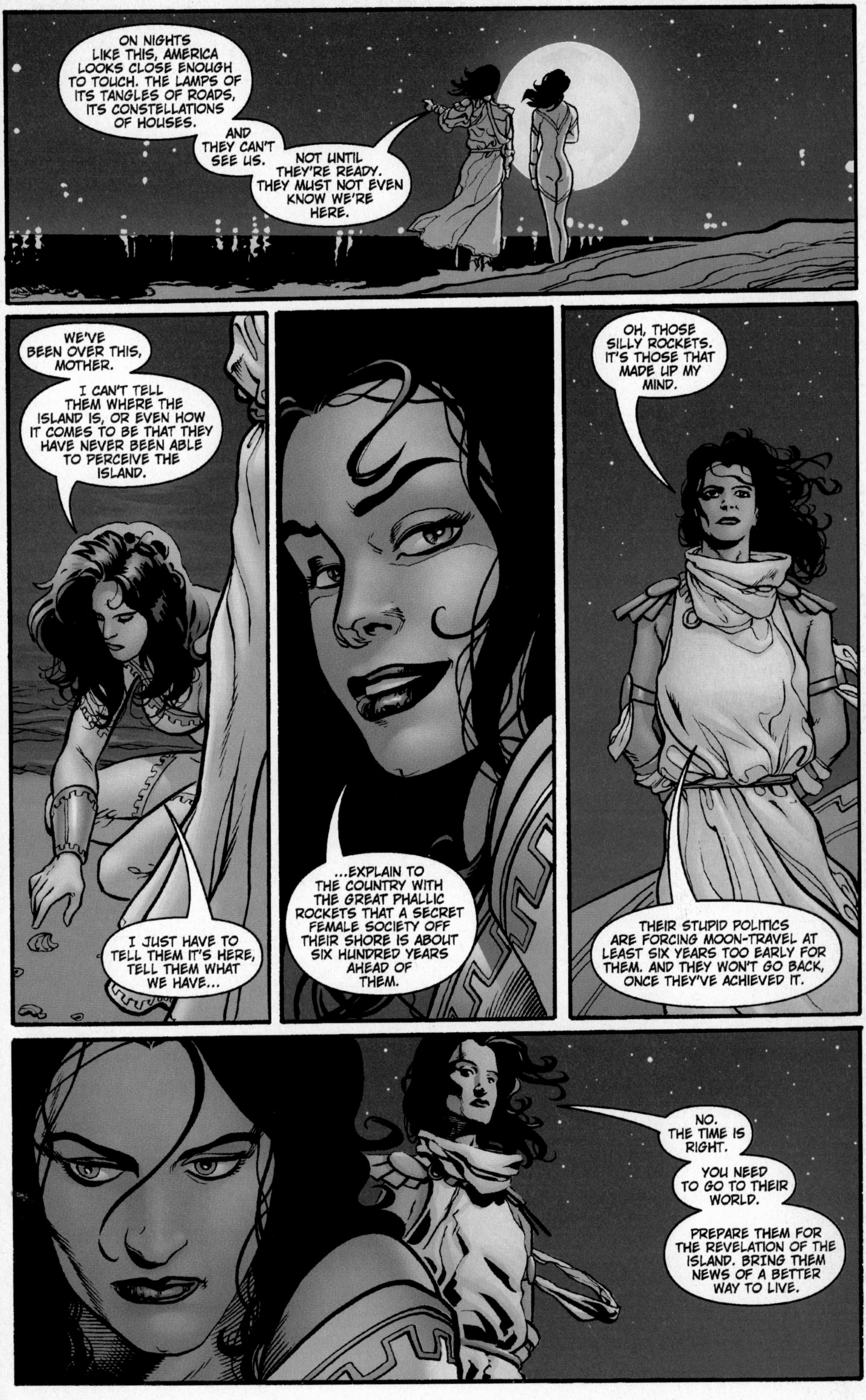
ON NIGHTS LIKE THIS, AMERICA LOOKS CLOSE ENOUGH TO TOUCH. THE LAMPS OF ITS TANGLES OF ROADS, ITS CONSTELLATIONS OF HOUSES.
AND THEY CAN'T SEE US.
NOT UNTIL THEY'RE READY. THEY MUST NOT EVEN KNOW WE'RE HERE.
WE'VE BEEN OVER THIS, MOTHER.
I CAN'T TELL THEM WHERE THE ISLAND IS, OR EVEN HOW IT COMES TO BE THAT THEY HAVE NEVER BEEN ABLE TO PERCEIVE THE ISLAND.
I JUST HAVE TO TELL THEM IT'S HERE, TELL THEM WHAT WE HAVE...
...EXPLAIN TO THE COUNTRY WITH THE GREAT PHALLIC ROCKETS THAT A SECRET FEMALE SOCIETY OFF THEIR SHORE IS ABOUT SIX HUNDRED YEARS AHEAD OF THEM.
OH, THOSE SILLY ROCKETS. IT'S THOSE THAT MADE UP MY MIND.
THEIR STUPID POLITICS ARE FORCING MOON-TRAVEL AT LEAST SIX YEARS TOO EARLY FOR THEM. AND THEY WON'T GO BACK, ONCE THEY'VE ACHIEVED IT.
NO. THE TIME IS RIGHT.
YOU NEED TO GO TO THEIR WORLD.
PREPARE THEM FOR THE REVELATION OF THE ISLAND. BRING THEM NEWS OF A BETTER WAY TO LIVE.

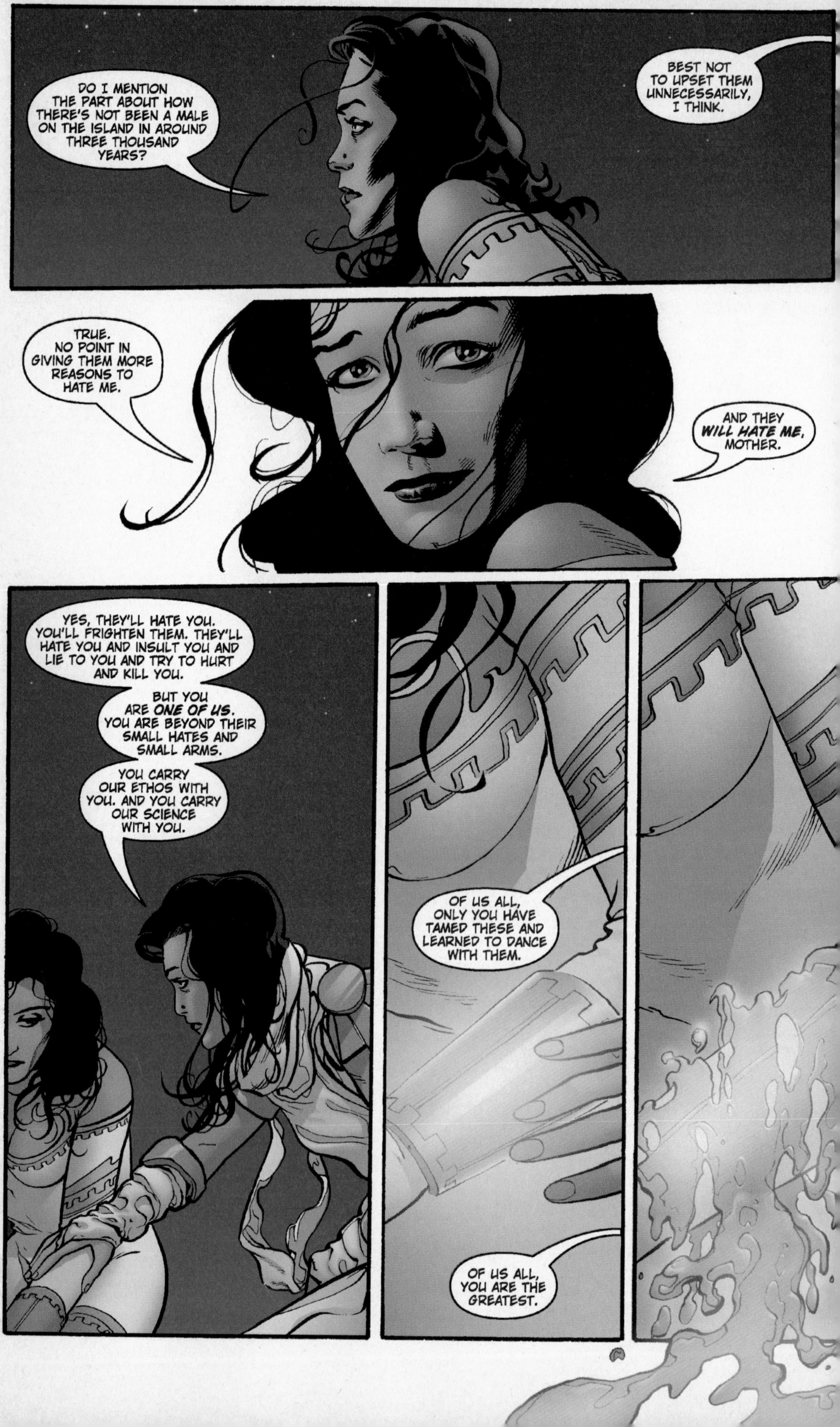
DO I MENTION THE PART ABOUT HOW THERE'S NOT BEEN A MALE ON THE ISLAND IN AROUND THREE THOUSAND YEARS?
BEST NOT TO UPSET THEM UNNECESSARILY, I THINK.
TRUE. NO POINT IN GIVING THEM MORE REASONS TO HATE ME.
AND THEY **WILL HATE ME**, MOTHER.
YES, THEY'LL HATE YOU. YOU'LL FRIGHTEN THEM. THEY'LL HATE YOU AND INSULT YOU AND LIE TO YOU AND TRY TO HURT AND KILL YOU.
BUT YOU ARE ***ONE OF US***. YOU ARE BEYOND THEIR SMALL HATES AND SMALL ARMS.
YOU CARRY OUR ETHOS WITH YOU. AND YOU CARRY OUR SCIENCE WITH YOU.
OF US ALL, ONLY YOU HAVE TAMED THESE AND LEARNED TO DANCE WITH THEM.
OF US ALL, YOU ARE THE GREATEST.

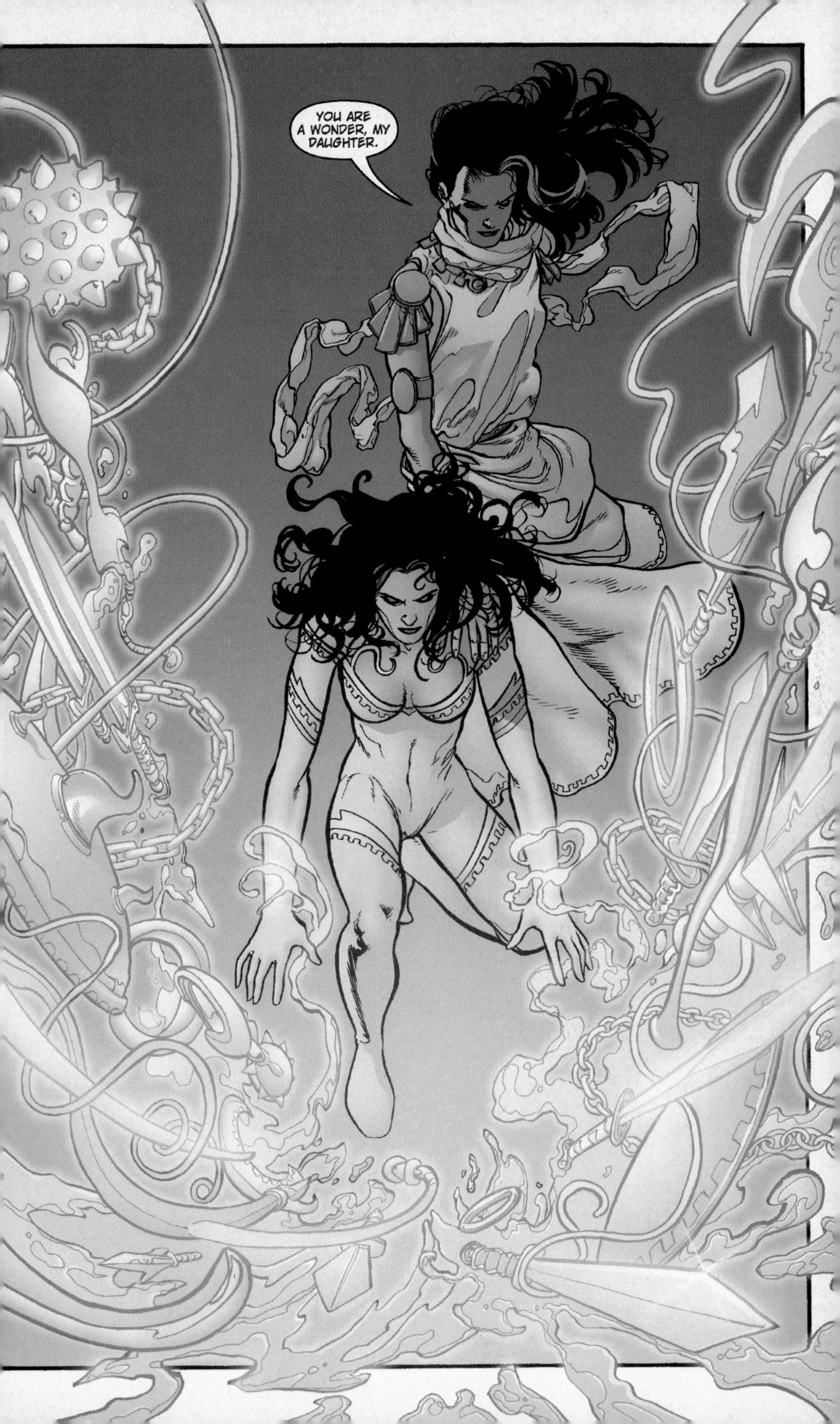
YOU ARE A WONDER, MY DAUGHTER.

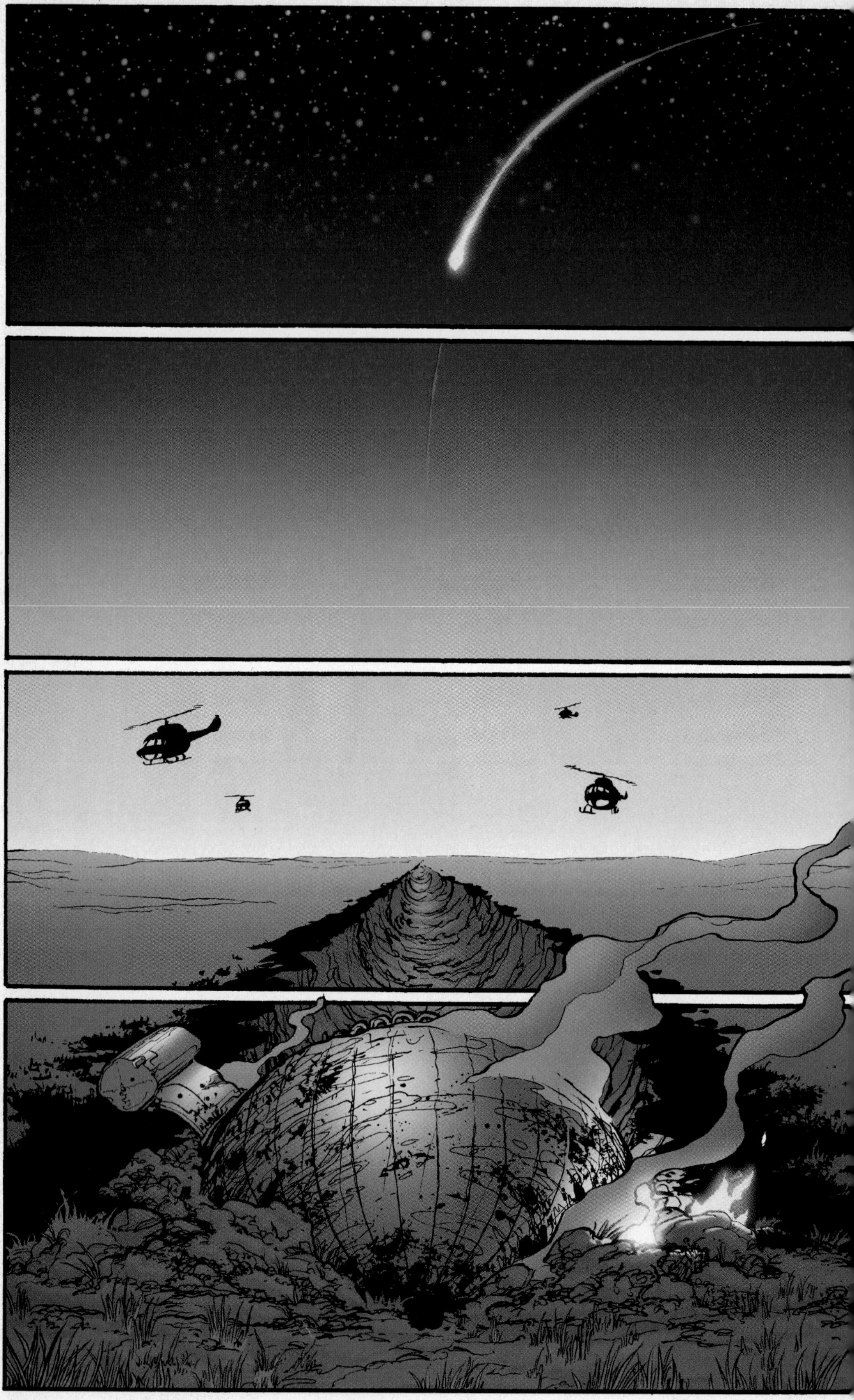

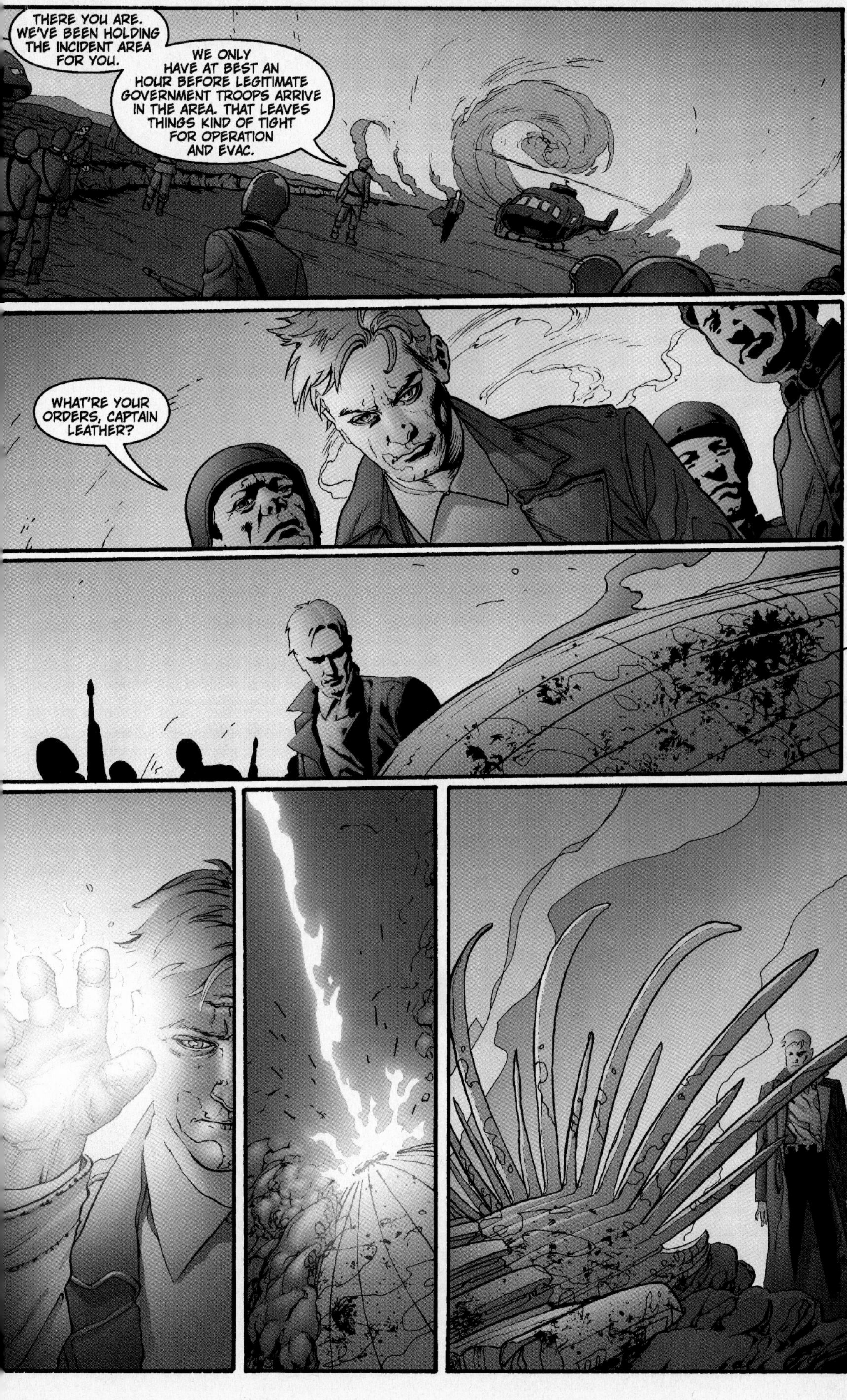
THERE YOU ARE. WE'VE BEEN HOLDING THE INCIDENT AREA FOR YOU.
WE ONLY HAVE AT BEST AN HOUR BEFORE LEGITIMATE GOVERNMENT TROOPS ARRIVE IN THE AREA. THAT LEAVES THINGS KIND OF TIGHT FOR OPERATION AND EVAC.
WHAT'RE YOUR ORDERS, CAPTAIN LEATHER?

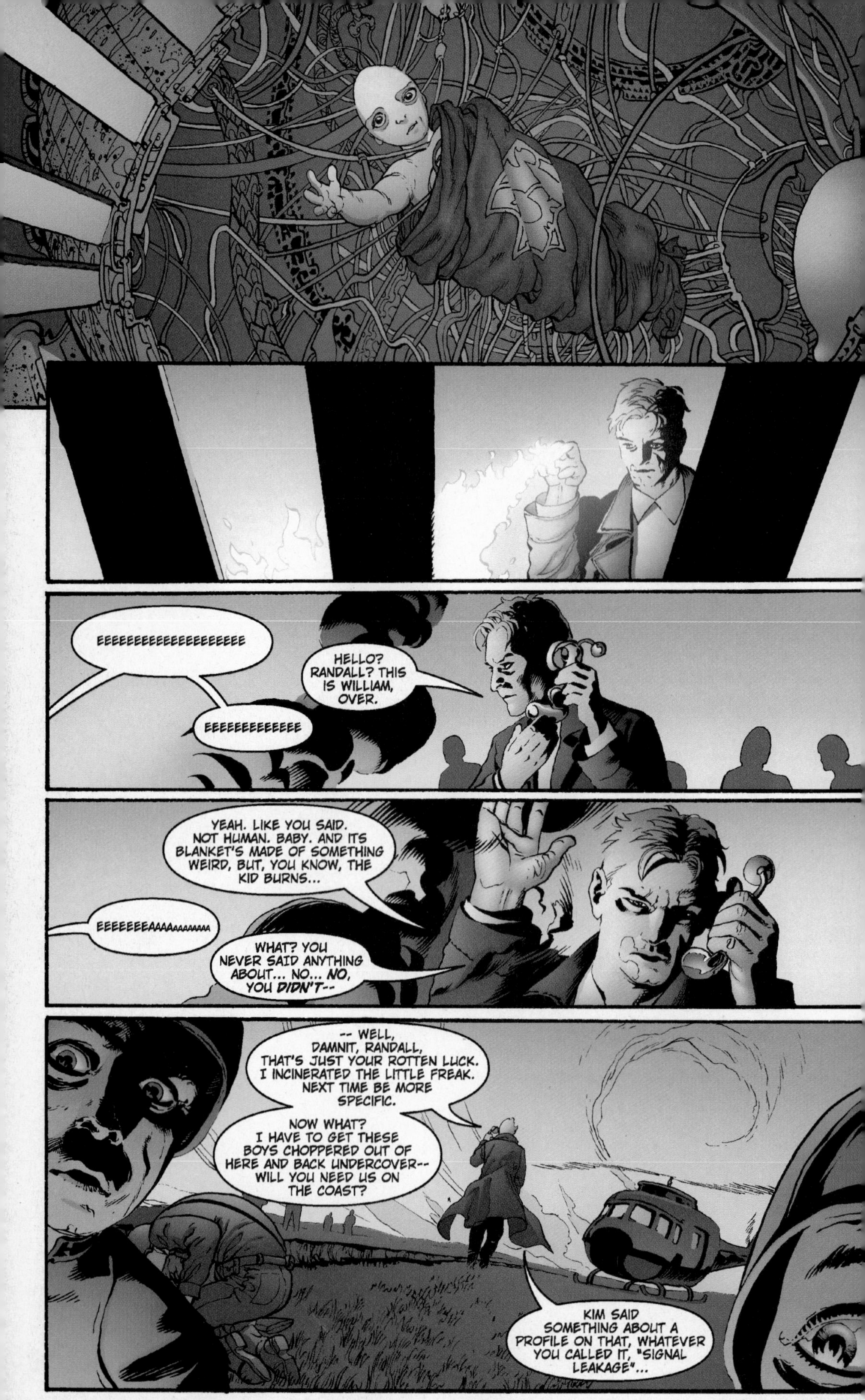
EEEEEEEEEEEEEEEEEEEE
HELLO? RANDALL? THIS IS WILLIAM, OVER.
EEEEEEEEEEEEE
YEAH. LIKE YOU SAID. NOT HUMAN. BABY. AND ITS BLANKET'S MADE OF SOMETHING WEIRD, BUT, YOU KNOW, THE KID BURNS...
EEEEEEEAAAAaaaaaaaa
WHAT? YOU NEVER SAID ANYTHING ABOUT... NO... NO, YOU DIDN'T--
-- WELL, DAMNIT, RANDALL, THAT'S JUST YOUR ROTTEN LUCK. I INCINERATED THE LITTLE FREAK. NEXT TIME BE MORE SPECIFIC.
NOW WHAT? I HAVE TO GET THESE BOYS CHOPPERED OUT OF HERE AND BACK UNDERCOVER-- WILL YOU NEED US ON THE COAST?
KIM SAID SOMETHING ABOUT A PROFILE ON THAT, WHATEVER YOU CALLED IT, "SIGNAL LEAKAGE"...

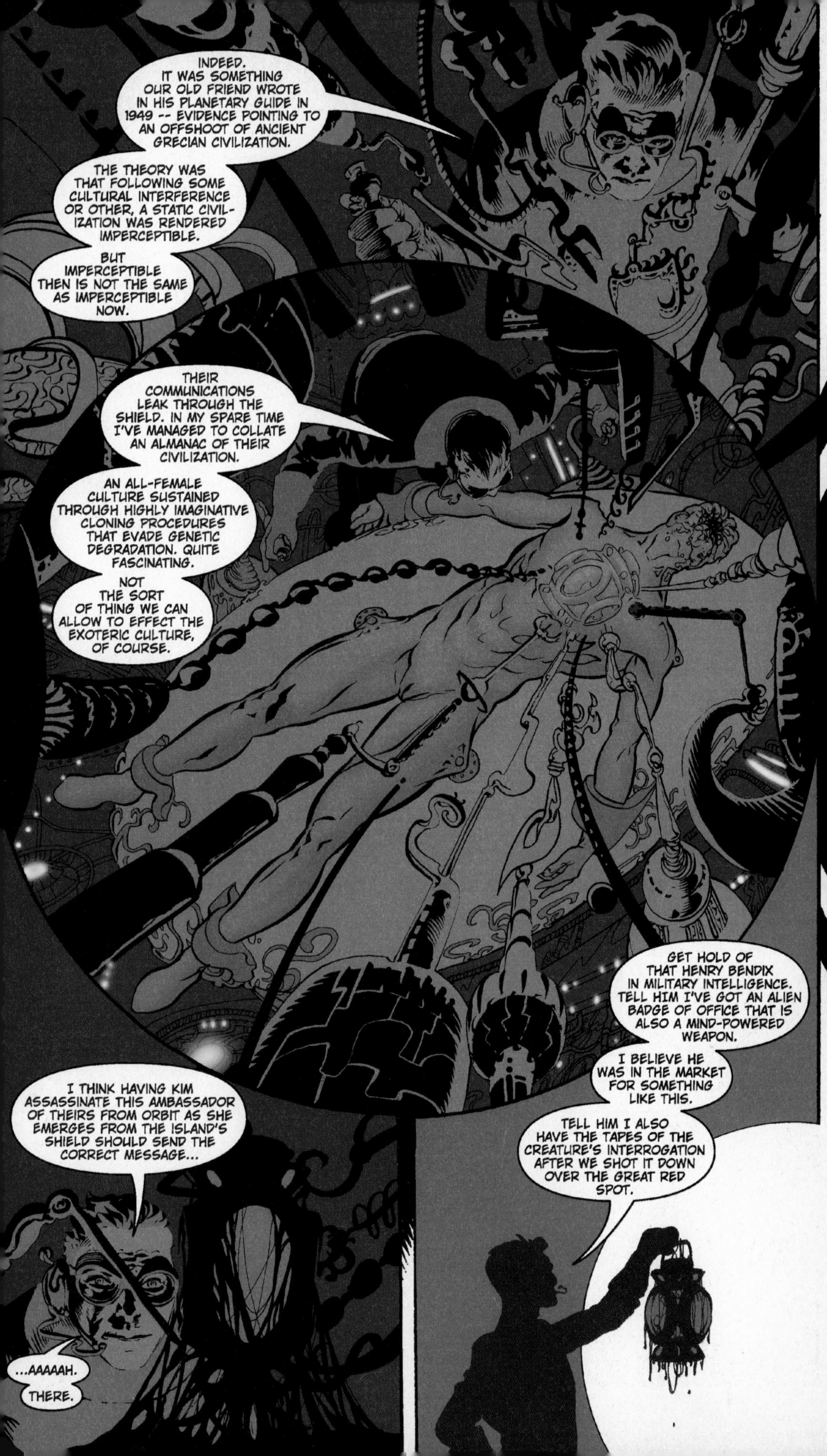
INDEED. IT WAS SOMETHING OUR OLD FRIEND WROTE IN HIS PLANETARY GUIDE IN 1949 -- EVIDENCE POINTING TO AN OFFSHOOT OF ANCIENT GRECIAN CIVILIZATION.
THE THEORY WAS THAT FOLLOWING SOME CULTURAL INTERFERENCE OR OTHER, A STATIC CIVILIZATION WAS RENDERED IMPERCEPTIBLE.
BUT IMPERCEPTIBLE THEN IS NOT THE SAME AS IMPERCEPTIBLE NOW.
THEIR COMMUNICATIONS LEAK THROUGH THE SHIELD. IN MY SPARE TIME I'VE MANAGED TO COLLATE AN ALMANAC OF THEIR CIVILIZATION.
AN ALL-FEMALE CULTURE SUSTAINED THROUGH HIGHLY IMAGINATIVE CLONING PROCEDURES THAT EVADE GENETIC DEGRADATION. QUITE FASCINATING.
NOT THE SORT OF THING WE CAN ALLOW TO EFFECT THE EXOTERIC CULTURE, OF COURSE.
I THINK HAVING KIM ASSASSINATE THIS AMBASSADOR OF THEIRS FROM ORBIT AS SHE EMERGES FROM THE ISLAND'S SHIELD SHOULD SEND THE CORRECT MESSAGE...
...AAAAAH.
THERE.
GET HOLD OF THAT HENRY BENDIX IN MILITARY INTELLIGENCE. TELL HIM I'VE GOT AN ALIEN BADGE OF OFFICE THAT IS ALSO A MIND-POWERED WEAPON.
I BELIEVE HE WAS IN THE MARKET FOR SOMETHING LIKE THIS.
TELL HIM I ALSO HAVE THE TAPES OF THE CREATURE'S INTERROGATION AFTER WE SHOT IT DOWN OVER THE GREAT RED SPOT.

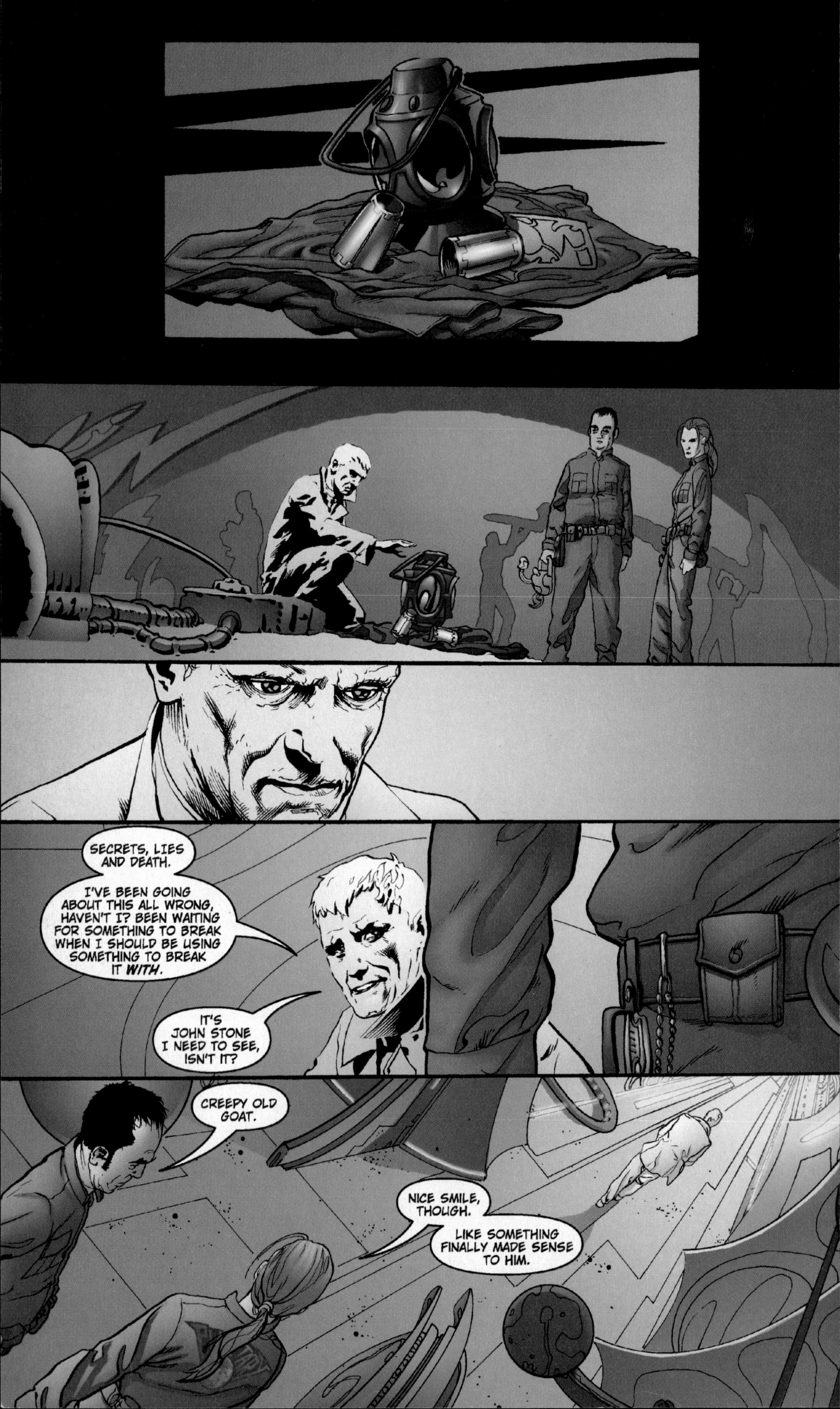
SECRETS, LIES AND DEATH.
I'VE BEEN GOING ABOUT THIS ALL WRONG, HAVEN'T I? BEEN WAITING FOR SOMETHING TO BREAK WHEN I SHOULD BE USING SOMETHING TO BREAK IT *WITH*.
IT'S JOHN STONE I NEED TO SEE, ISN'T IT?
CREEPY OLD GOAT.
NICE SMILE, THOUGH.
LIKE SOMETHING FINALLY MADE SENSE TO HIM.

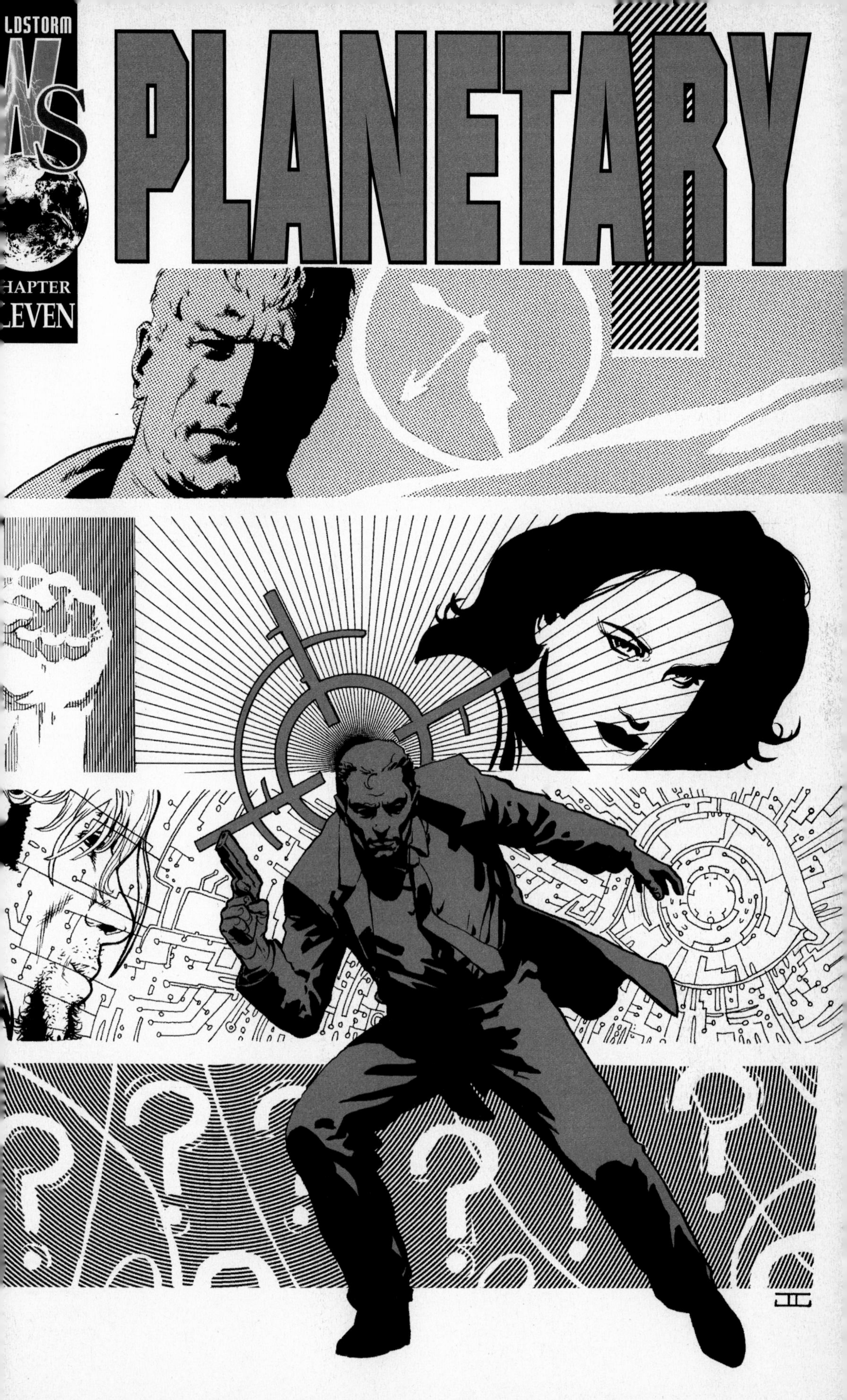
LDSTORM
PLANETARY
HAPTER
LEVEN

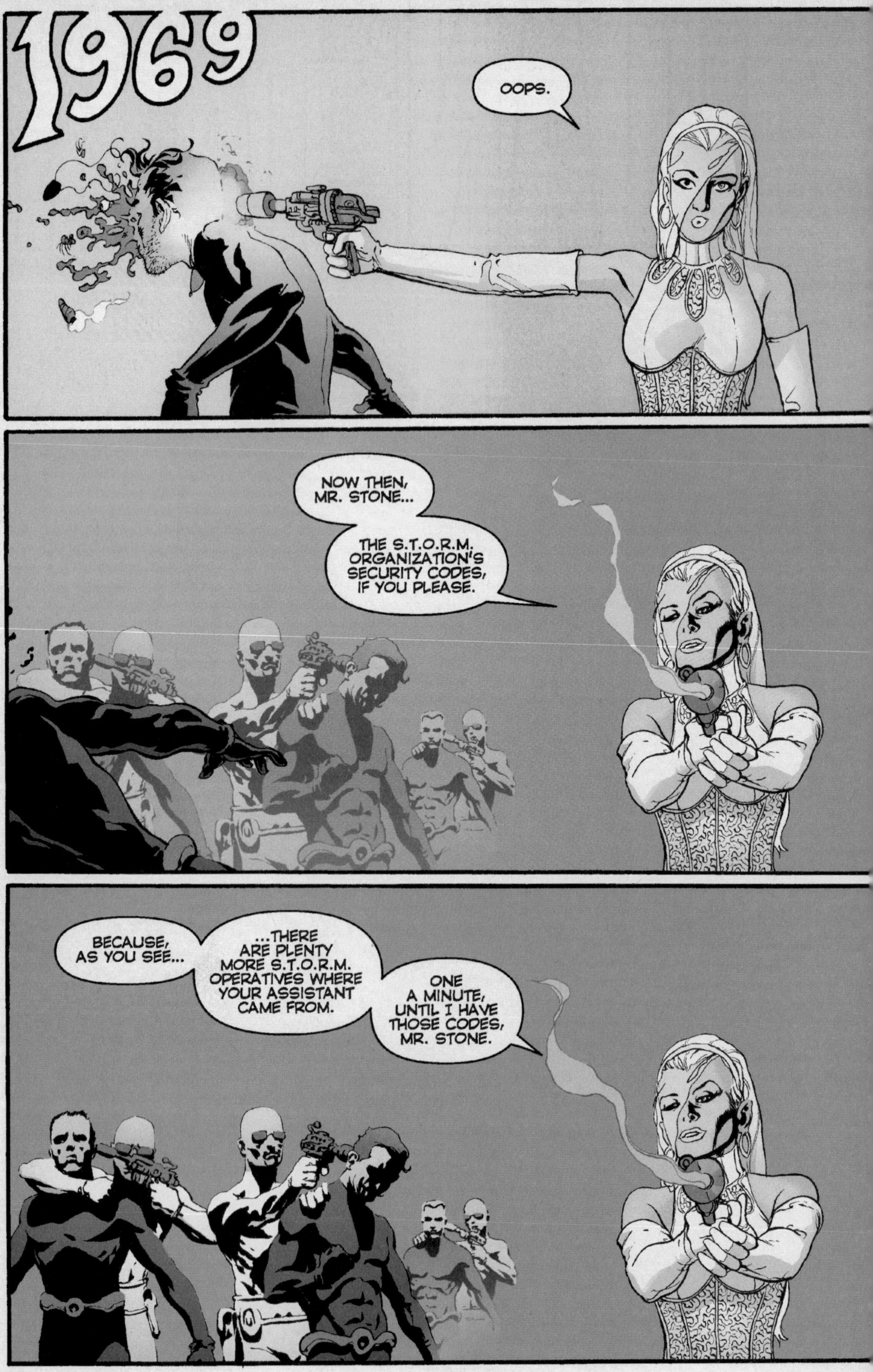
1969
OOPS.
NOW THEN, MR. STONE...
THE S.T.O.R.M. ORGANIZATION'S SECURITY CODES, IF YOU PLEASE.
BECAUSE, AS YOU SEE...
...THERE ARE PLENTY MORE S.T.O.R.M. OPERATIVES WHERE YOUR ASSISTANT CAME FROM.
ONE A MINUTE, UNTIL I HAVE THOSE CODES, MR. STONE.

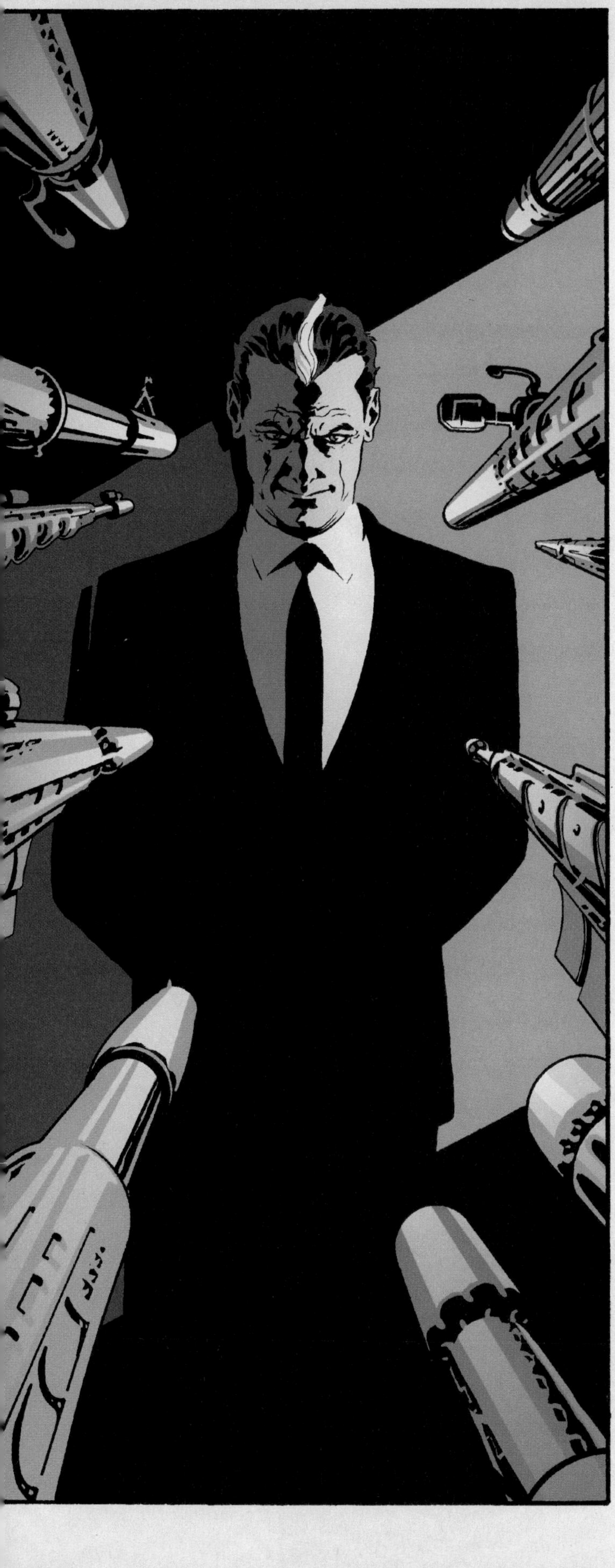

COLD WORLD

by WARREN ELLIS
and JOHN CASSADAY
with LAURA DEPUY
and BILL O'NEIL
as produced by JOHN LAYMAN

Planetary created by
Warren Ellis and John Cassaday

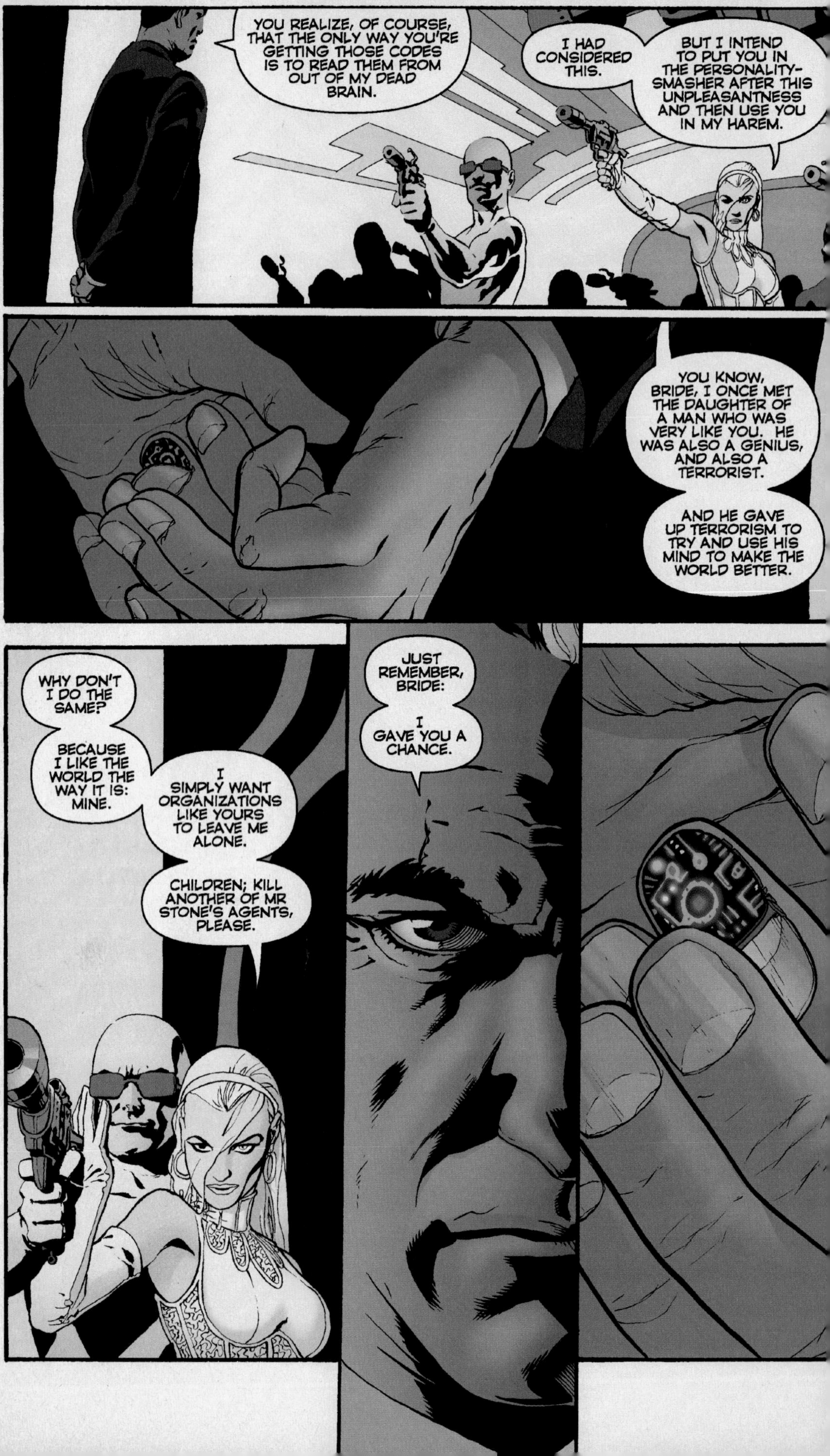
YOU REALIZE, OF COURSE, THAT THE ONLY WAY YOU'RE GETTING THOSE CODES IS TO READ THEM FROM OUT OF MY DEAD BRAIN.
I HAD CONSIDERED THIS.
BUT I INTEND TO PUT YOU IN THE PERSONALITY-SMASHER AFTER THIS UNPLEASANTNESS AND THEN USE YOU IN MY HAREM.
YOU KNOW, BRIDE, I ONCE MET THE DAUGHTER OF A MAN WHO WAS VERY LIKE YOU. HE WAS ALSO A GENIUS, AND ALSO A TERRORIST.
AND HE GAVE UP TERRORISM TO TRY AND USE HIS MIND TO MAKE THE WORLD BETTER.
WHY DON'T I DO THE SAME?
BECAUSE I LIKE THE WORLD THE WAY IT IS: MINE.
I SIMPLY WANT ORGANIZATIONS LIKE YOURS TO LEAVE ME ALONE.
CHILDREN; KILL ANOTHER OF MR STONE'S AGENTS, PLEASE.
JUST REMEMBER, BRIDE:
I GAVE YOU A CHANCE.

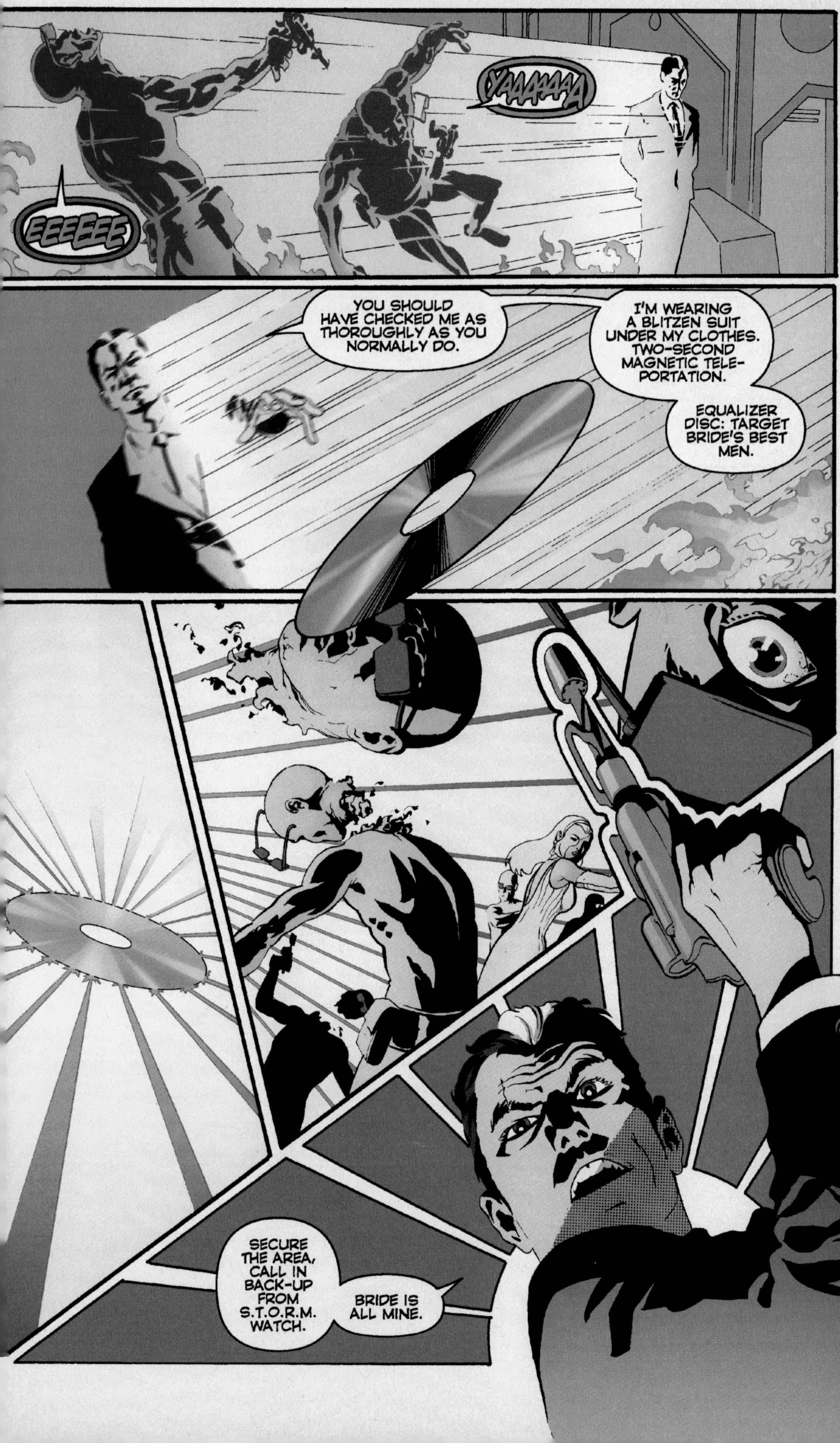
YAAAAAA
EEEEEE
YOU SHOULD HAVE CHECKED ME AS THOROUGHLY AS YOU NORMALLY DO.
I'M WEARING A BLITZEN SUIT UNDER MY CLOTHES. TWO-SECOND MAGNETIC TELE-PORTATION.
EQUALIZER DISC: TARGET BRIDE'S BEST MEN.
SECURE THE AREA, CALL IN BACK-UP FROM S.T.O.R.M. WATCH.
BRIDE IS ALL MINE.

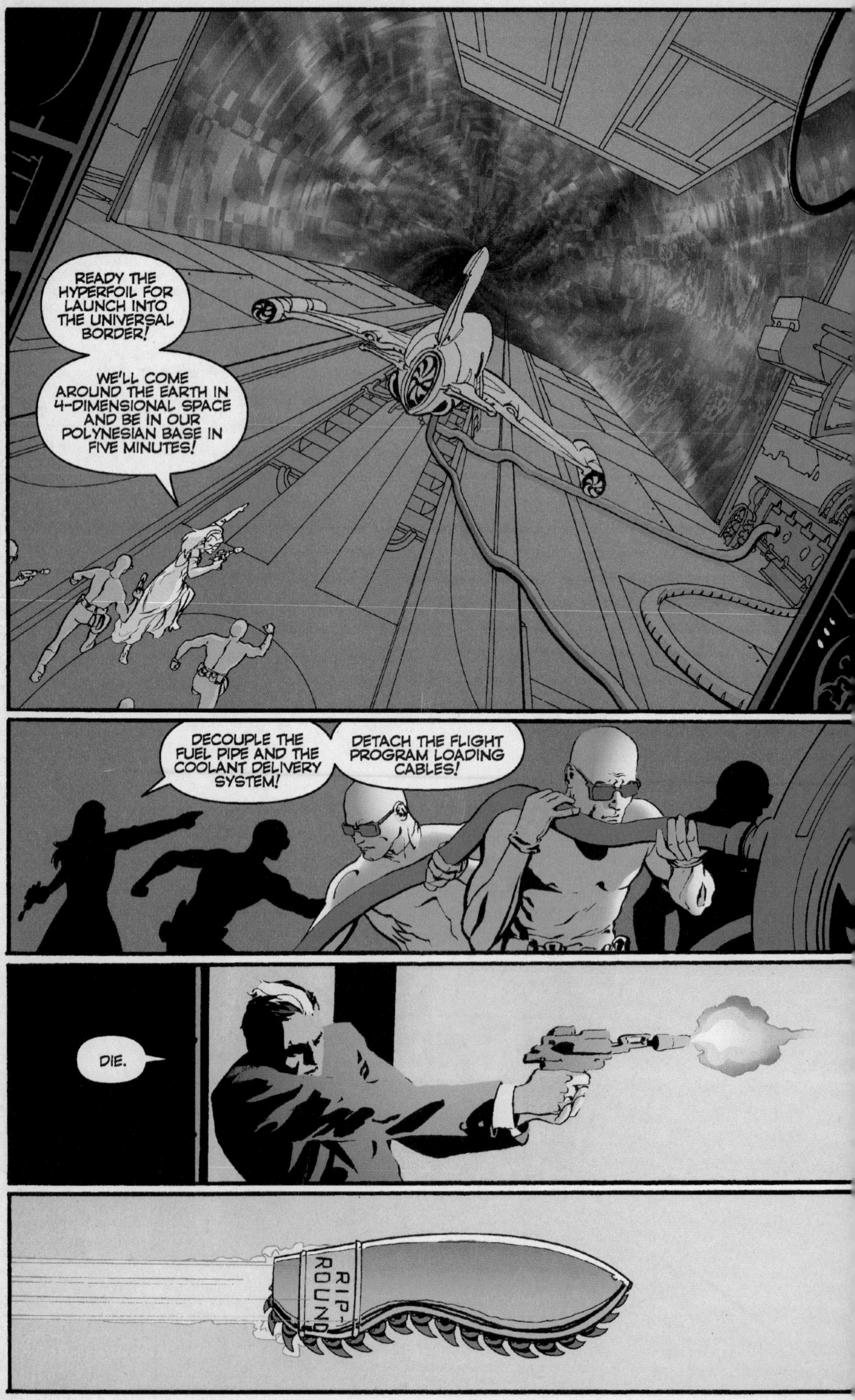
READY THE HYPERFOIL FOR LAUNCH INTO THE UNIVERSAL BORDER!
WE'LL COME AROUND THE EARTH IN 4-DIMENSIONAL SPACE AND BE IN OUR POLYNESIAN BASE IN FIVE MINUTES!
DECOUPLE THE FUEL PIPE AND THE COOLANT DELIVERY SYSTEM!
DETACH THE FLIGHT PROGRAM LOADING CABLES!
DIE.
RIP-ROUND

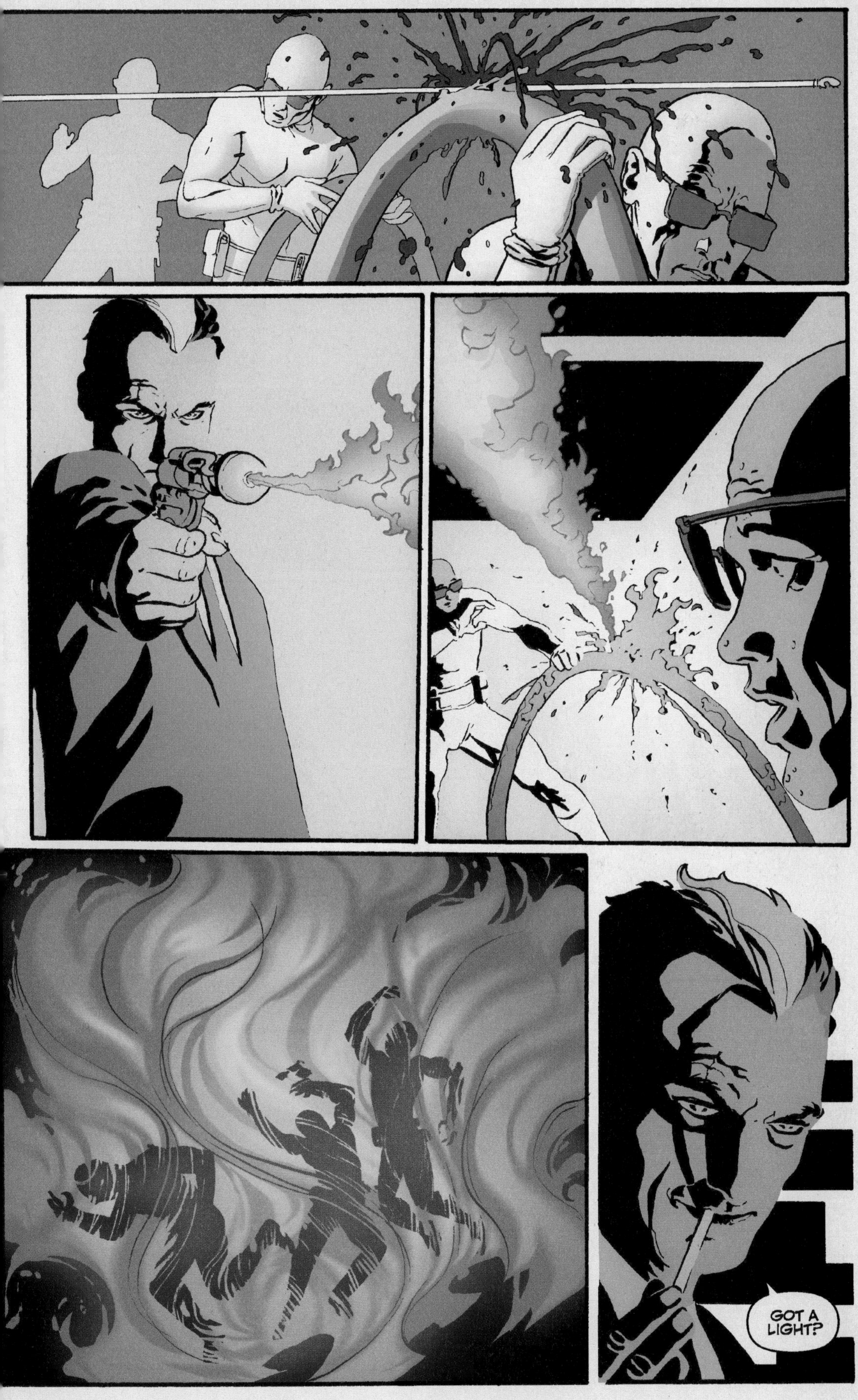
GOT A LIGHT?

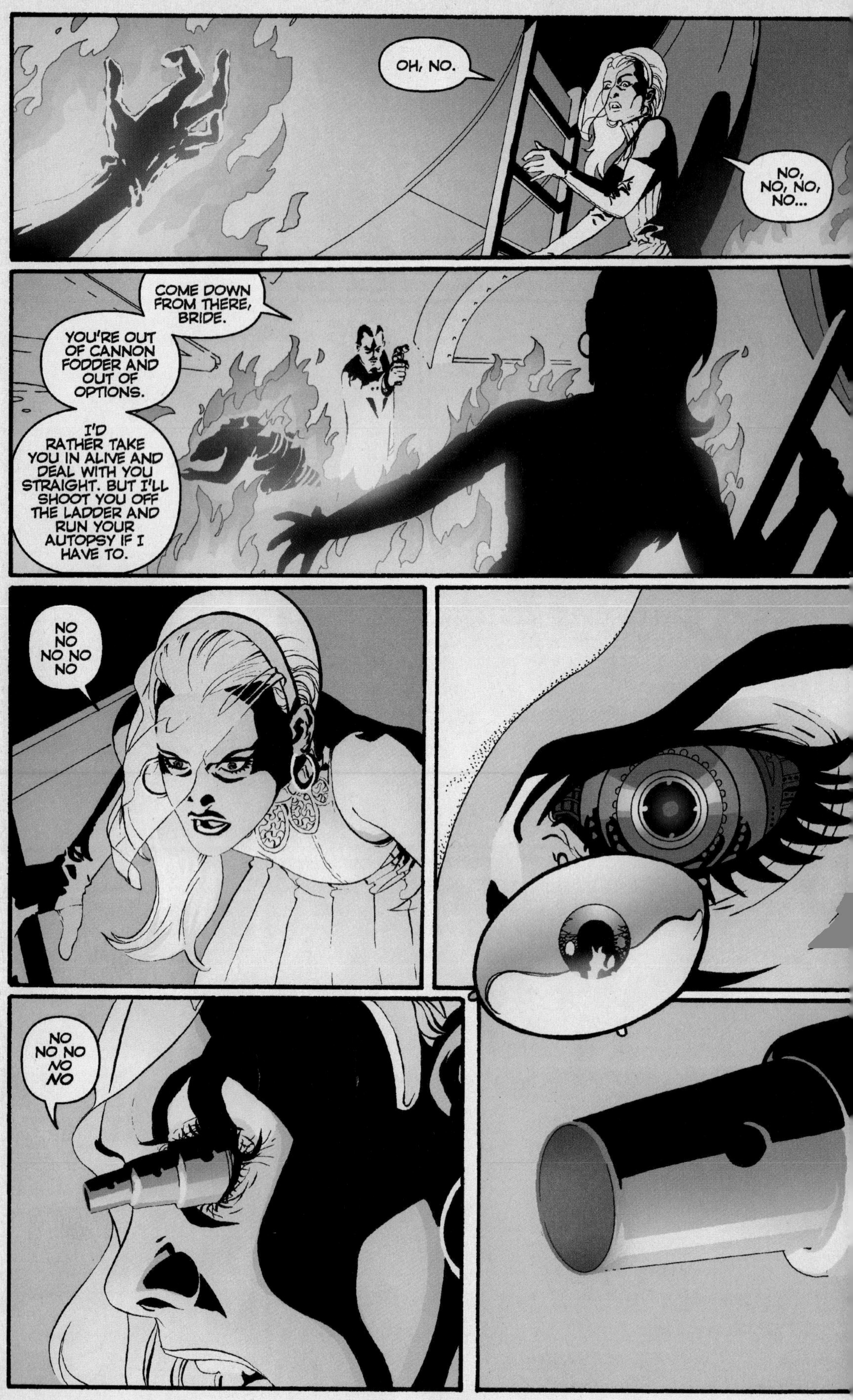
OH, NO.
NO, NO, NO, NO...
COME DOWN FROM THERE, BRIDE.
YOU'RE OUT OF CANNON FODDER AND OUT OF OPTIONS.
I'D RATHER TAKE YOU IN ALIVE AND DEAL WITH YOU STRAIGHT. BUT I'LL SHOOT YOU OFF THE LADDER AND RUN YOUR AUTOPSY IF I HAVE TO.
NO NO NO NO NO
NO NO NO NO NO

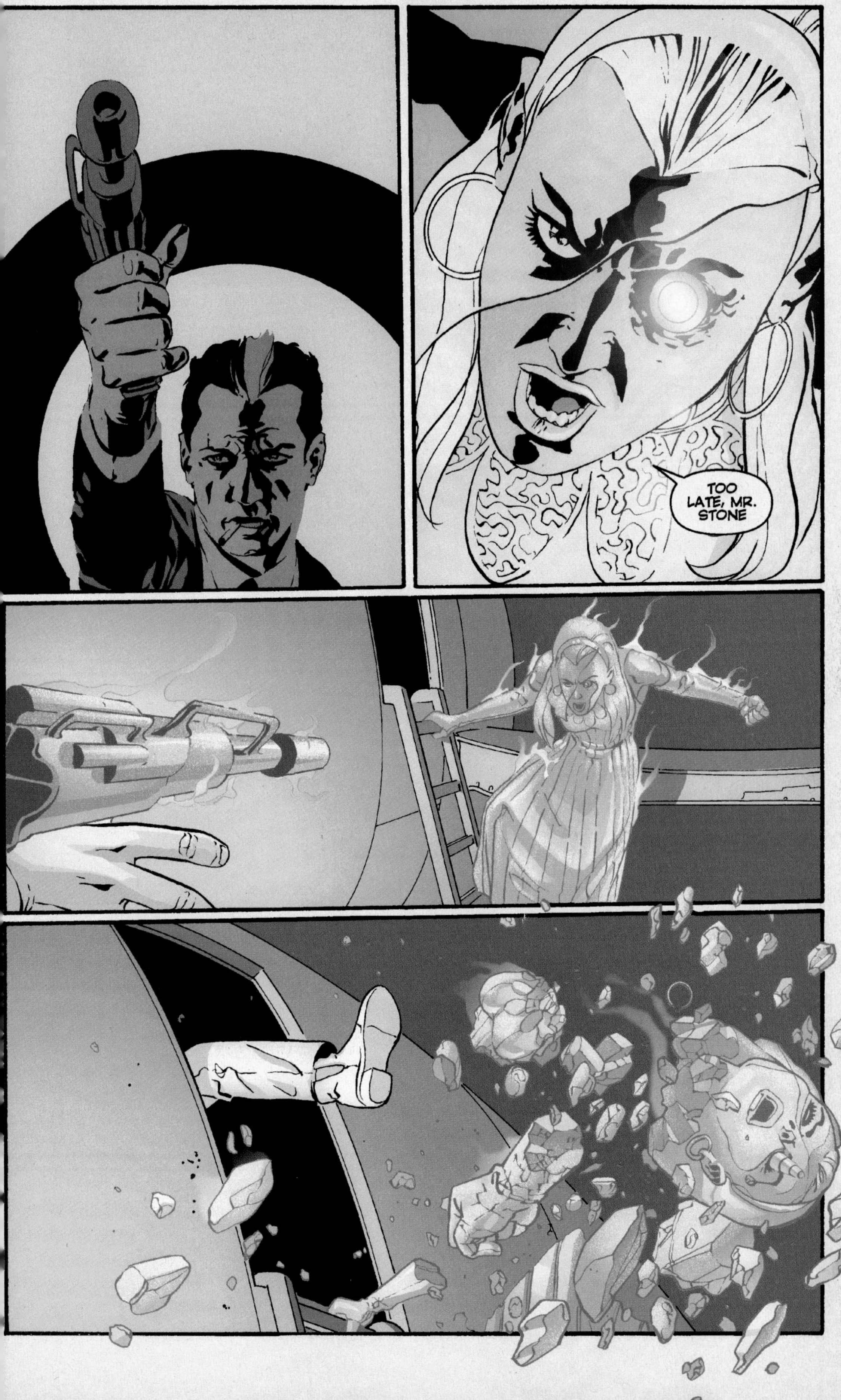
TOO LATE, MR. STONE

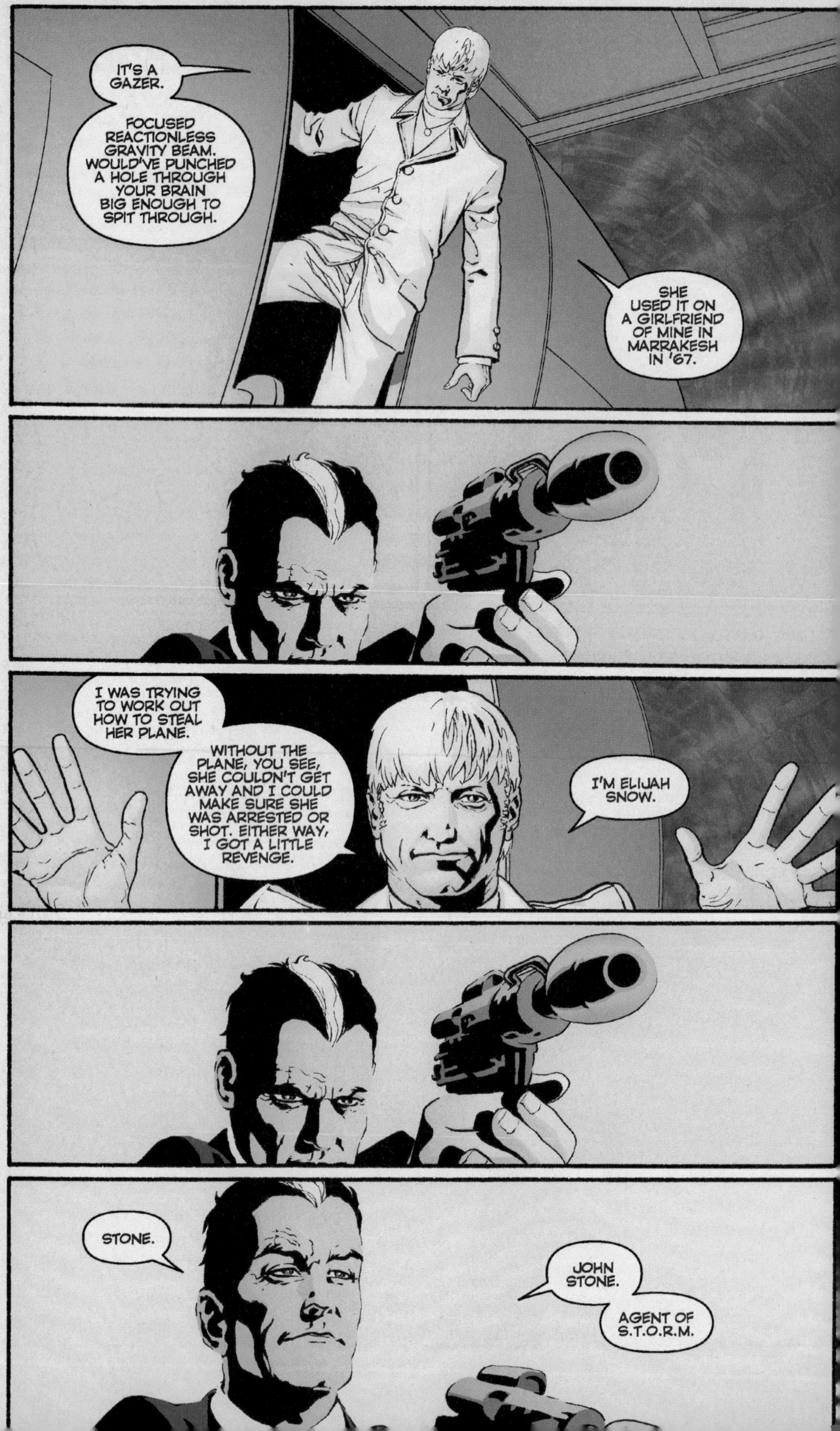
IT'S A GAZER.
FOCUSED REACTIONLESS GRAVITY BEAM. WOULD'VE PUNCHED A HOLE THROUGH YOUR BRAIN BIG ENOUGH TO SPIT THROUGH.
SHE USED IT ON A GIRLFRIEND OF MINE IN MARRAKESH IN '67.
I WAS TRYING TO WORK OUT HOW TO STEAL HER PLANE.
WITHOUT THE PLANE, YOU SEE, SHE COULDN'T GET AWAY AND I COULD MAKE SURE SHE WAS ARRESTED OR SHOT. EITHER WAY, I GOT A LITTLE REVENGE.
I'M ELIJAH SNOW.
STONE.
JOHN STONE.
AGENT OF S.T.O.R.M.

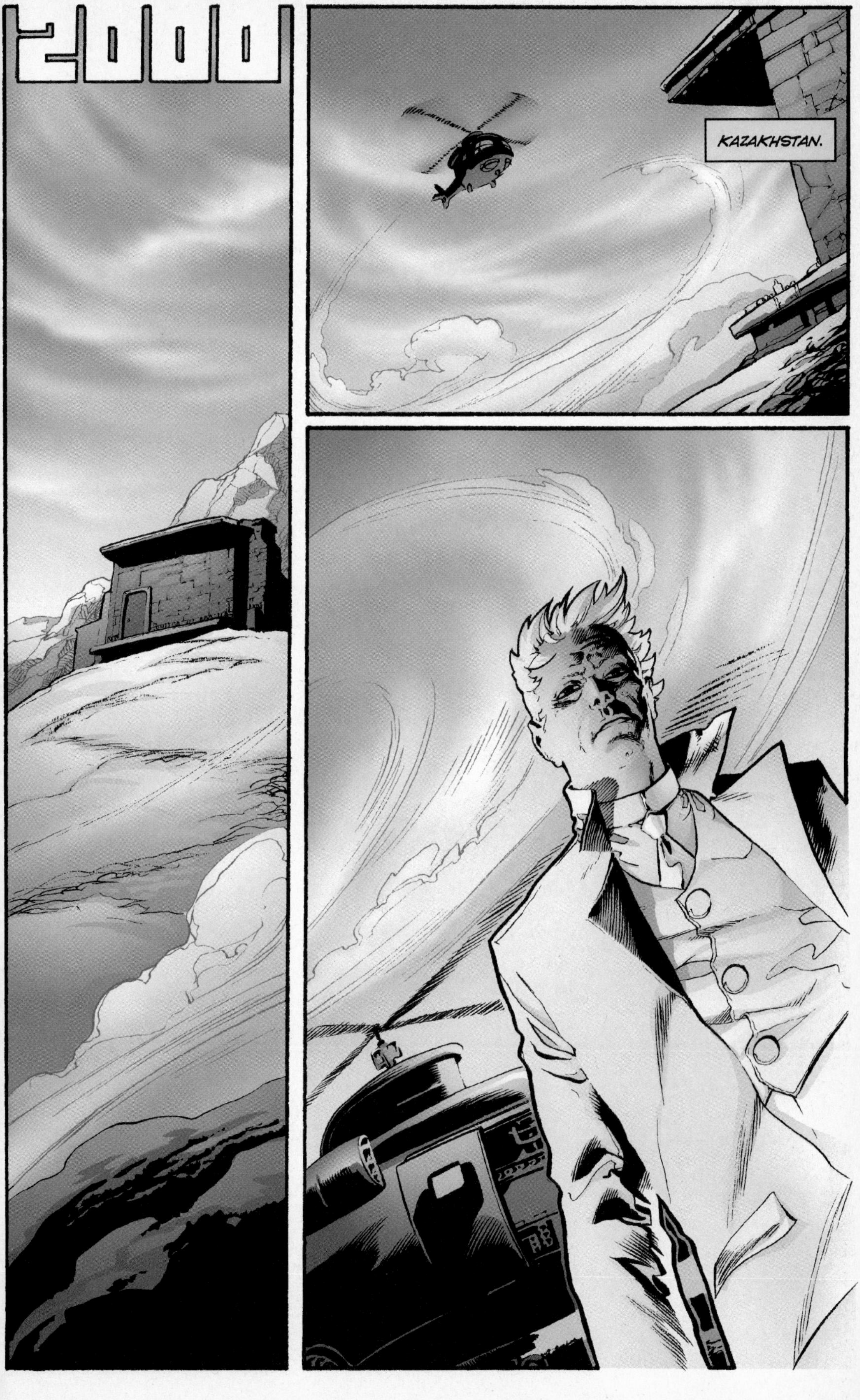
2000
KAZAKHSTAN.

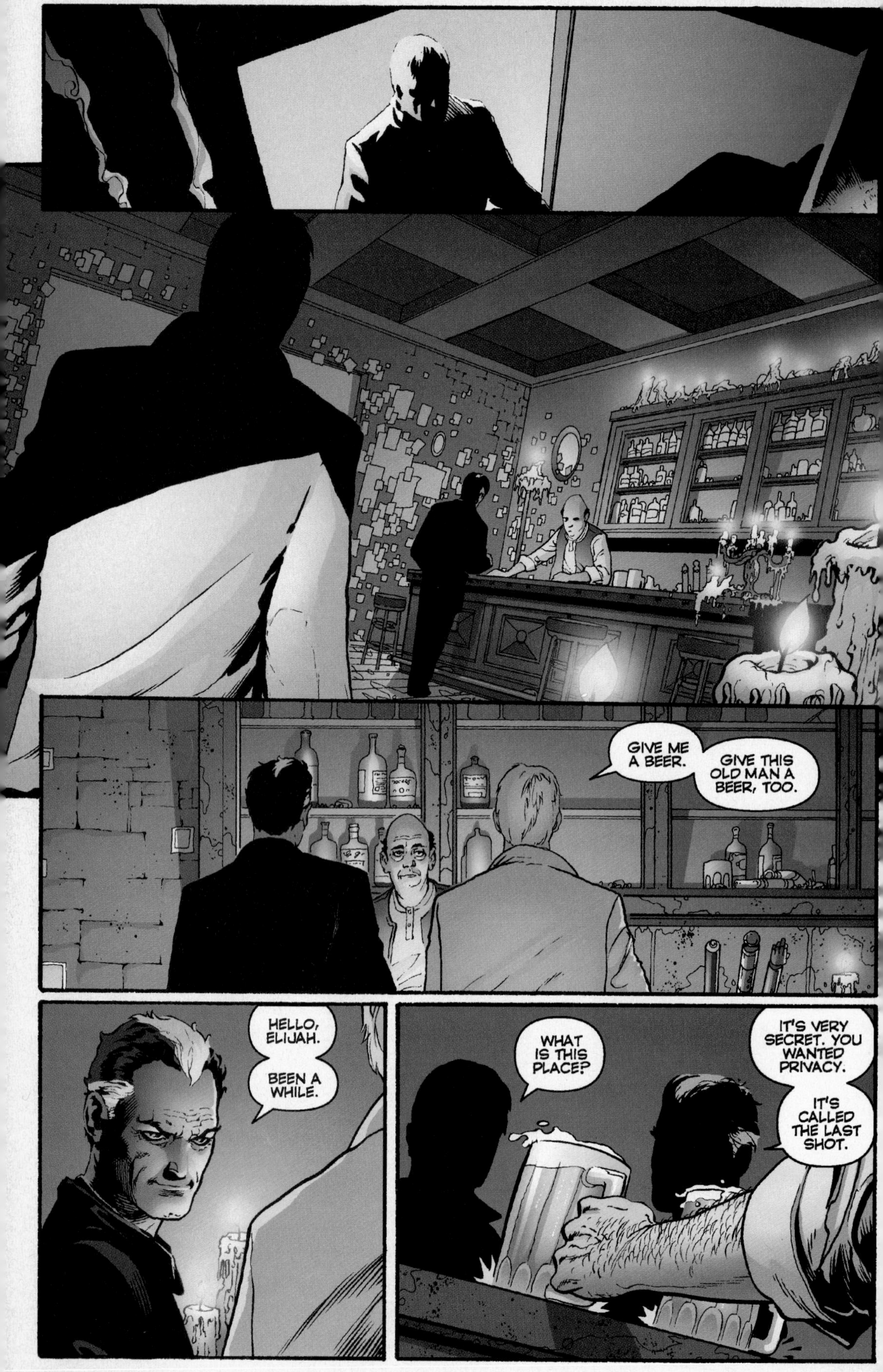
GIVE ME A BEER.
GIVE THIS OLD MAN A BEER, TOO.
HELLO, ELIJAH.
BEEN A WHILE.
WHAT IS THIS PLACE?
IT'S VERY SECRET. YOU WANTED PRIVACY.
IT'S CALLED THE LAST SHOT.

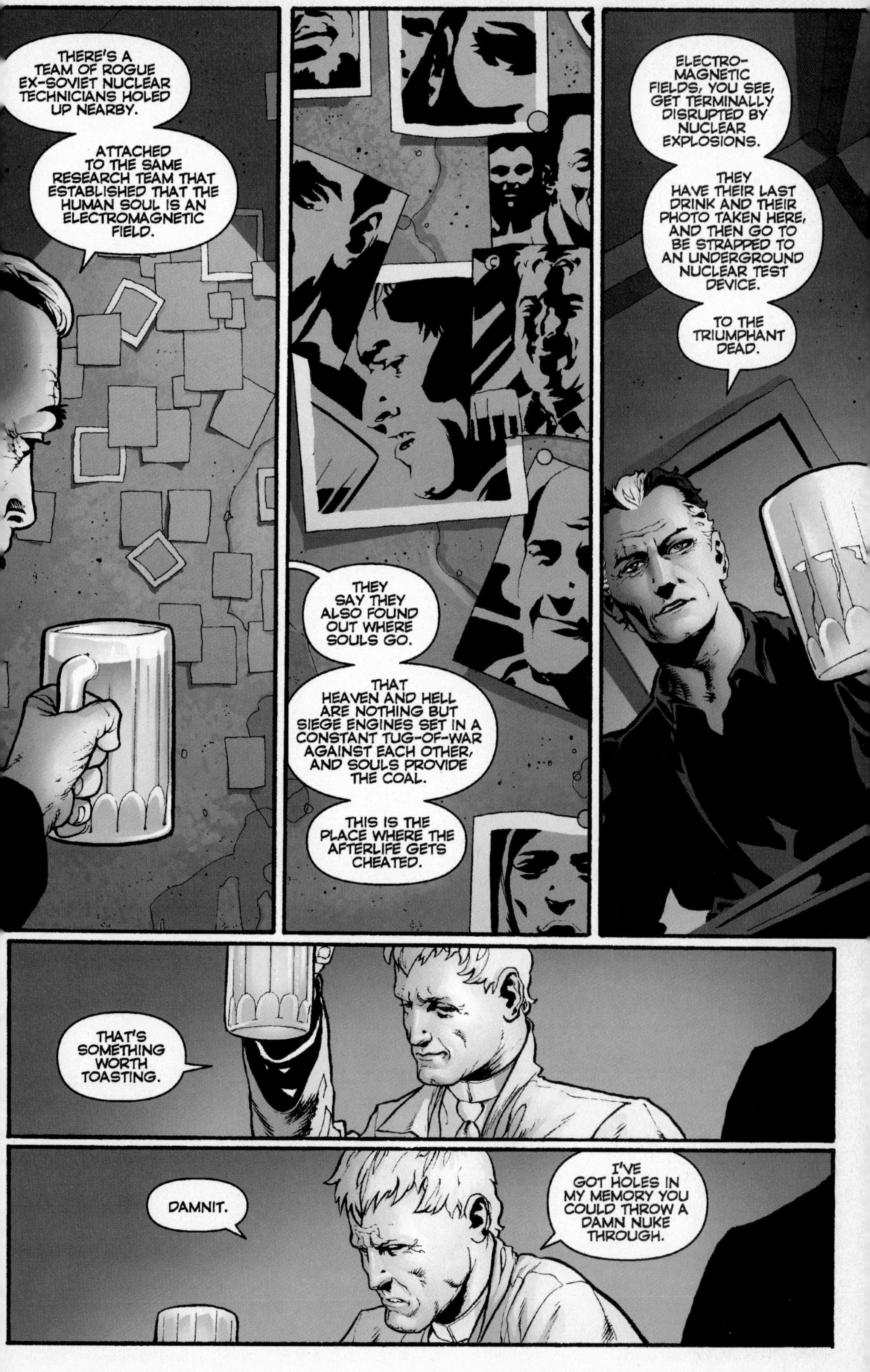
THERE'S A TEAM OF ROGUE EX-SOVIET NUCLEAR TECHNICIANS HOLED UP NEARBY.
ATTACHED TO THE SAME RESEARCH TEAM THAT ESTABLISHED THAT THE HUMAN SOUL IS AN ELECTROMAGNETIC FIELD.
THEY SAY THEY ALSO FOUND OUT WHERE SOULS GO.
THAT HEAVEN AND HELL ARE NOTHING BUT SIEGE ENGINES SET IN A CONSTANT TUG-OF-WAR AGAINST EACH OTHER, AND SOULS PROVIDE THE COAL.
THIS IS THE PLACE WHERE THE AFTERLIFE GETS CHEATED.
ELECTRO-MAGNETIC FIELDS, YOU SEE, GET TERMINALLY DISRUPTED BY NUCLEAR EXPLOSIONS.
THEY HAVE THEIR LAST DRINK AND THEIR PHOTO TAKEN HERE, AND THEN GO TO BE STRAPPED TO AN UNDERGROUND NUCLEAR TEST DEVICE.
TO THE TRIUMPHANT DEAD.
THAT'S SOMETHING WORTH TOASTING.
DAMNIT.
I'VE GOT HOLES IN MY MEMORY YOU COULD THROW A DAMN NUKE THROUGH.

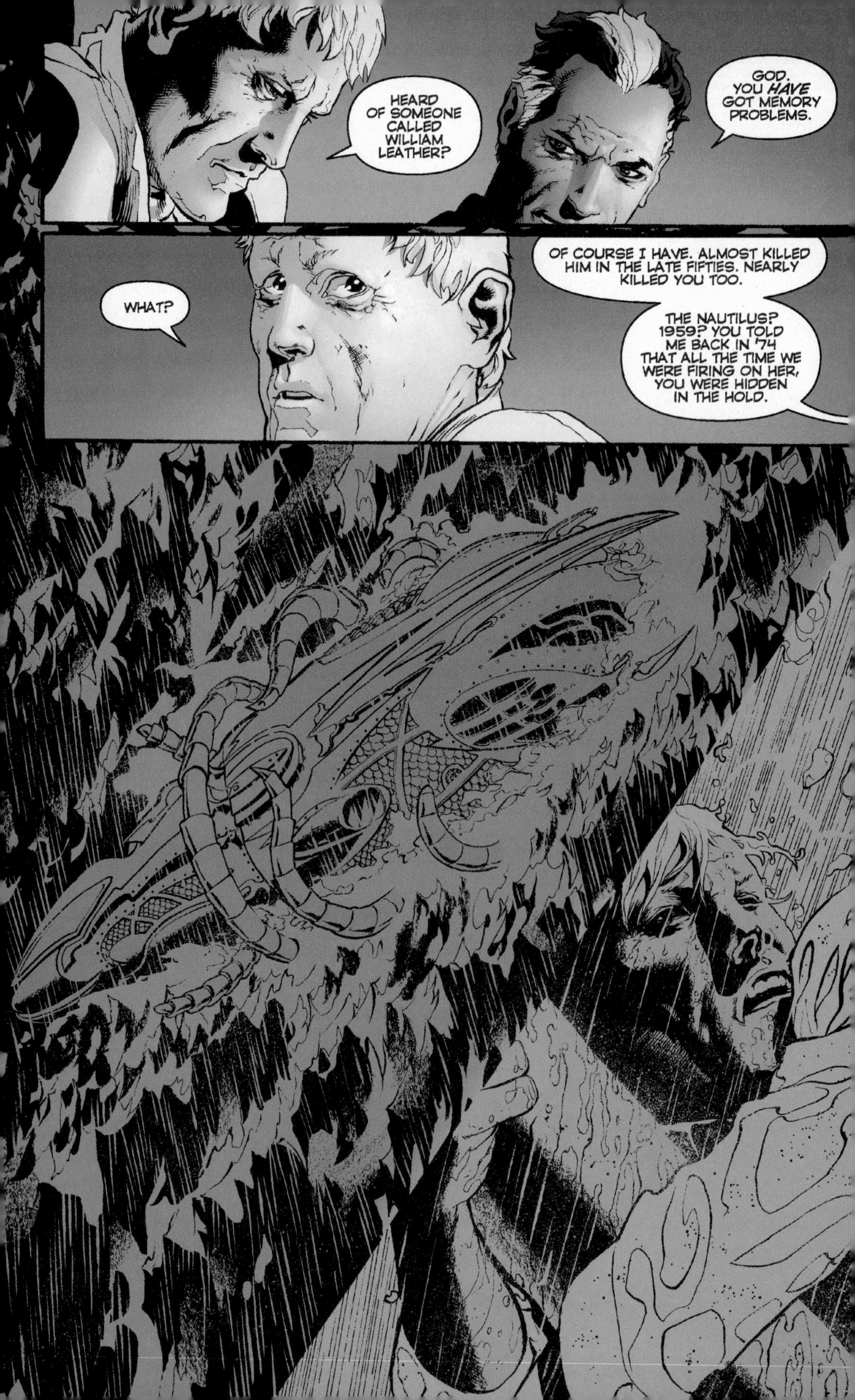
HEARD OF SOMEONE CALLED WILLIAM LEATHER?
GOD. YOU HAVE GOT MEMORY PROBLEMS.
WHAT?
OF COURSE I HAVE. ALMOST KILLED HIM IN THE LATE FIFTIES. NEARLY KILLED YOU TOO.
THE NAUTILUS? 1959? YOU TOLD ME BACK IN '74 THAT ALL THE TIME WE WERE FIRING ON HER, YOU WERE HIDDEN IN THE HOLD.

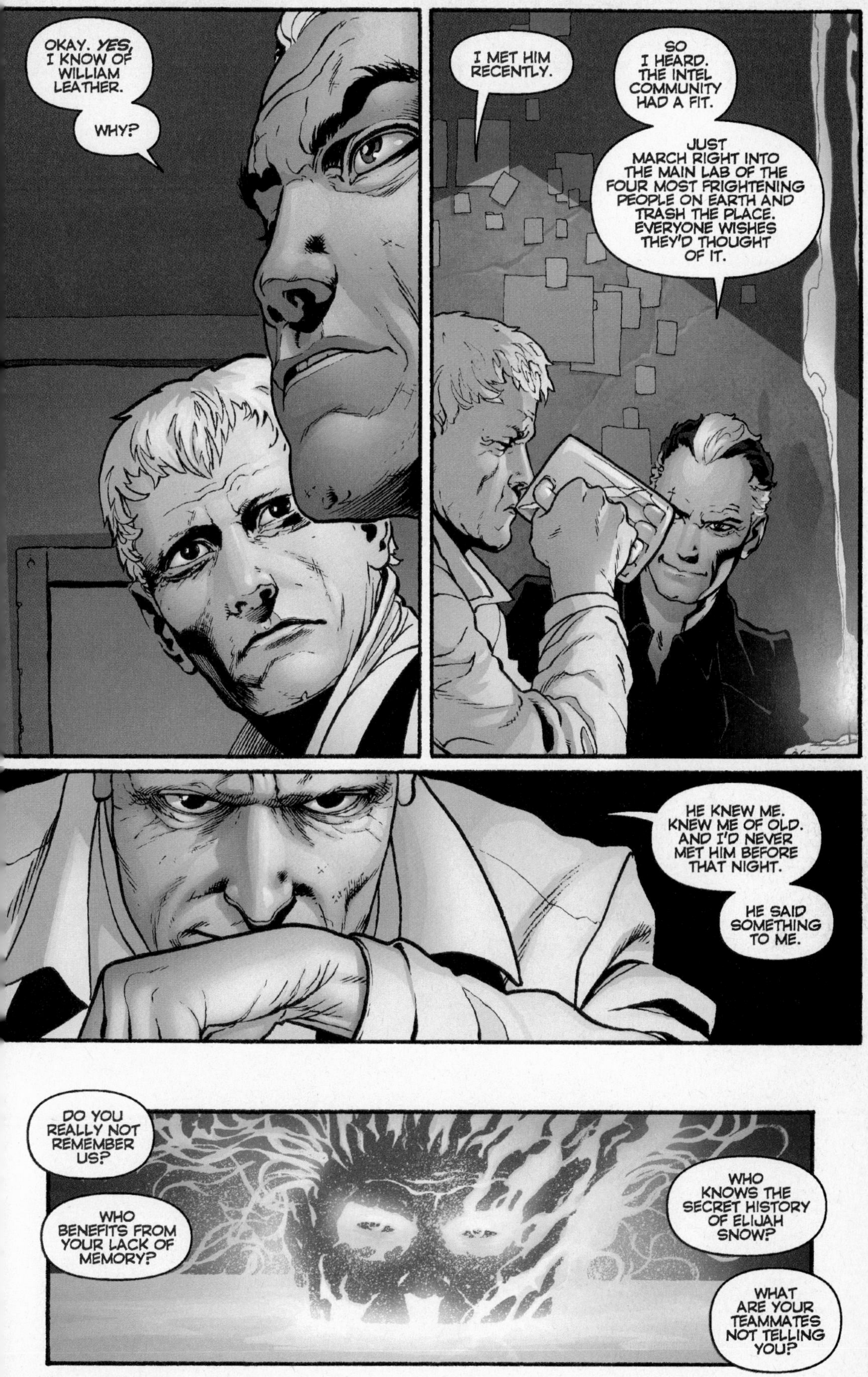
OKAY. *YES,* I KNOW OF WILLIAM LEATHER.
WHY?
I MET HIM RECENTLY.
SO I HEARD. THE INTEL COMMUNITY HAD A FIT.
JUST MARCH RIGHT INTO THE MAIN LAB OF THE FOUR MOST FRIGHTENING PEOPLE ON EARTH AND TRASH THE PLACE. EVERYONE WISHES THEY'D THOUGHT OF IT.
HE KNEW ME. KNEW ME OF OLD. AND I'D NEVER MET HIM BEFORE THAT NIGHT.
HE SAID SOMETHING TO ME.
DO YOU REALLY NOT REMEMBER US?
WHO BENEFITS FROM YOUR LACK OF MEMORY?
WHO KNOWS THE SECRET HISTORY OF ELIJAH SNOW?
WHAT ARE YOUR TEAMMATES NOT TELLING YOU?

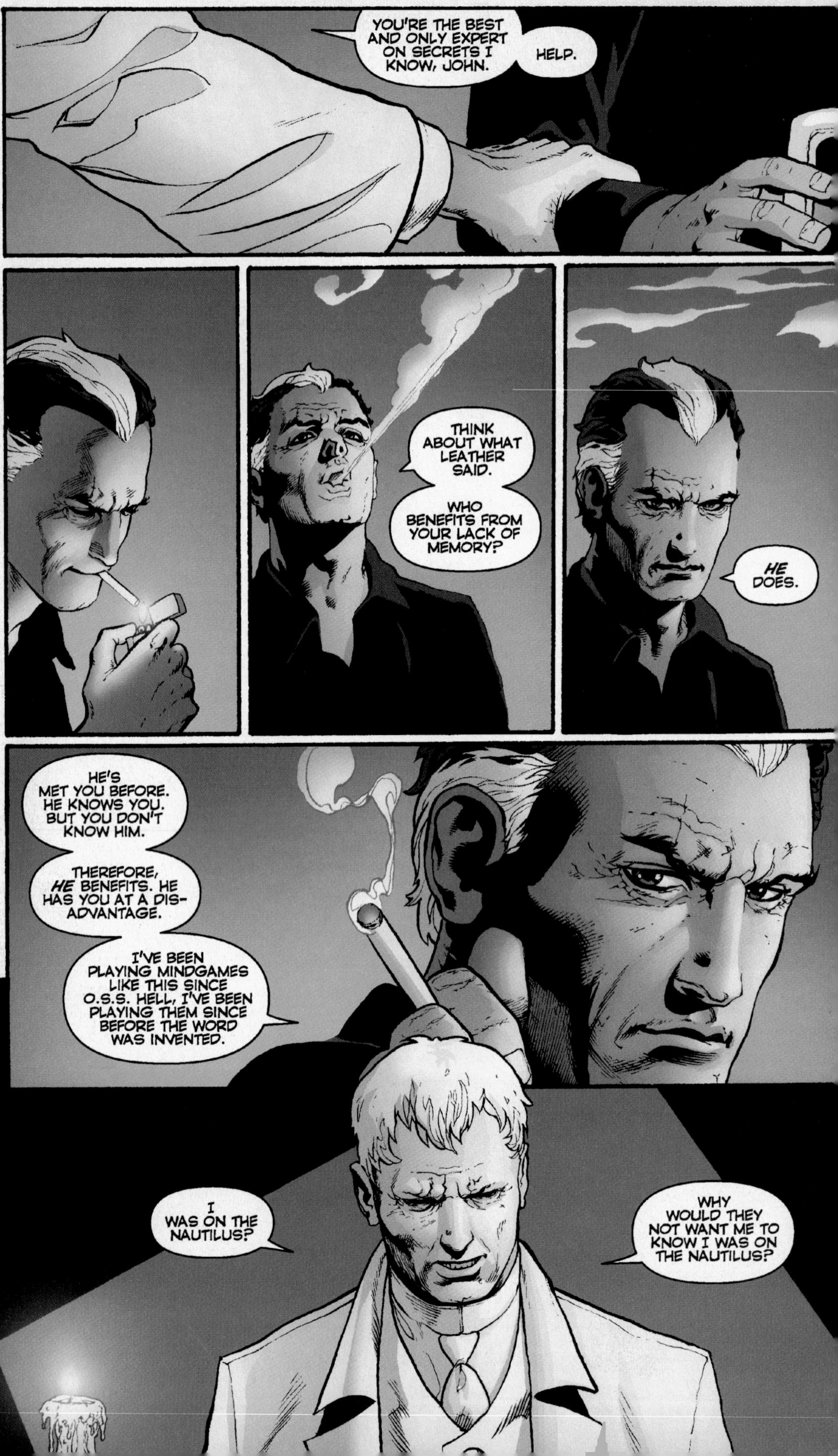
YOU'RE THE BEST AND ONLY EXPERT ON SECRETS I KNOW, JOHN.
HELP.
THINK ABOUT WHAT LEATHER SAID.
WHO BENEFITS FROM YOUR LACK OF MEMORY?
HE DOES.
HE'S MET YOU BEFORE. HE KNOWS YOU. BUT YOU DON'T KNOW HIM.
THEREFORE, HE BENEFITS. HE HAS YOU AT A DIS-ADVANTAGE.
I'VE BEEN PLAYING MINDGAMES LIKE THIS SINCE O.S.S. HELL, I'VE BEEN PLAYING THEM SINCE BEFORE THE WORD WAS INVENTED.
I WAS ON THE NAUTILUS?
WHY WOULD THEY NOT WANT ME TO KNOW I WAS ON THE NAUTILUS?

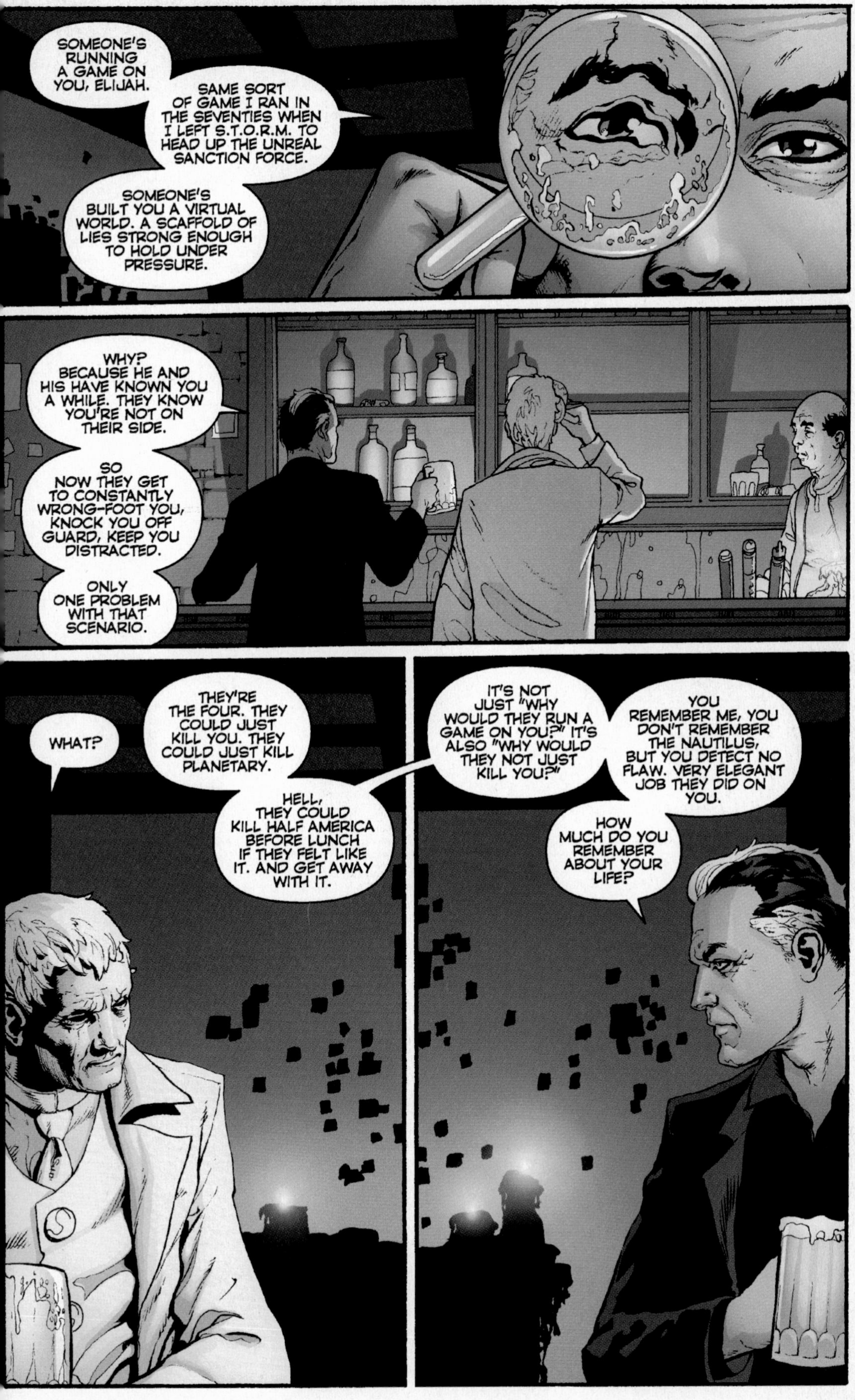
SOMEONE'S RUNNING A GAME ON YOU, ELIJAH.
SAME SORT OF GAME I RAN IN THE SEVENTIES WHEN I LEFT S.T.O.R.M. TO HEAD UP THE UNREAL SANCTION FORCE.
SOMEONE'S BUILT YOU A VIRTUAL WORLD. A SCAFFOLD OF LIES STRONG ENOUGH TO HOLD UNDER PRESSURE.
WHY? BECAUSE HE AND HIS HAVE KNOWN YOU A WHILE. THEY KNOW YOU'RE NOT ON THEIR SIDE.
SO NOW THEY GET TO CONSTANTLY WRONG-FOOT YOU, KNOCK YOU OFF GUARD, KEEP YOU DISTRACTED.
ONLY ONE PROBLEM WITH THAT SCENARIO.
WHAT?
THEY'RE THE FOUR. THEY COULD JUST KILL YOU. THEY COULD JUST KILL PLANETARY.
HELL, THEY COULD KILL HALF AMERICA BEFORE LUNCH IF THEY FELT LIKE IT. AND GET AWAY WITH IT.
IT'S NOT JUST "WHY WOULD THEY RUN A GAME ON YOU?" IT'S ALSO "WHY WOULD THEY NOT JUST KILL YOU?"
YOU REMEMBER ME, YOU DON'T REMEMBER THE NAUTILUS, BUT YOU DETECT NO FLAW. VERY ELEGANT JOB THEY DID ON YOU.
HOW MUCH DO YOU REMEMBER ABOUT YOUR LIFE?

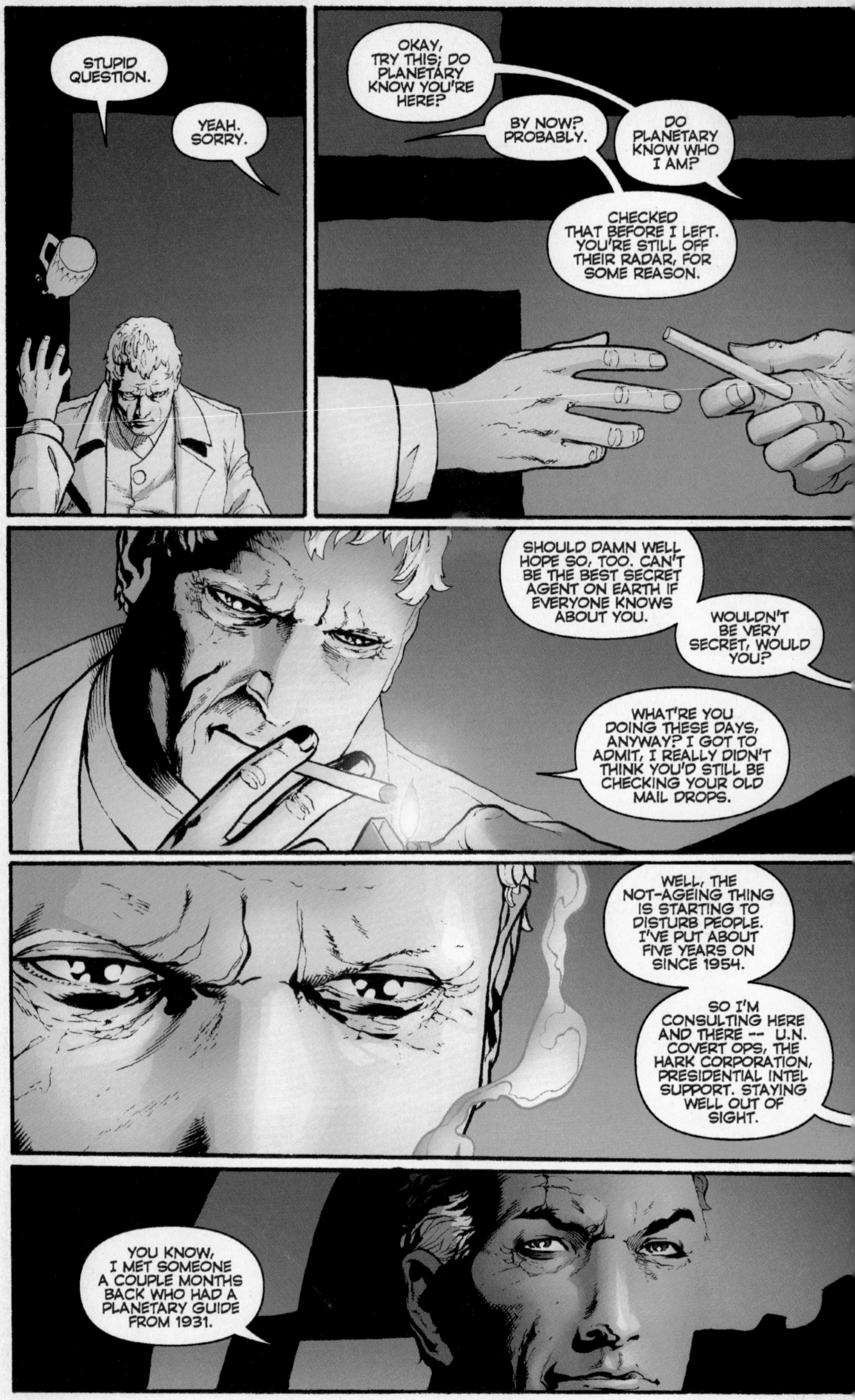
STUPID QUESTION.
YEAH. SORRY.
OKAY, TRY THIS; DO PLANETARY KNOW YOU'RE HERE?
BY NOW? PROBABLY.
DO PLANETARY KNOW WHO I AM?
CHECKED THAT BEFORE I LEFT. YOU'RE STILL OFF THEIR RADAR, FOR SOME REASON.
SHOULD DAMN WELL HOPE SO, TOO. CAN'T BE THE BEST SECRET AGENT ON EARTH IF EVERYONE KNOWS ABOUT YOU.
WOULDN'T BE VERY SECRET, WOULD YOU?
WHAT'RE YOU DOING THESE DAYS, ANYWAY? I GOT TO ADMIT, I REALLY DIDN'T THINK YOU'D STILL BE CHECKING YOUR OLD MAIL DROPS.
WELL, THE NOT-AGEING THING IS STARTING TO DISTURB PEOPLE. I'VE PUT ABOUT FIVE YEARS ON SINCE 1954.
SO I'M CONSULTING HERE AND THERE -- U.N. COVERT OPS, THE HARK CORPORATION, PRESIDENTIAL INTEL SUPPORT. STAYING WELL OUT OF SIGHT.
YOU KNOW, I MET SOMEONE A COUPLE MONTHS BACK WHO HAD A PLANETARY GUIDE FROM 1931.

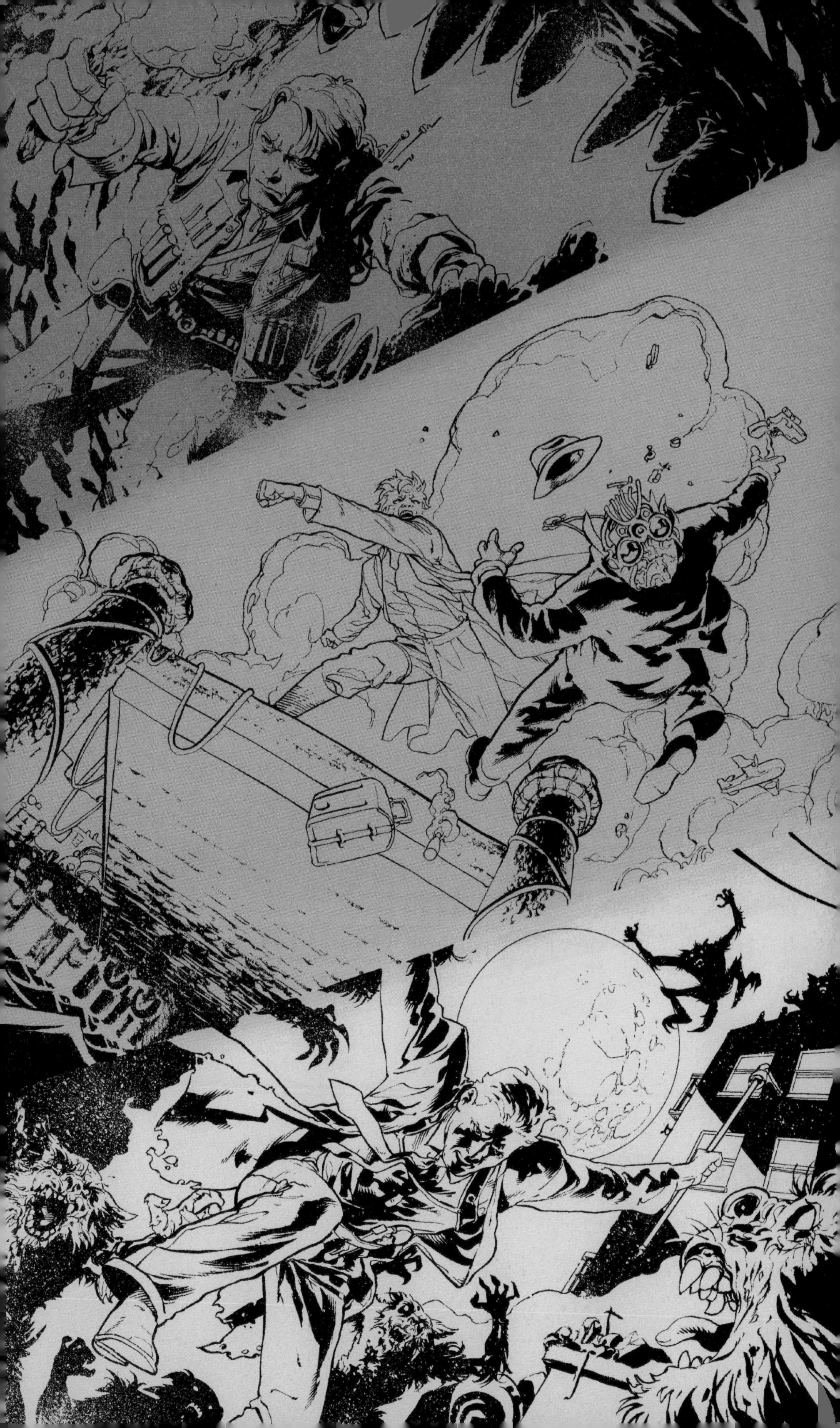

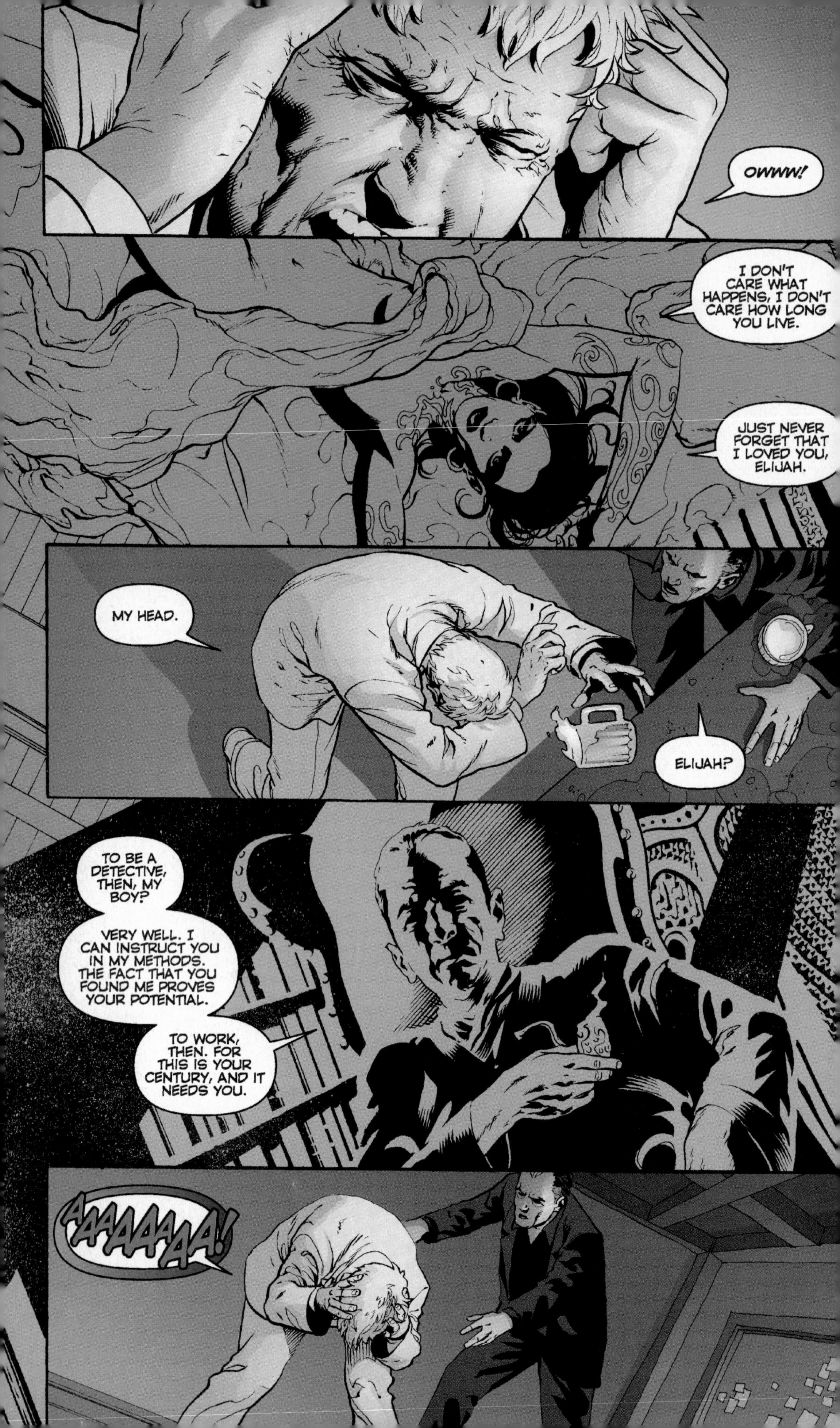
OWWW!
I DON'T CARE WHAT HAPPENS, I DON'T CARE HOW LONG YOU LIVE.
JUST NEVER FORGET THAT I LOVED YOU, ELIJAH.
MY HEAD.
ELIJAH?
TO BE A DETECTIVE, THEN, MY BOY?
VERY WELL. I CAN INSTRUCT YOU IN MY METHODS. THE FACT THAT YOU FOUND ME PROVES YOUR POTENTIAL.
TO WORK, THEN. FOR THIS IS YOUR CENTURY, AND IT NEEDS YOU.
AAAAAAAA!

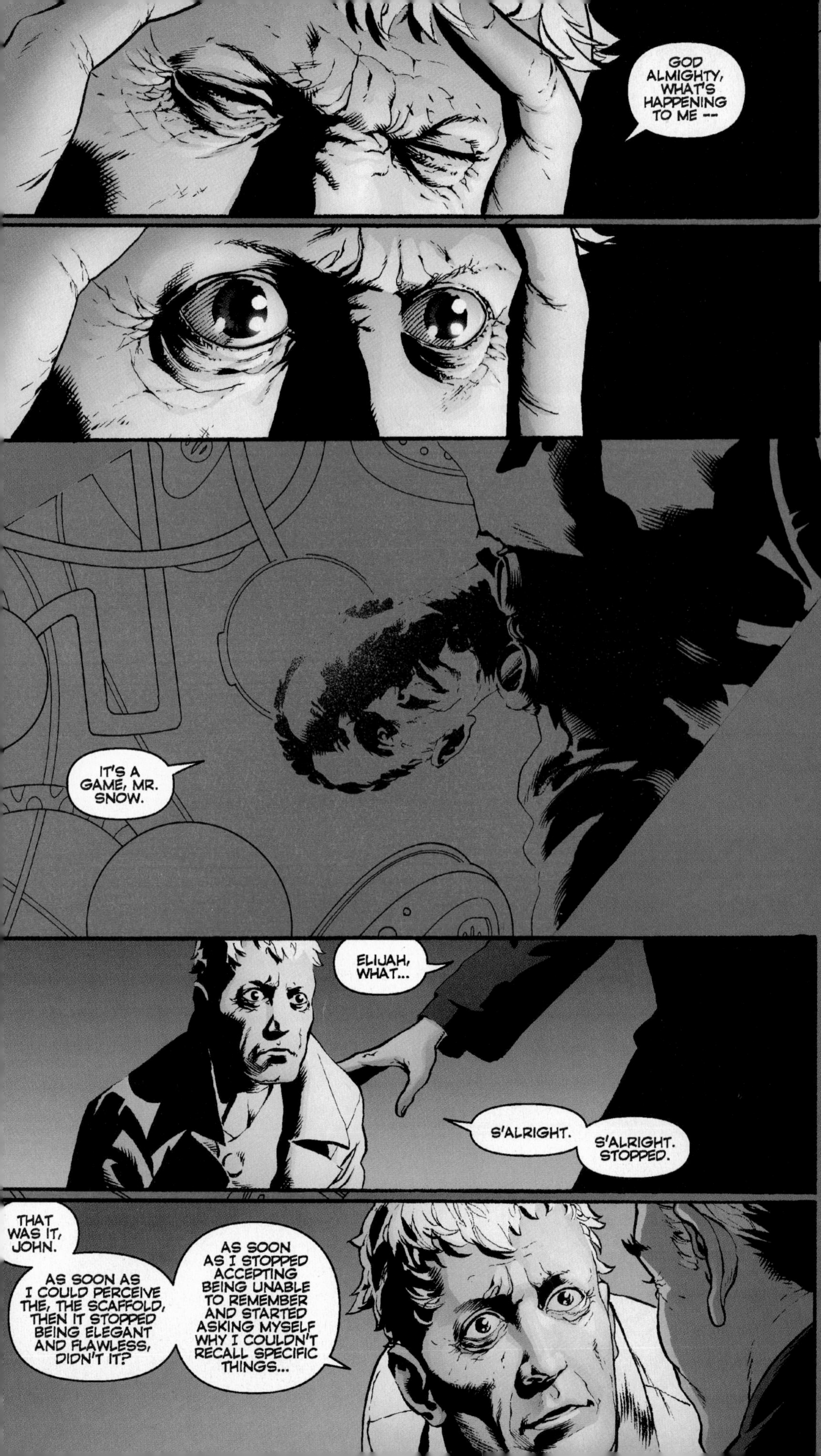
GOD ALMIGHTY, WHAT'S HAPPENING TO ME --
IT'S A GAME, MR. SNOW.
ELIJAH, WHAT...
S'ALRIGHT.
S'ALRIGHT. STOPPED.
THAT WAS IT, JOHN.
AS SOON AS I COULD PERCEIVE THE, THE SCAFFOLD, THEN IT STOPPED BEING ELEGANT AND FLAWLESS, DIDN'T IT?
AS SOON AS I STOPPED ACCEPTING BEING UNABLE TO REMEMBER AND STARTED ASKING MYSELF WHY I COULDN'T RECALL SPECIFIC THINGS...

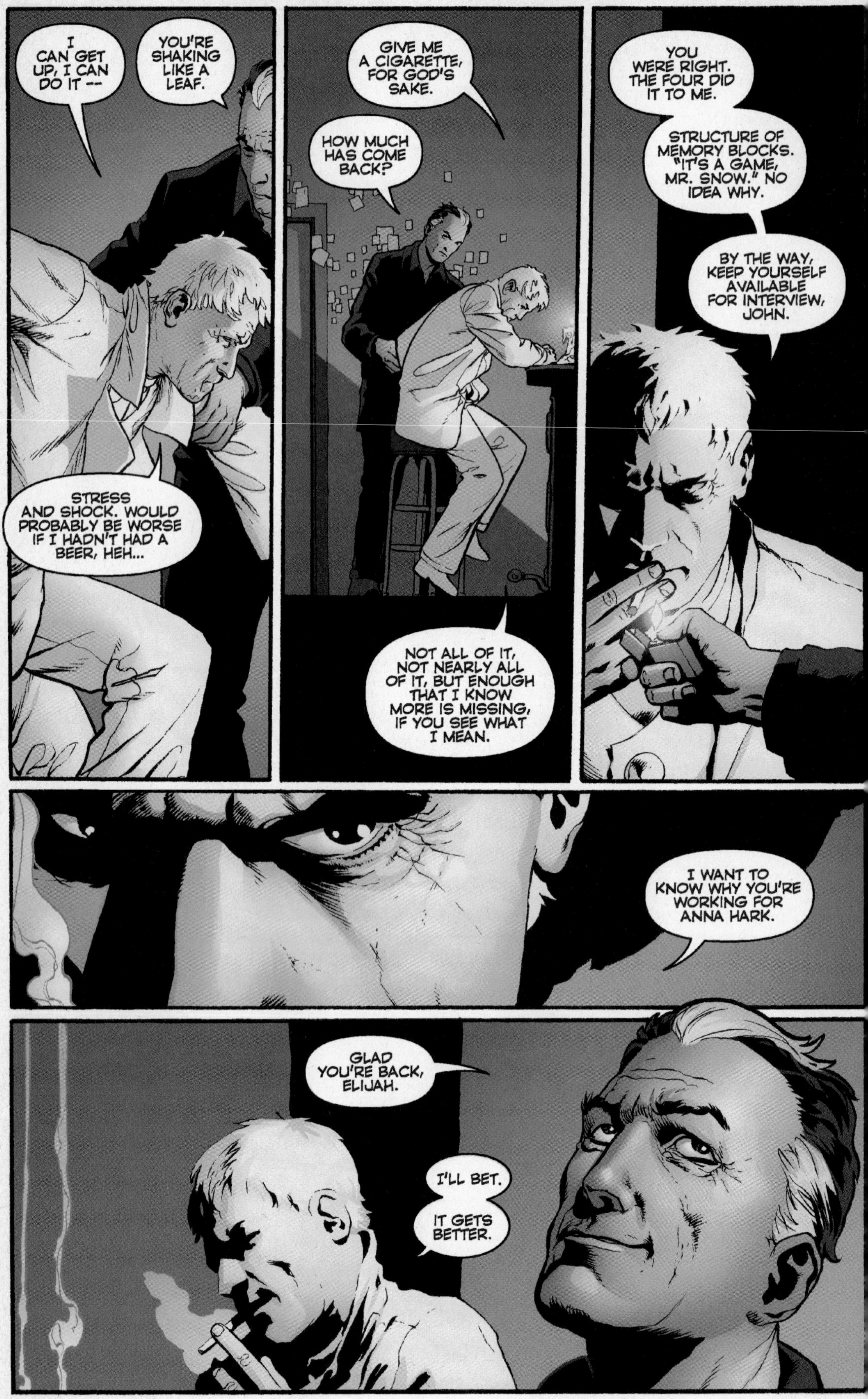
I CAN GET UP, I CAN DO IT --
YOU'RE SHAKING LIKE A LEAF.
STRESS AND SHOCK. WOULD PROBABLY BE WORSE IF I HADN'T HAD A BEER, HEH...
GIVE ME A CIGARETTE, FOR GOD'S SAKE.
HOW MUCH HAS COME BACK?
NOT ALL OF IT, NOT NEARLY ALL OF IT, BUT ENOUGH THAT I KNOW MORE IS MISSING, IF YOU SEE WHAT I MEAN.
YOU WERE RIGHT. THE FOUR DID IT TO ME.
STRUCTURE OF MEMORY BLOCKS. "IT'S A GAME, MR. SNOW." NO IDEA WHY.
BY THE WAY, KEEP YOURSELF AVAILABLE FOR INTERVIEW, JOHN.
I WANT TO KNOW WHY YOU'RE WORKING FOR ANNA HARK.
GLAD YOU'RE BACK, ELIJAH.
I'LL BET.
IT GETS BETTER.

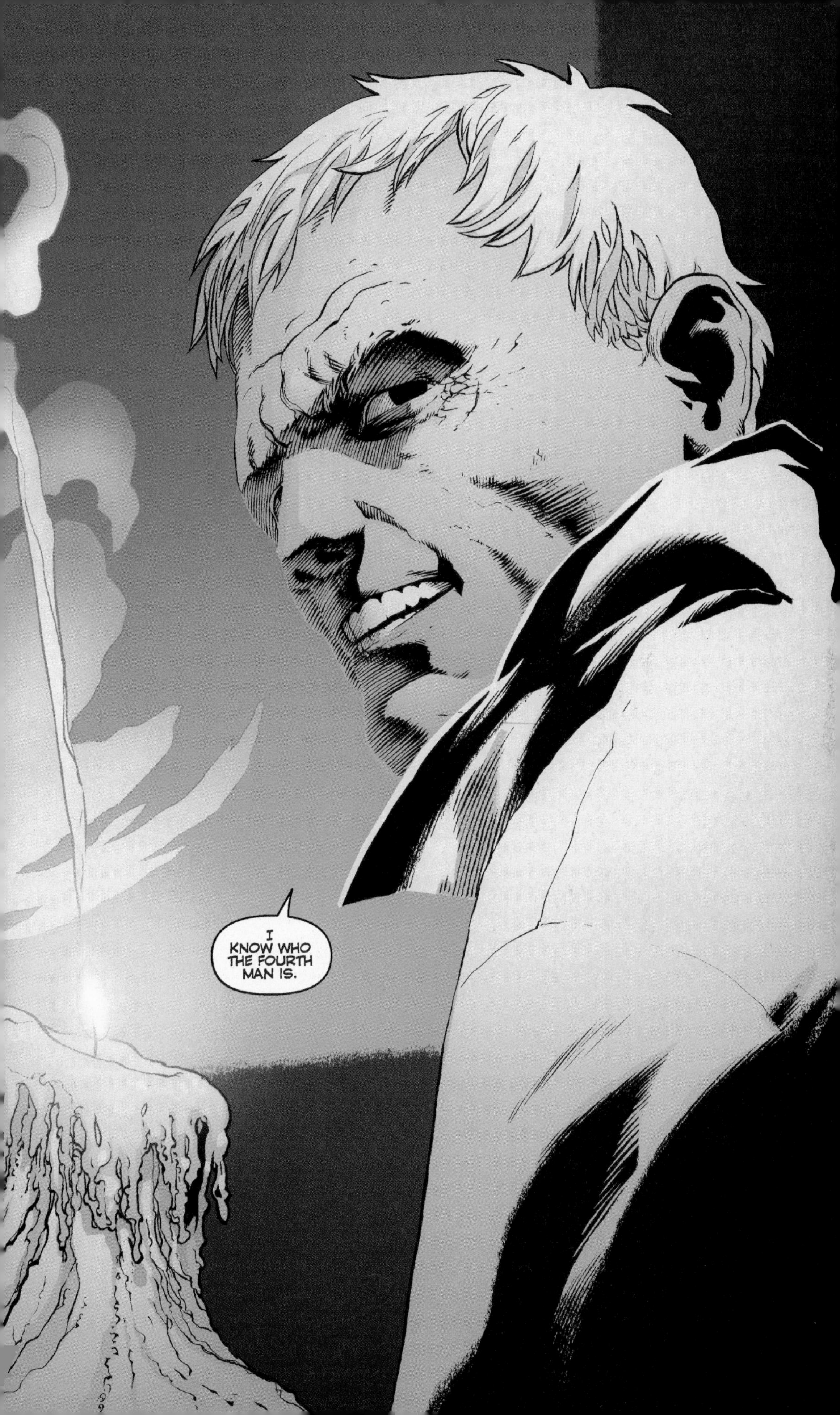
I KNOW WHO THE FOURTH MAN IS.

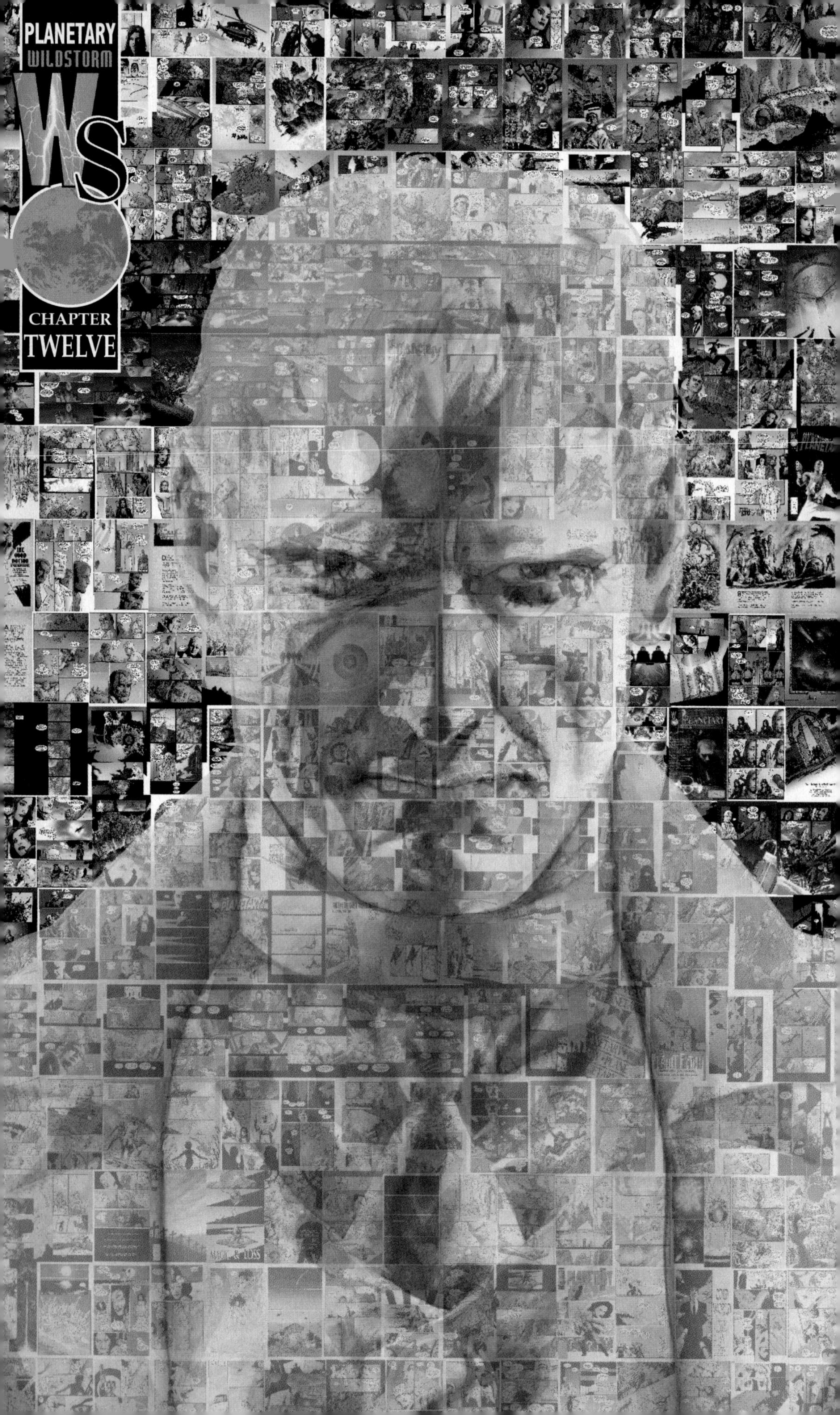
PLANETARY
WILDSTORM
WS
CHAPTER
TWELVE

MEMORY CLOUD

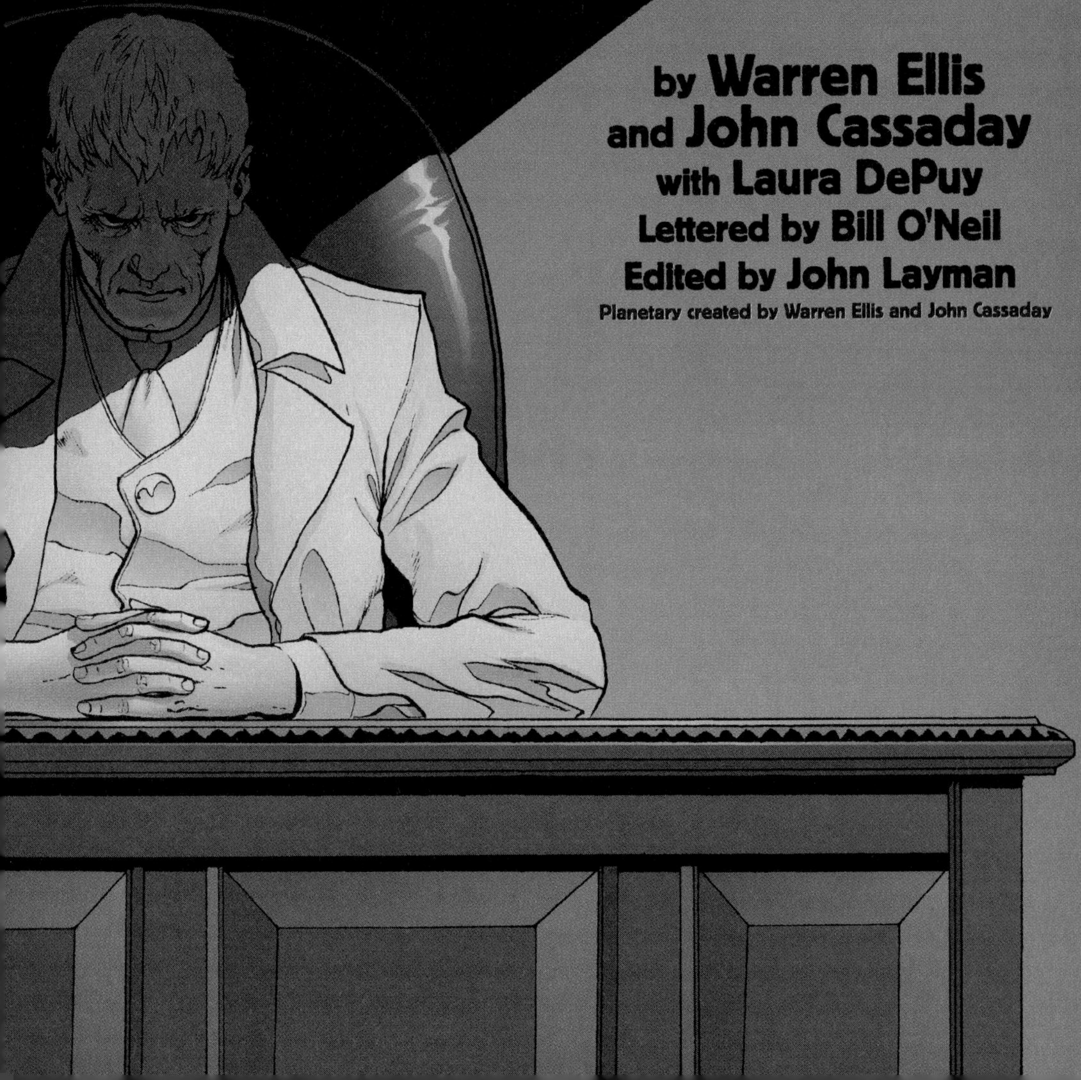

by Warren Ellis
and John Cassaday
with Laura DePuy
Lettered by Bill O'Neil
Edited by John Layman
Planetary created by Warren Ellis and John Cassaday

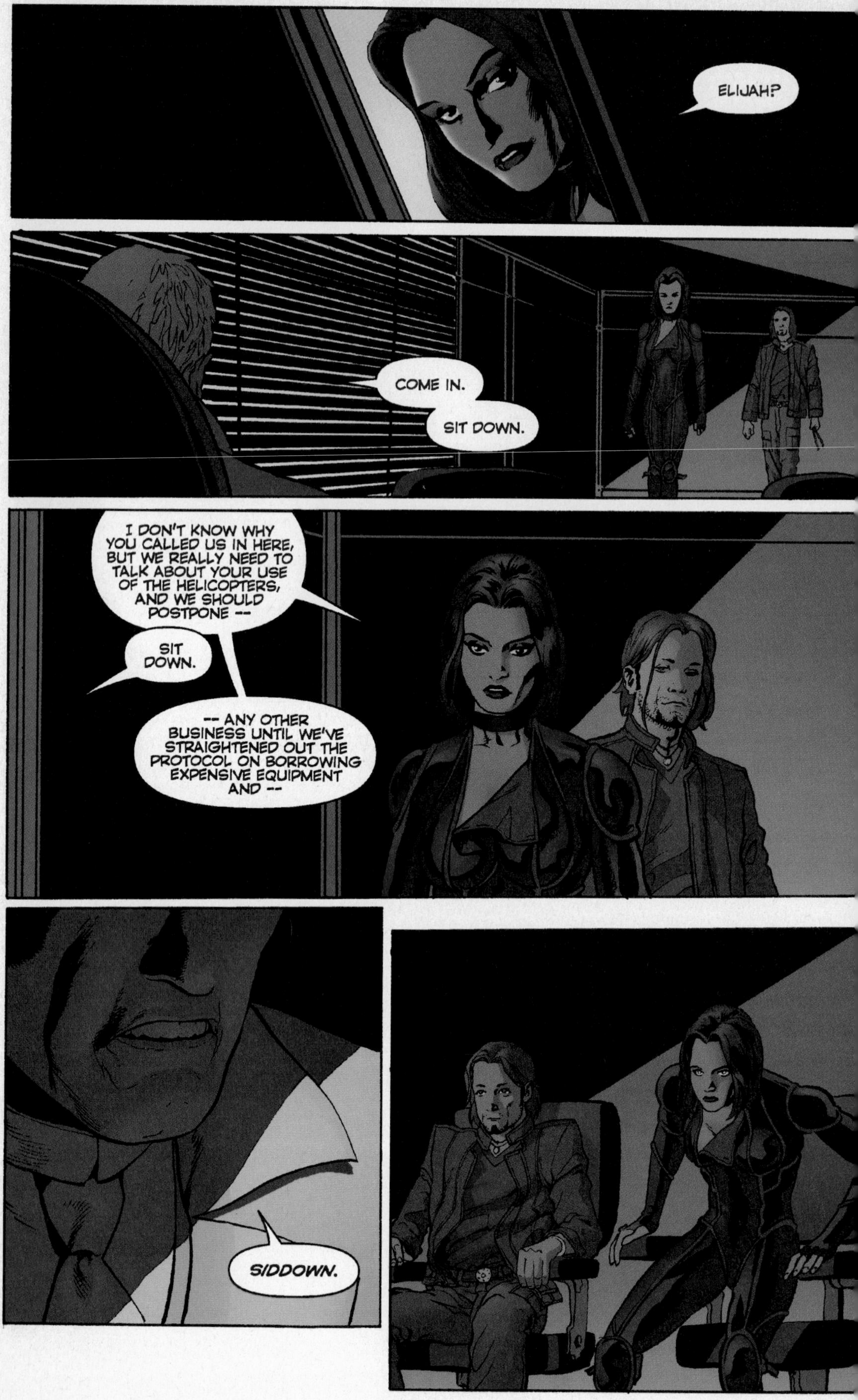
ELIJAH?
COME IN.
SIT DOWN.
I DON'T KNOW WHY YOU CALLED US IN HERE, BUT WE REALLY NEED TO TALK ABOUT YOUR USE OF THE HELICOPTERS, AND WE SHOULD POSTPONE --
SIT DOWN.
-- ANY OTHER BUSINESS UNTIL WE'VE STRAIGHTENED OUT THE PROTOCOL ON BORROWING EXPENSIVE EQUIPMENT AND --
SIDDOWN.

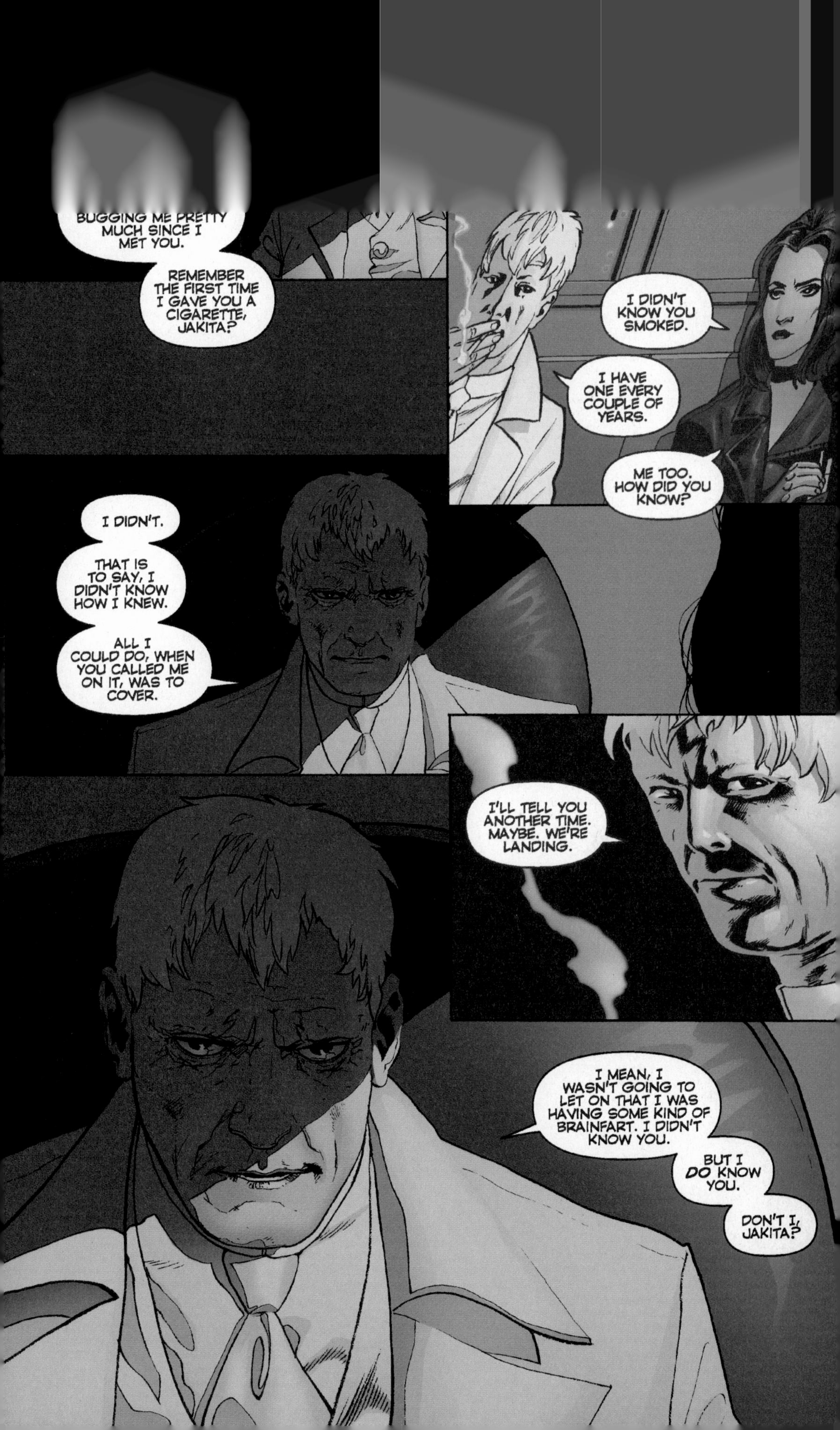
BUGGING ME PRETTY MUCH SINCE I MET YOU.
REMEMBER THE FIRST TIME I GAVE YOU A CIGARETTE, JAKITA?
I DIDN'T KNOW YOU SMOKED.
I HAVE ONE EVERY COUPLE OF YEARS.
ME TOO. HOW DID YOU KNOW?
I DIDN'T.
THAT IS TO SAY, I DIDN'T KNOW HOW I KNEW.
ALL I COULD DO, WHEN YOU CALLED ME ON IT, WAS TO COVER.
I'LL TELL YOU ANOTHER TIME. MAYBE. WE'RE LANDING.
I MEAN, I WASN'T GOING TO LET ON THAT I WAS HAVING SOME KIND OF BRAINFART. I DIDN'T KNOW YOU.
BUT I DO KNOW YOU.
DON'T I, JAKITA?

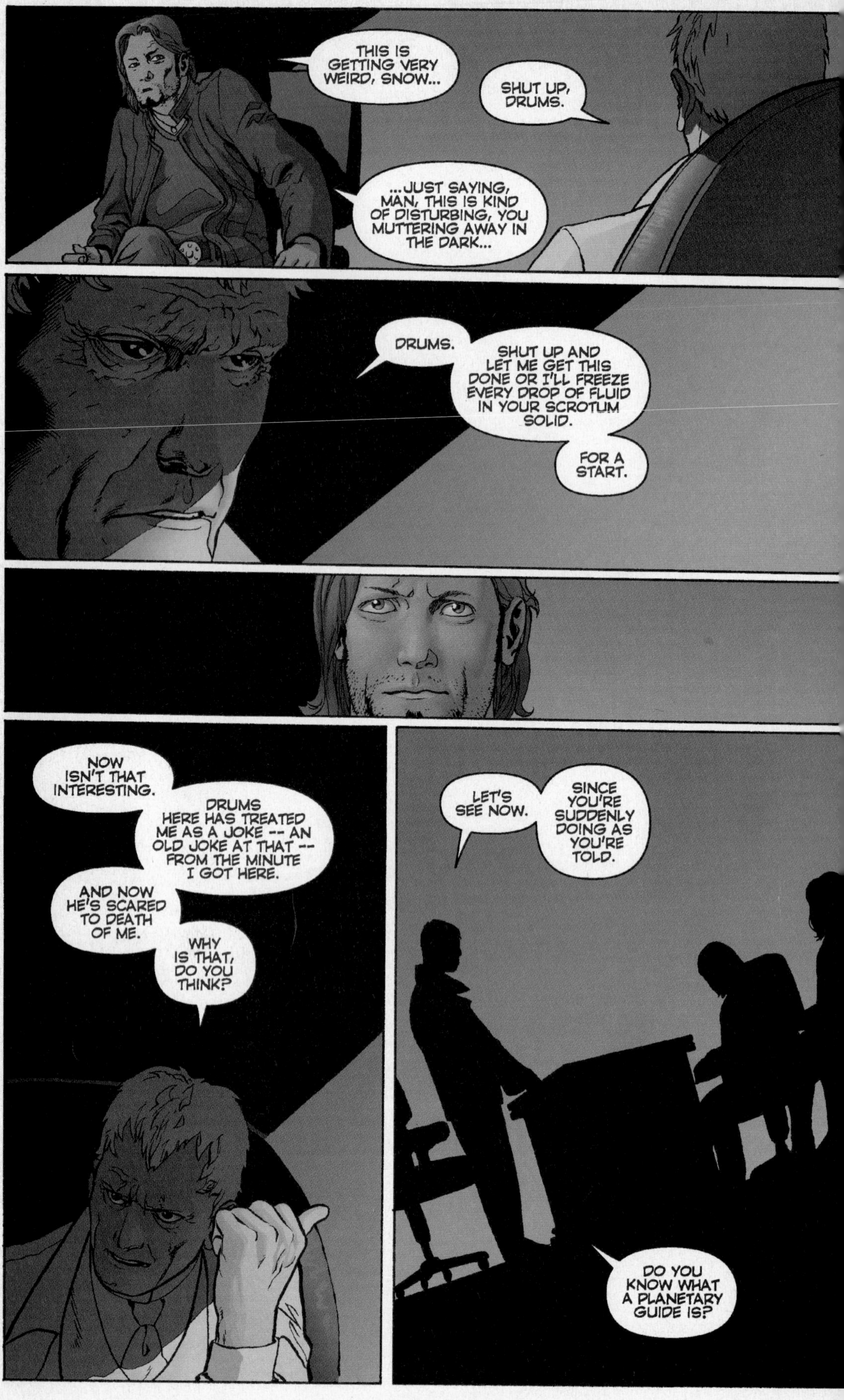
THIS IS GETTING VERY WEIRD, SNOW...
SHUT UP, DRUMS.
...JUST SAYING, MAN, THIS IS KIND OF DISTURBING, YOU MUTTERING AWAY IN THE DARK...
DRUMS.
SHUT UP AND LET ME GET THIS DONE OR I'LL FREEZE EVERY DROP OF FLUID IN YOUR SCROTUM SOLID.
FOR A START.
NOW ISN'T THAT INTERESTING.
DRUMS HERE HAS TREATED ME AS A JOKE -- AN OLD JOKE AT THAT -- FROM THE MINUTE I GOT HERE.
AND NOW HE'S SCARED TO DEATH OF ME.
WHY IS THAT, DO YOU THINK?
LET'S SEE NOW.
SINCE YOU'RE SUDDENLY DOING AS YOU'RE TOLD.
DO YOU KNOW WHAT A PLANETARY GUIDE IS?

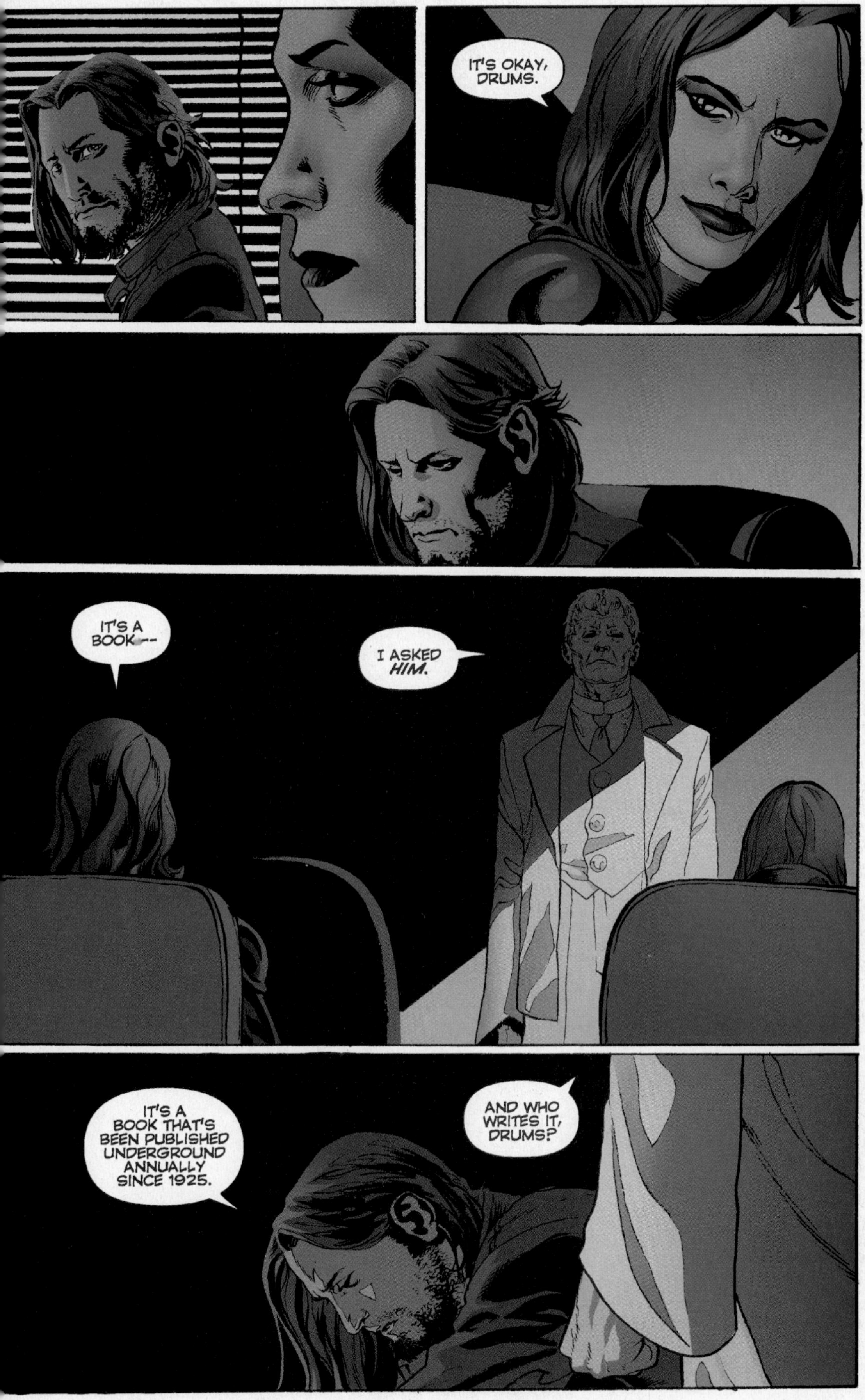
IT'S OKAY, DRUMS.
IT'S A BOOK--
I ASKED *HIM*.
IT'S A BOOK THAT'S BEEN PUBLISHED UNDERGROUND ANNUALLY SINCE 1925.
AND WHO WRITES IT, DRUMS?

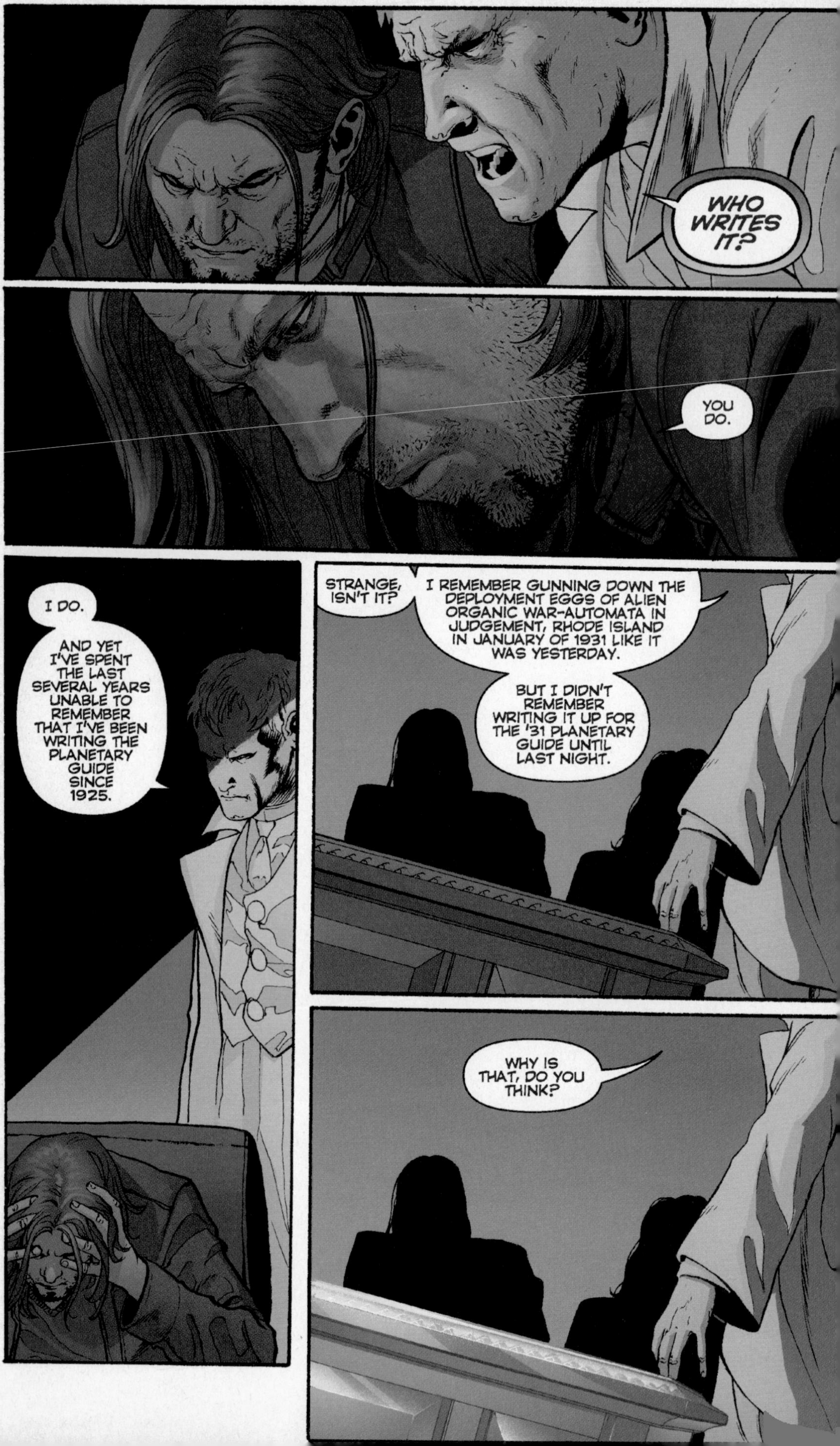
WHO WRITES IT?
YOU DO.
I DO.
AND YET I'VE SPENT THE LAST SEVERAL YEARS UNABLE TO REMEMBER THAT I'VE BEEN WRITING THE PLANETARY GUIDE SINCE 1925.
STRANGE, ISN'T IT?
I REMEMBER GUNNING DOWN THE DEPLOYMENT EGGS OF ALIEN ORGANIC WAR-AUTOMATA IN JUDGEMENT, RHODE ISLAND IN JANUARY OF 1931 LIKE IT WAS YESTERDAY.
BUT I DIDN'T REMEMBER WRITING IT UP FOR THE '31 PLANETARY GUIDE UNTIL LAST NIGHT.
WHY IS THAT, DO YOU THINK?

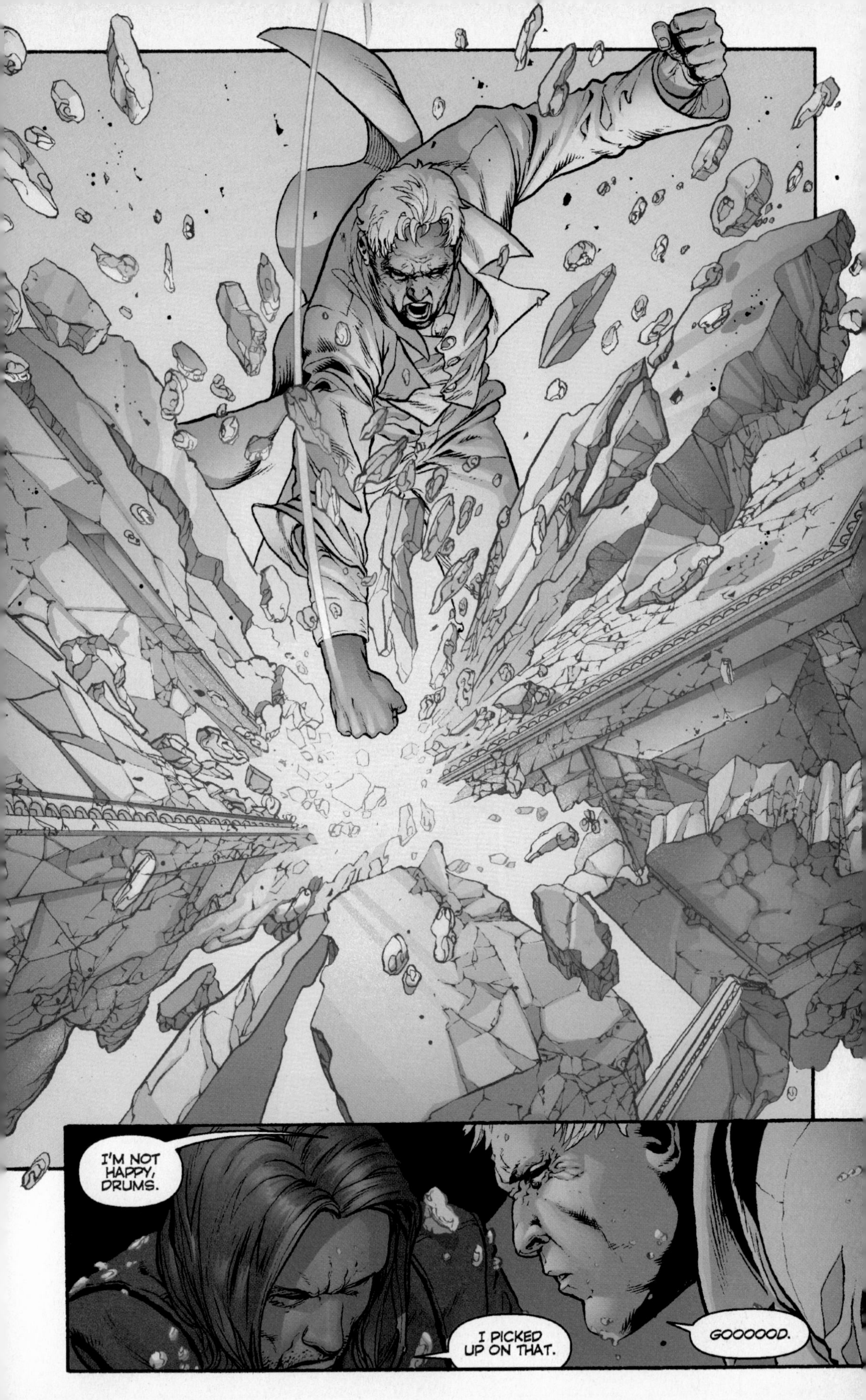
I'M NOT HAPPY, DRUMS.
I PICKED UP ON THAT.
GOOOOOD.

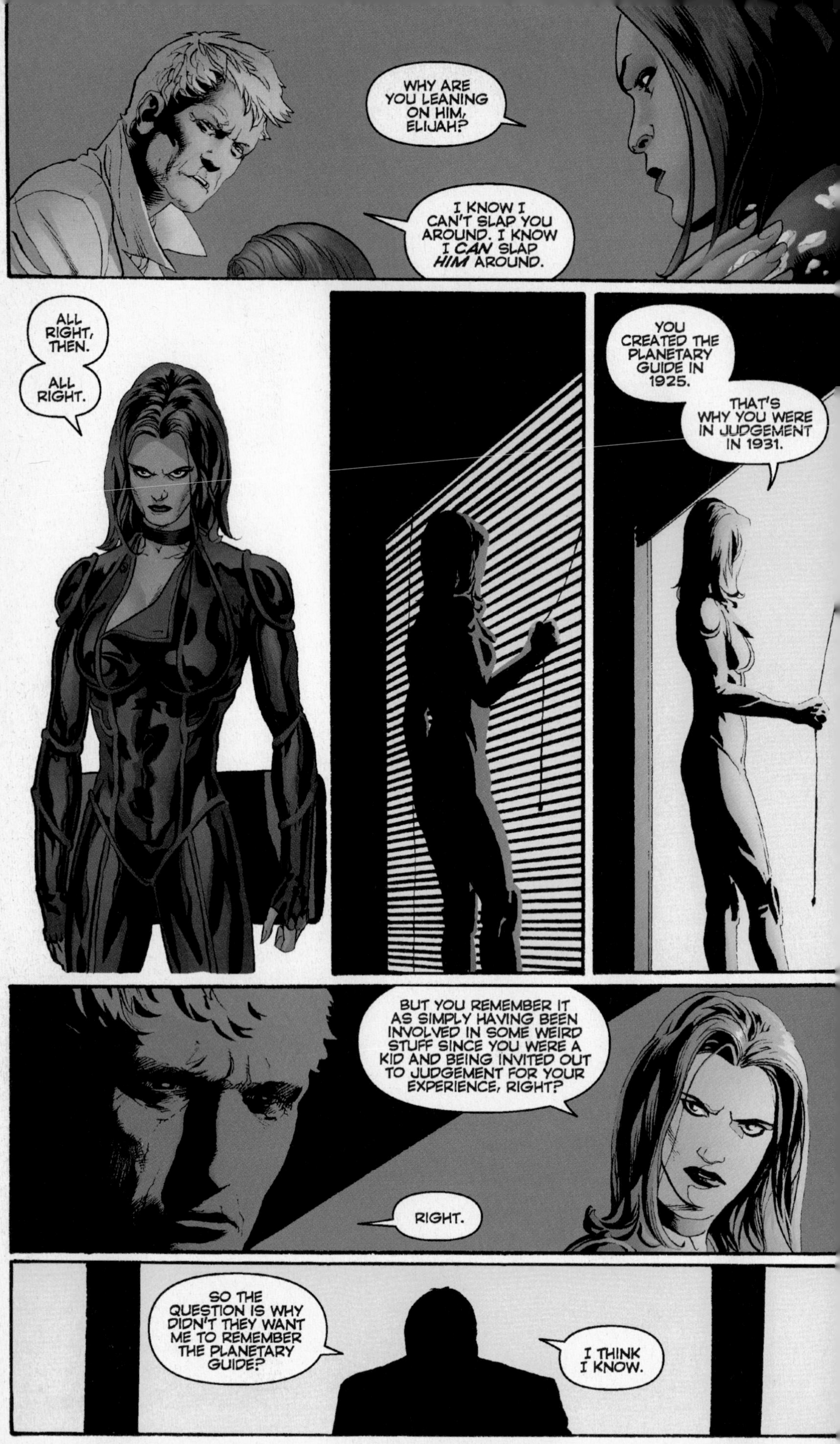
WHY ARE YOU LEANING ON HIM, ELIJAH?
I KNOW I CAN'T SLAP YOU AROUND. I KNOW I *CAN* SLAP *HIM* AROUND.
ALL RIGHT, THEN.
ALL RIGHT.
YOU CREATED THE PLANETARY GUIDE IN 1925.
THAT'S WHY YOU WERE IN JUDGEMENT IN 1931.
BUT YOU REMEMBER IT AS SIMPLY HAVING BEEN INVOLVED IN SOME WEIRD STUFF SINCE YOU WERE A KID AND BEING INVITED OUT TO JUDGEMENT FOR YOUR EXPERIENCE, RIGHT?
RIGHT.
SO THE QUESTION IS WHY DIDN'T THEY WANT ME TO REMEMBER THE PLANETARY GUIDE?
I THINK I KNOW.

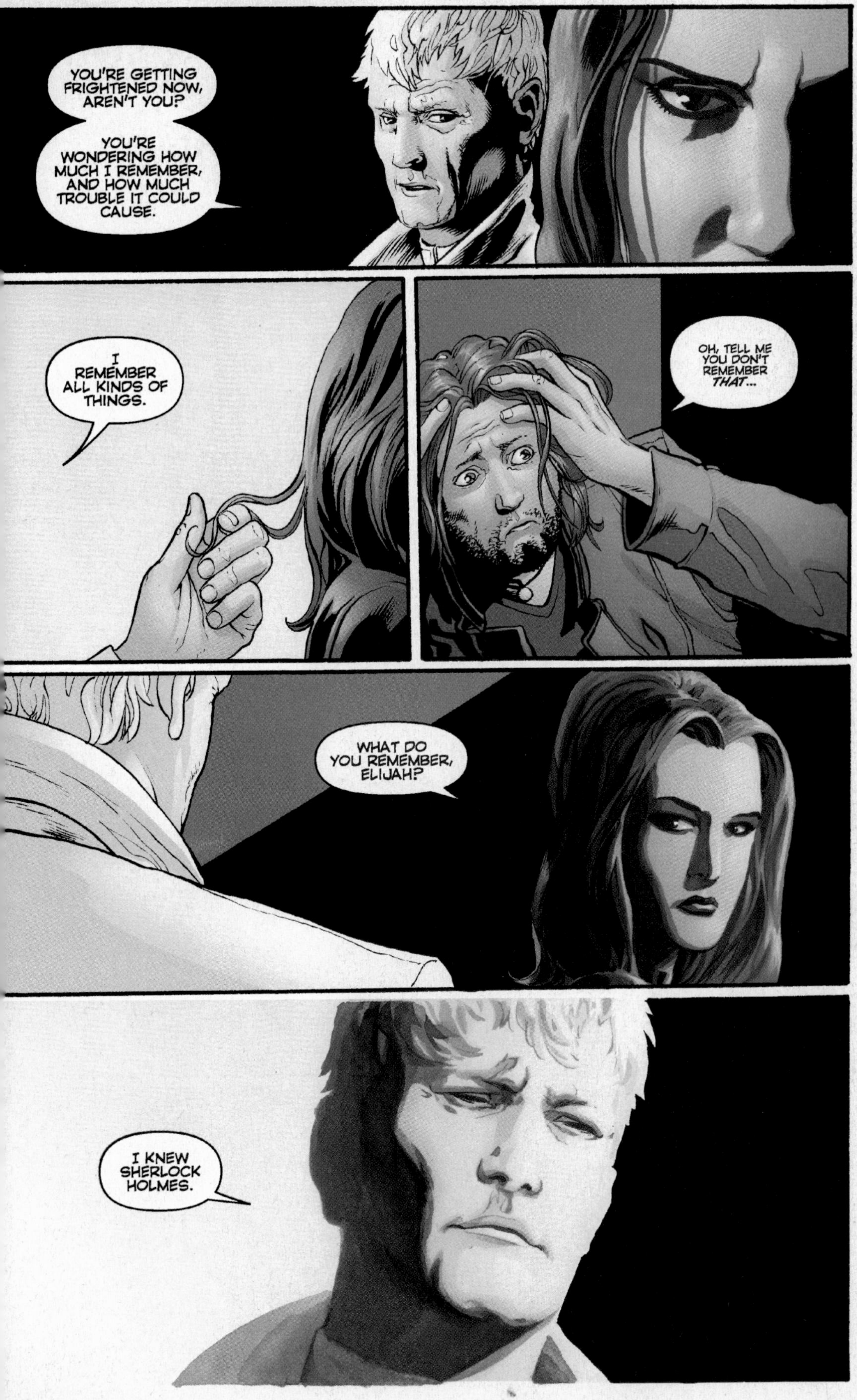
YOU'RE GETTING FRIGHTENED NOW, AREN'T YOU?
YOU'RE WONDERING HOW MUCH I REMEMBER, AND HOW MUCH TROUBLE IT COULD CAUSE.
I REMEMBER ALL KINDS OF THINGS.
OH, TELL ME YOU DON'T REMEMBER *THAT*...
WHAT DO YOU REMEMBER, ELIJAH?
I KNEW SHERLOCK HOLMES.

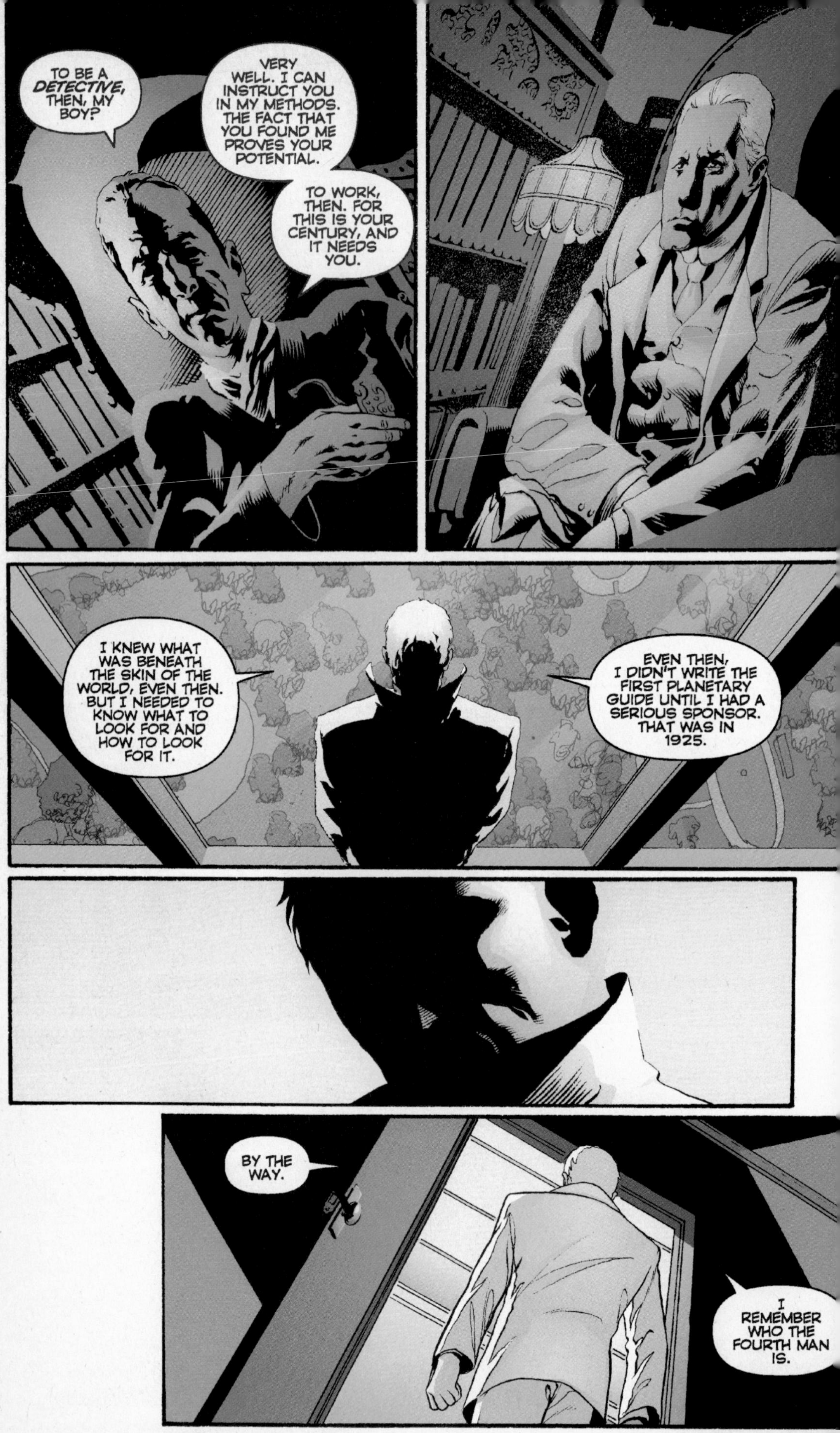
TO BE A *DETECTIVE,* THEN, MY BOY?
VERY WELL. I CAN INSTRUCT YOU IN MY METHODS. THE FACT THAT YOU FOUND ME PROVES YOUR POTENTIAL.
TO WORK, THEN. FOR THIS IS YOUR CENTURY, AND IT NEEDS YOU.
I KNEW WHAT WAS BENEATH THE SKIN OF THE WORLD, EVEN THEN. BUT I NEEDED TO KNOW WHAT TO LOOK FOR AND HOW TO LOOK FOR IT.
EVEN THEN, I DIDN'T WRITE THE FIRST PLANETARY GUIDE UNTIL I HAD A SERIOUS SPONSOR. THAT WAS IN 1925.
BY THE WAY.
I REMEMBER WHO THE FOURTH MAN IS.

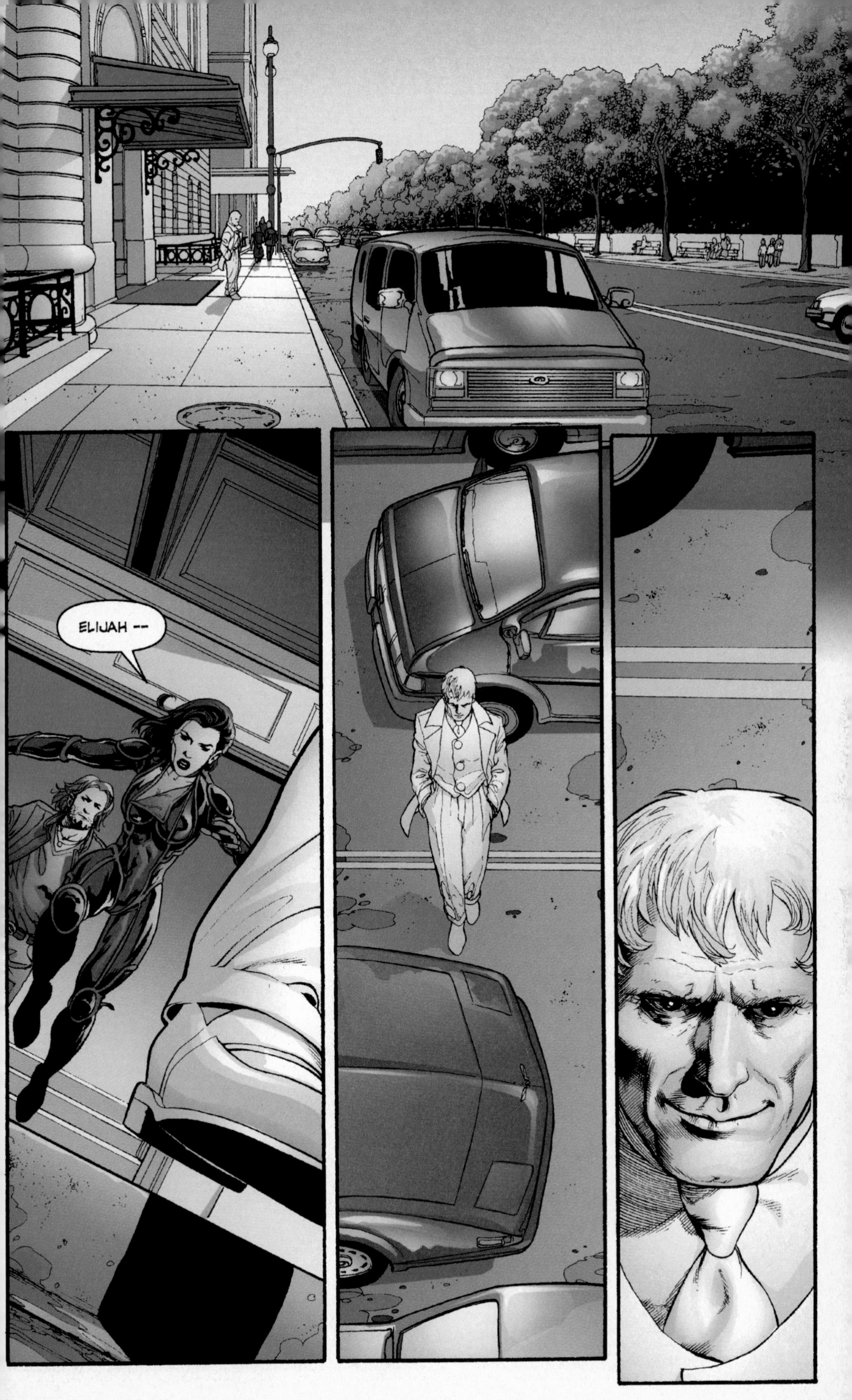
ELIJAH --

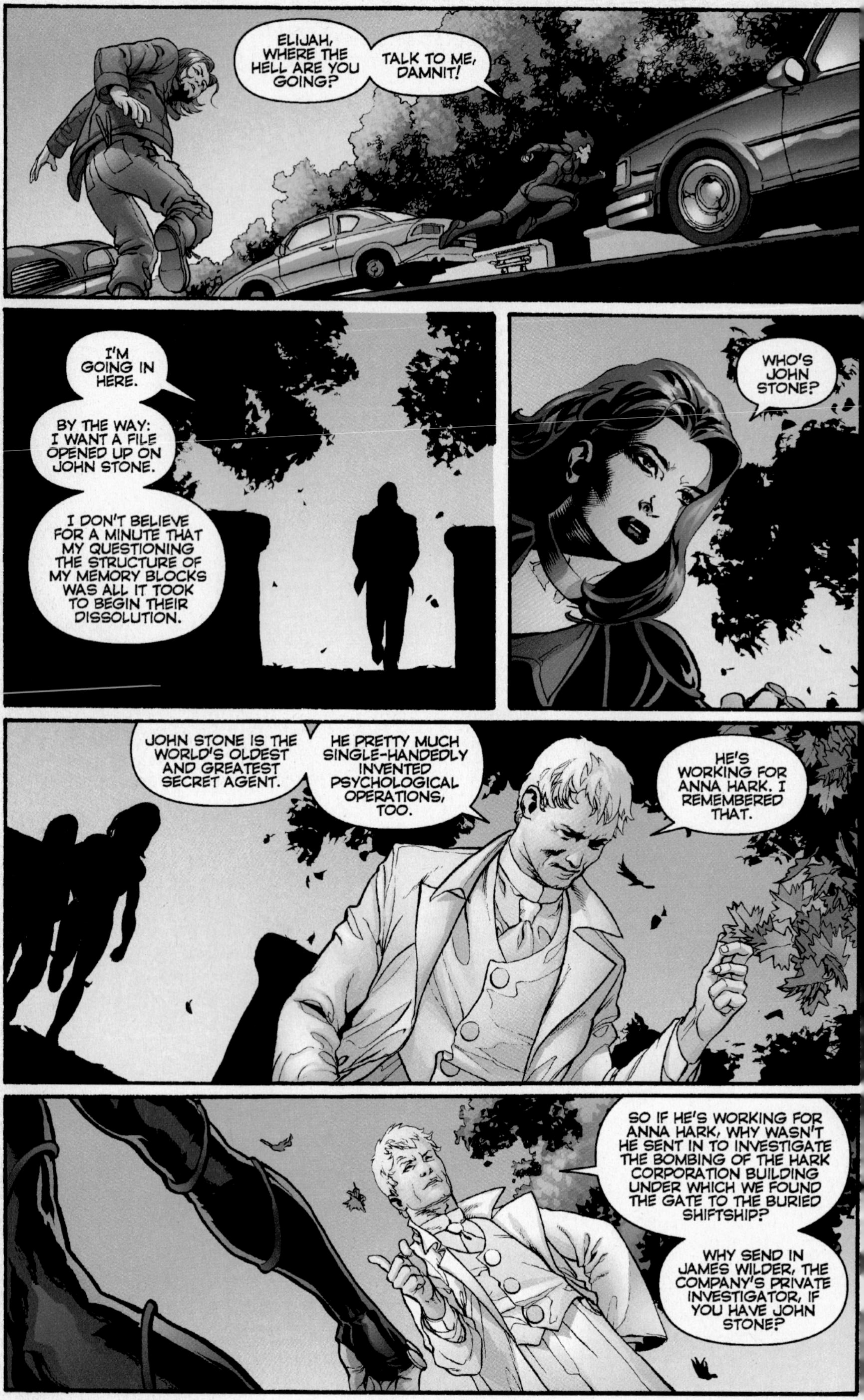
ELIJAH, WHERE THE HELL ARE YOU GOING?
TALK TO ME, DAMNIT!
I'M GOING IN HERE.
BY THE WAY: I WANT A FILE OPENED UP ON JOHN STONE.
I DON'T BELIEVE FOR A MINUTE THAT MY QUESTIONING THE STRUCTURE OF MY MEMORY BLOCKS WAS ALL IT TOOK TO BEGIN THEIR DISSOLUTION.
WHO'S JOHN STONE?
JOHN STONE IS THE WORLD'S OLDEST AND GREATEST SECRET AGENT.
HE PRETTY MUCH SINGLE-HANDEDLY INVENTED PSYCHOLOGICAL OPERATIONS, TOO.
HE'S WORKING FOR ANNA HARK. I REMEMBERED THAT.
SO IF HE'S WORKING FOR ANNA HARK, WHY WASN'T HE SENT IN TO INVESTIGATE THE BOMBING OF THE HARK CORPORATION BUILDING UNDER WHICH WE FOUND THE GATE TO THE BURIED SHIFTSHIP?
WHY SEND IN JAMES WILDER, THE COMPANY'S PRIVATE INVESTIGATOR, IF YOU HAVE JOHN STONE?

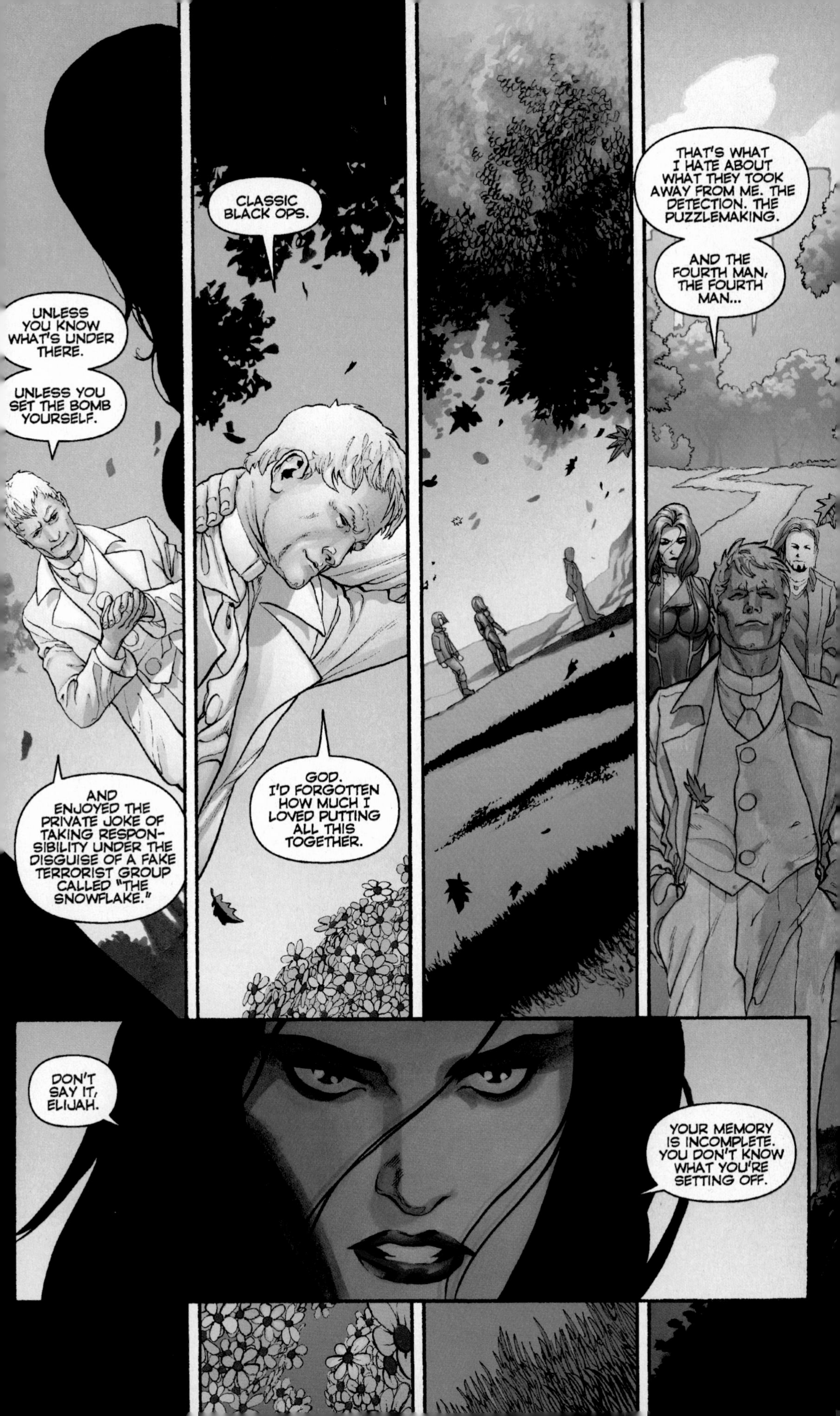
UNLESS YOU KNOW WHAT'S UNDER THERE.
UNLESS YOU SET THE BOMB YOURSELF.
AND ENJOYED THE PRIVATE JOKE OF TAKING RESPON-SIBILITY UNDER THE DISGUISE OF A FAKE TERRORIST GROUP CALLED "THE SNOWFLAKE."
CLASSIC BLACK OPS.
GOD. I'D FORGOTTEN HOW MUCH I LOVED PUTTING ALL THIS TOGETHER.
THAT'S WHAT I HATE ABOUT WHAT THEY TOOK AWAY FROM ME. THE DETECTION. THE PUZZLEMAKING.
AND THE FOURTH MAN, THE FOURTH MAN...
DON'T SAY IT, ELIJAH.
YOUR MEMORY IS INCOMPLETE. YOU DON'T KNOW WHAT YOU'RE SETTING OFF.

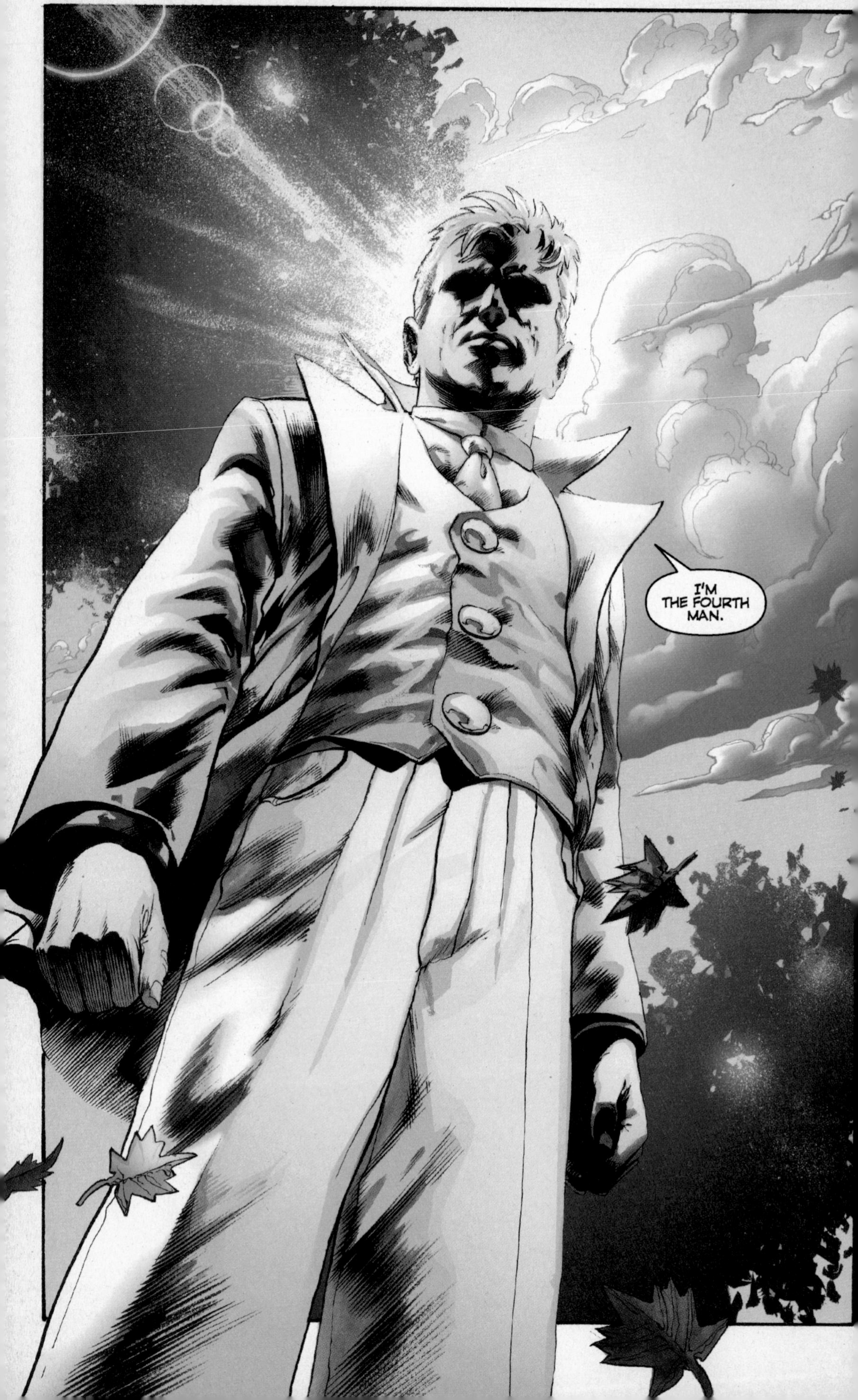
I'M
THE FOURTH
MAN.

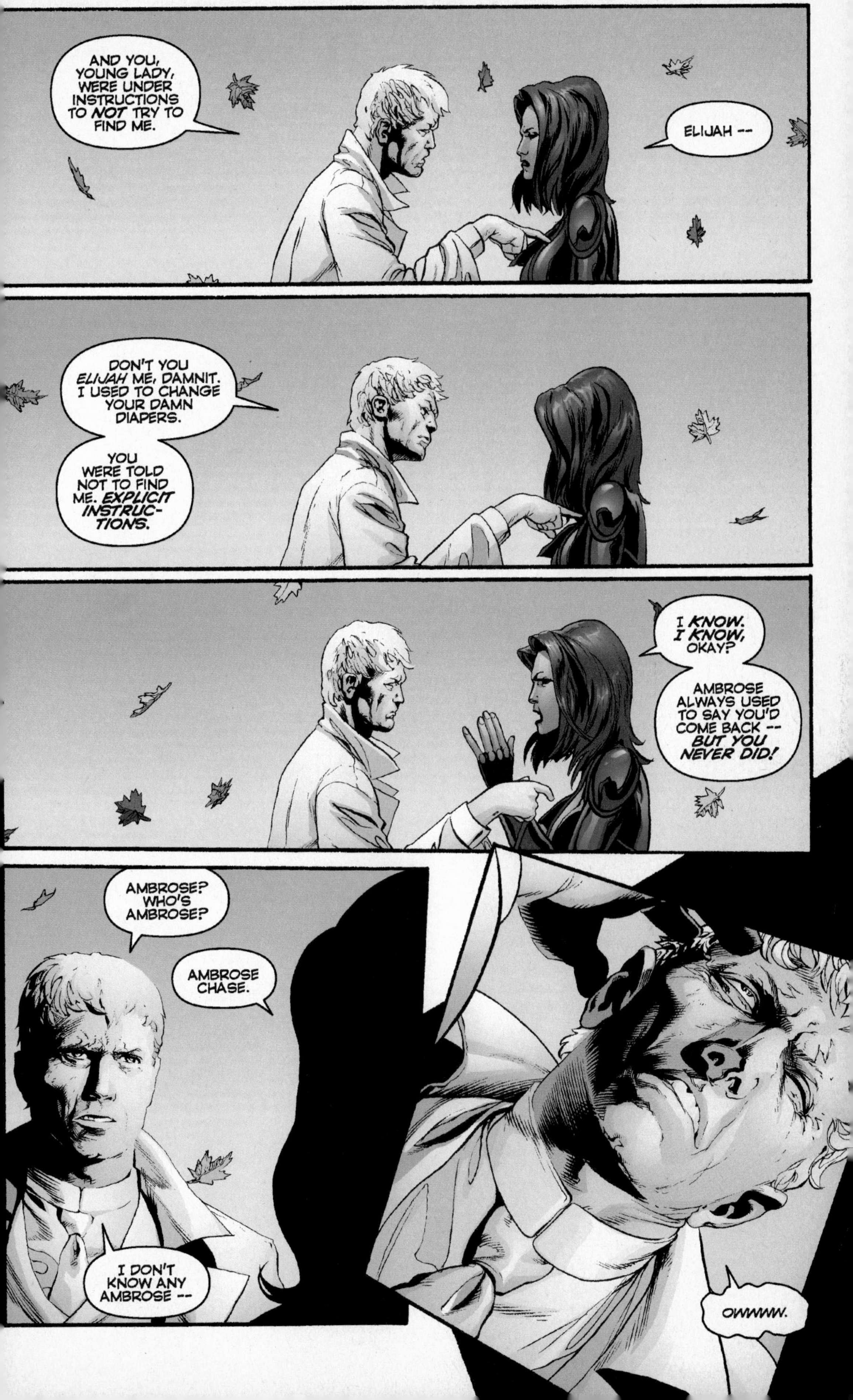

AND YOU, YOUNG LADY, WERE UNDER INSTRUCTIONS TO *NOT* TRY TO FIND ME.
ELIJAH --
DON'T YOU *ELIJAH* ME, DAMNIT. I USED TO CHANGE YOUR DAMN DIAPERS.
YOU WERE TOLD NOT TO FIND ME. *EXPLICIT INSTRUCTIONS.*
I *KNOW.* *I KNOW,* OKAY?
AMBROSE ALWAYS USED TO SAY YOU'D COME BACK -- *BUT YOU NEVER DID!*
AMBROSE? WHO'S AMBROSE?
AMBROSE CHASE.
I DON'T KNOW ANY AMBROSE --
OWWWW.

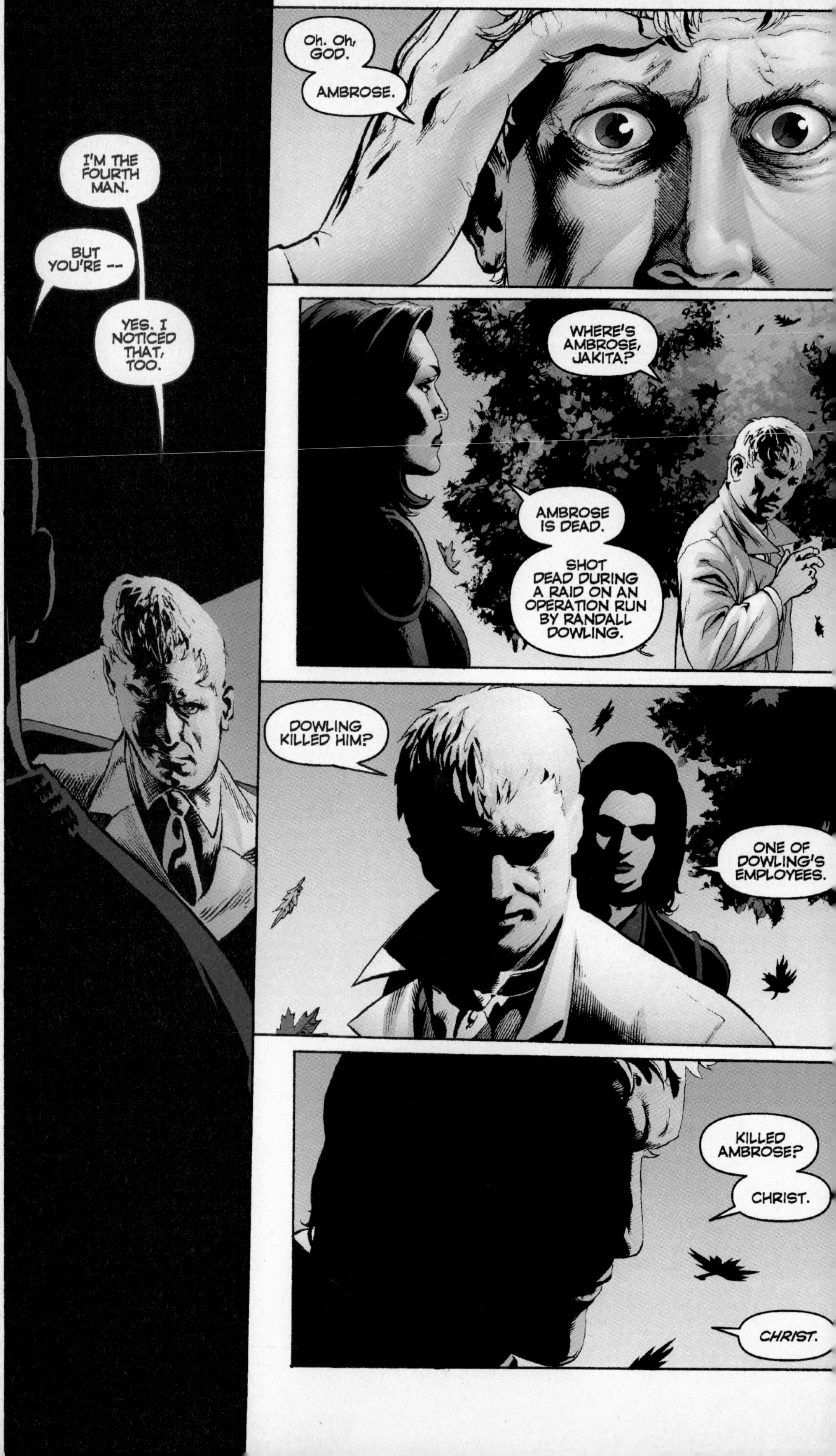

Oh. Oh, GOD.
AMBROSE.
I'M THE FOURTH MAN.
BUT YOU'RE --
YES. I NOTICED THAT, TOO.
WHERE'S AMBROSE, JAKITA?
AMBROSE IS DEAD.
SHOT DEAD DURING A RAID ON AN OPERATION RUN BY RANDALL DOWLING.
DOWLING KILLED HIM?
ONE OF DOWLING'S EMPLOYEES.
KILLED AMBROSE?
CHRIST.
CHRIST.

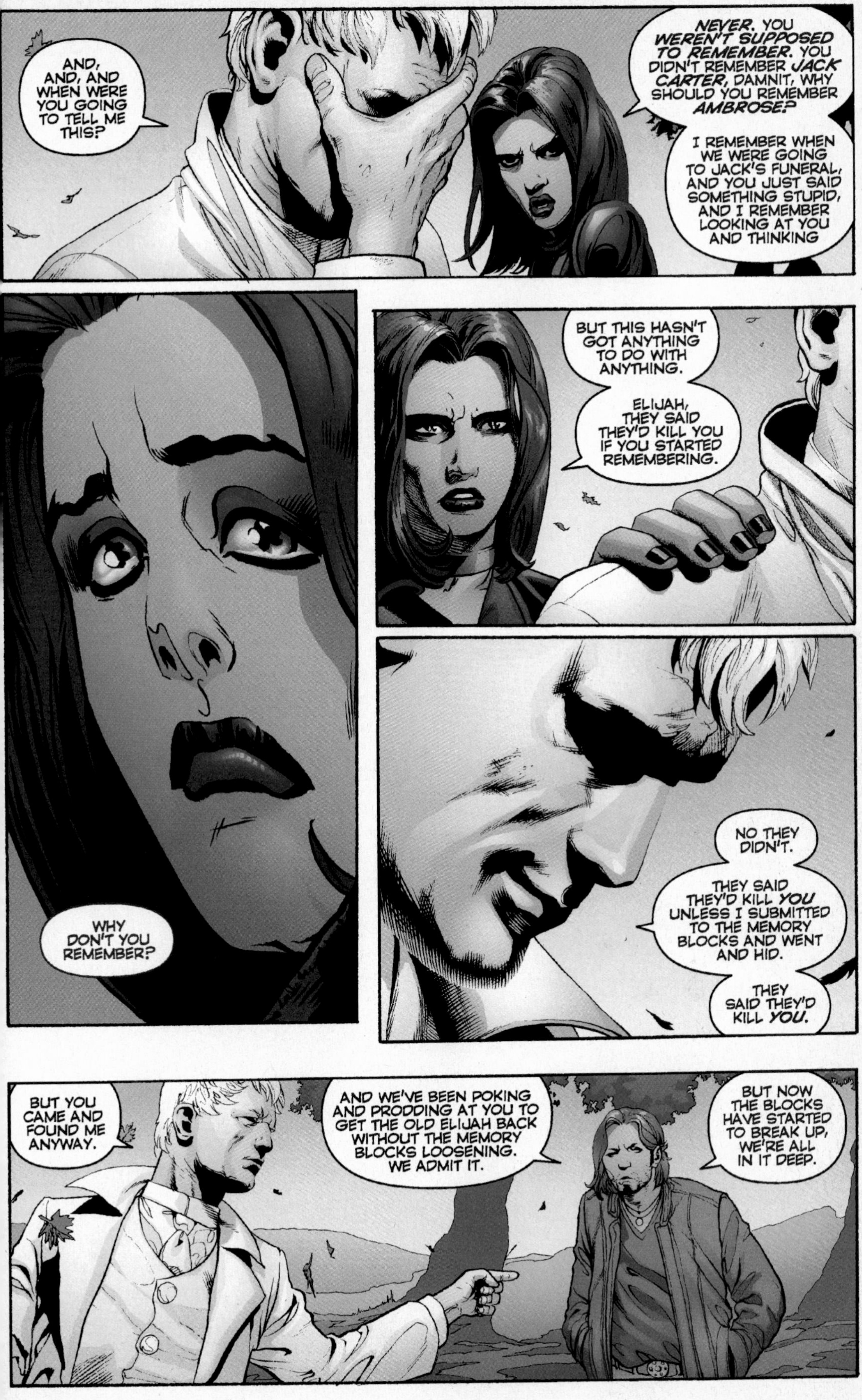

AND, AND, AND WHEN WERE YOU GOING TO TELL ME THIS?
NEVER. YOU WEREN'T SUPPOSED TO REMEMBER. YOU DIDN'T REMEMBER JACK CARTER, DAMNIT, WHY SHOULD YOU REMEMBER AMBROSE?
I REMEMBER WHEN WE WERE GOING TO JACK'S FUNERAL, AND YOU JUST SAID SOMETHING STUPID, AND I REMEMBER LOOKING AT YOU AND THINKING
WHY DON'T YOU REMEMBER?
BUT THIS HASN'T GOT ANYTHING TO DO WITH ANYTHING.
ELIJAH, THEY SAID THEY'D KILL YOU IF YOU STARTED REMEMBERING.
NO THEY DIDN'T.
THEY SAID THEY'D KILL YOU UNLESS I SUBMITTED TO THE MEMORY BLOCKS AND WENT AND HID.
THEY SAID THEY'D KILL YOU.
BUT YOU CAME AND FOUND ME ANYWAY.
AND WE'VE BEEN POKING AND PRODDING AT YOU TO GET THE OLD ELIJAH BACK WITHOUT THE MEMORY BLOCKS LOOSENING. WE ADMIT IT.
BUT NOW THE BLOCKS HAVE STARTED TO BREAK UP, WE'RE ALL IN IT DEEP.

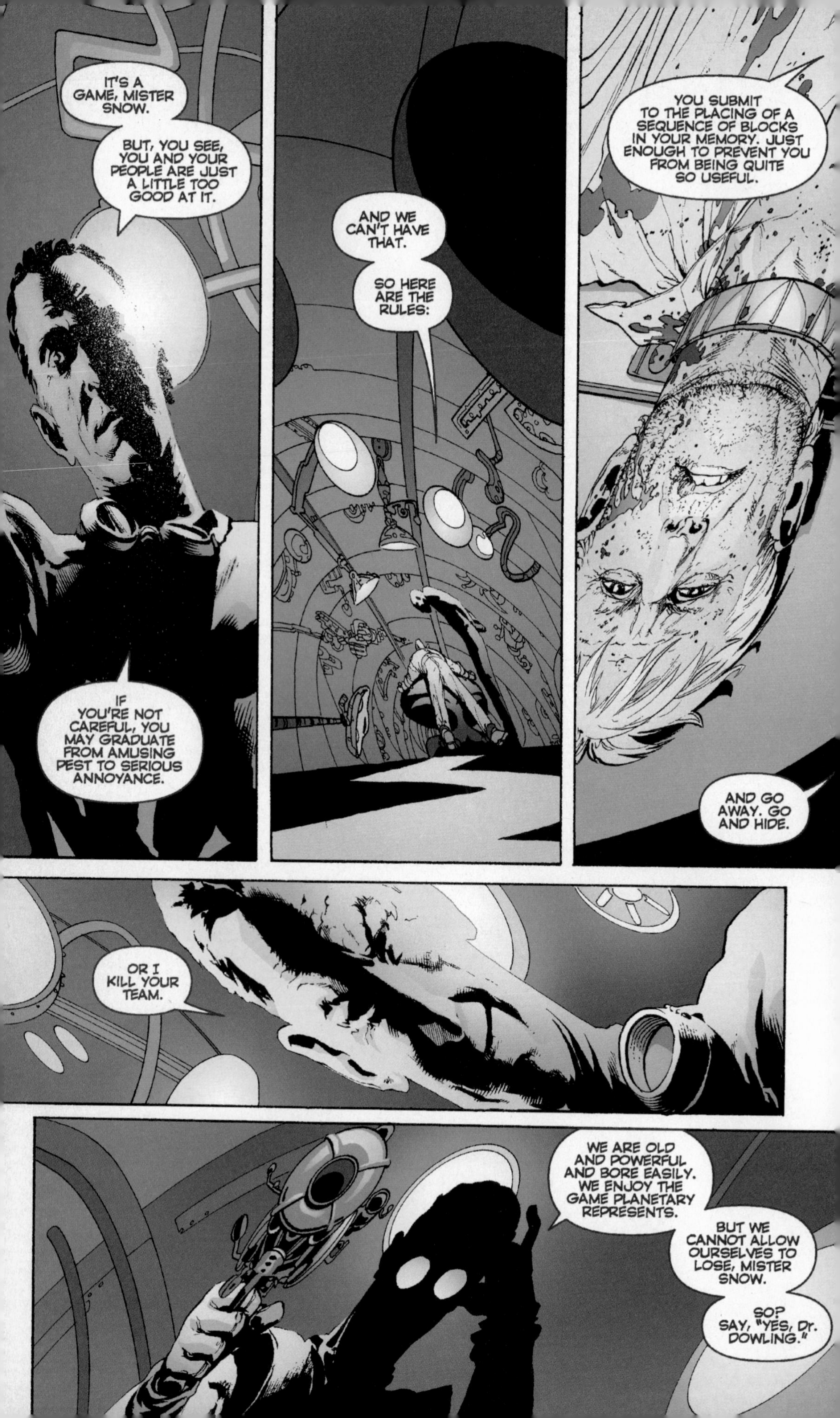
IT'S A GAME, MISTER SNOW.
BUT, YOU SEE, YOU AND YOUR PEOPLE ARE JUST A LITTLE TOO GOOD AT IT.
IF YOU'RE NOT CAREFUL, YOU MAY GRADUATE FROM AMUSING PEST TO SERIOUS ANNOYANCE.
AND WE CAN'T HAVE THAT.
SO HERE ARE THE RULES:
YOU SUBMIT TO THE PLACING OF A SEQUENCE OF BLOCKS IN YOUR MEMORY. JUST ENOUGH TO PREVENT YOU FROM BEING QUITE SO USEFUL.
AND GO AWAY. GO AND HIDE.
OR I KILL YOUR TEAM.
WE ARE OLD AND POWERFUL AND BORE EASILY. WE ENJOY THE GAME PLANETARY REPRESENTS.
BUT WE CANNOT ALLOW OURSELVES TO LOSE, MISTER SNOW.
SO? SAY, "YES, Dr. DOWLING."

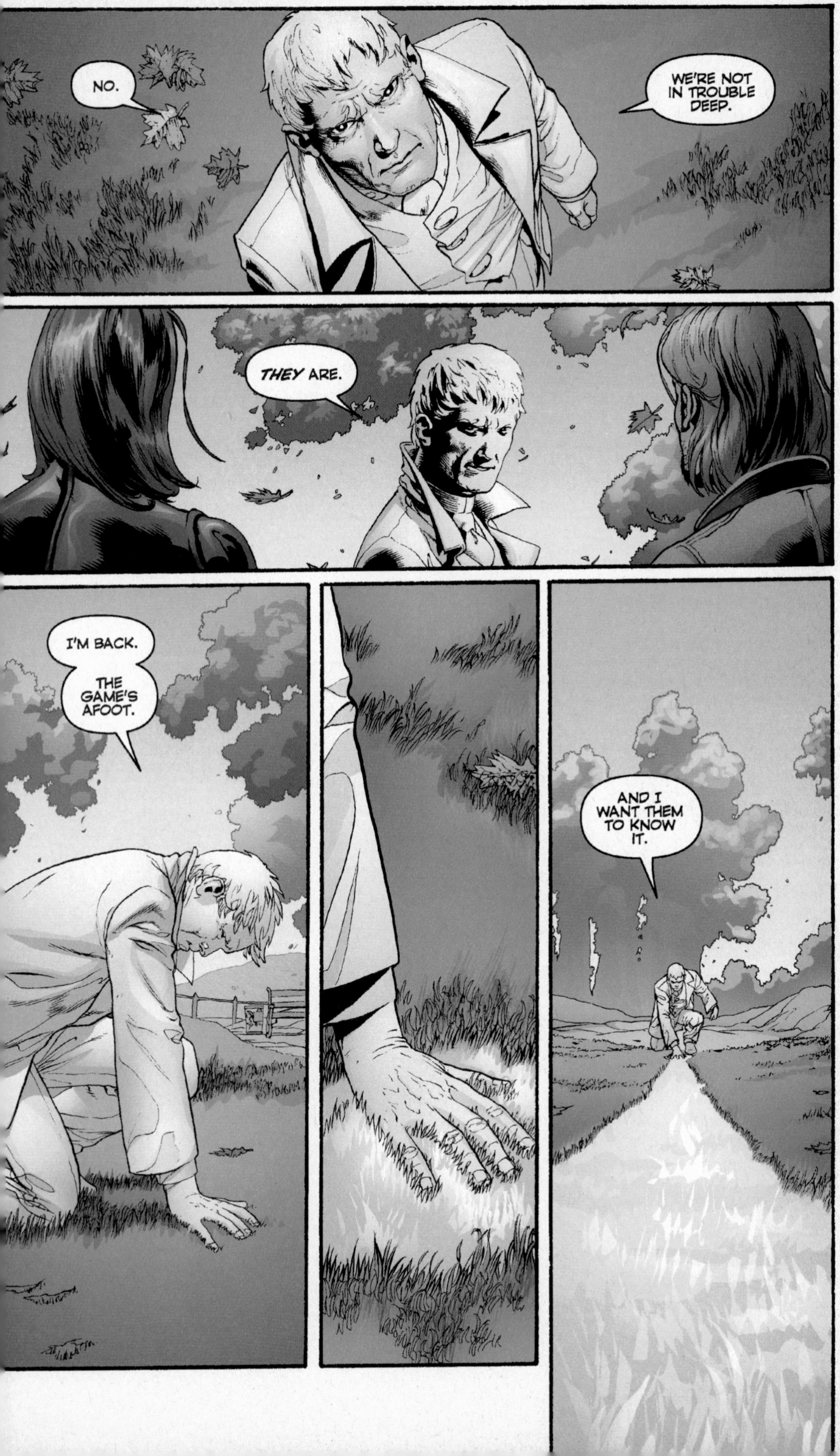
NO.
WE'RE NOT IN TROUBLE DEEP.
THEY ARE.
I'M BACK.
THE GAME'S AFOOT.
AND I WANT THEM TO KNOW IT.

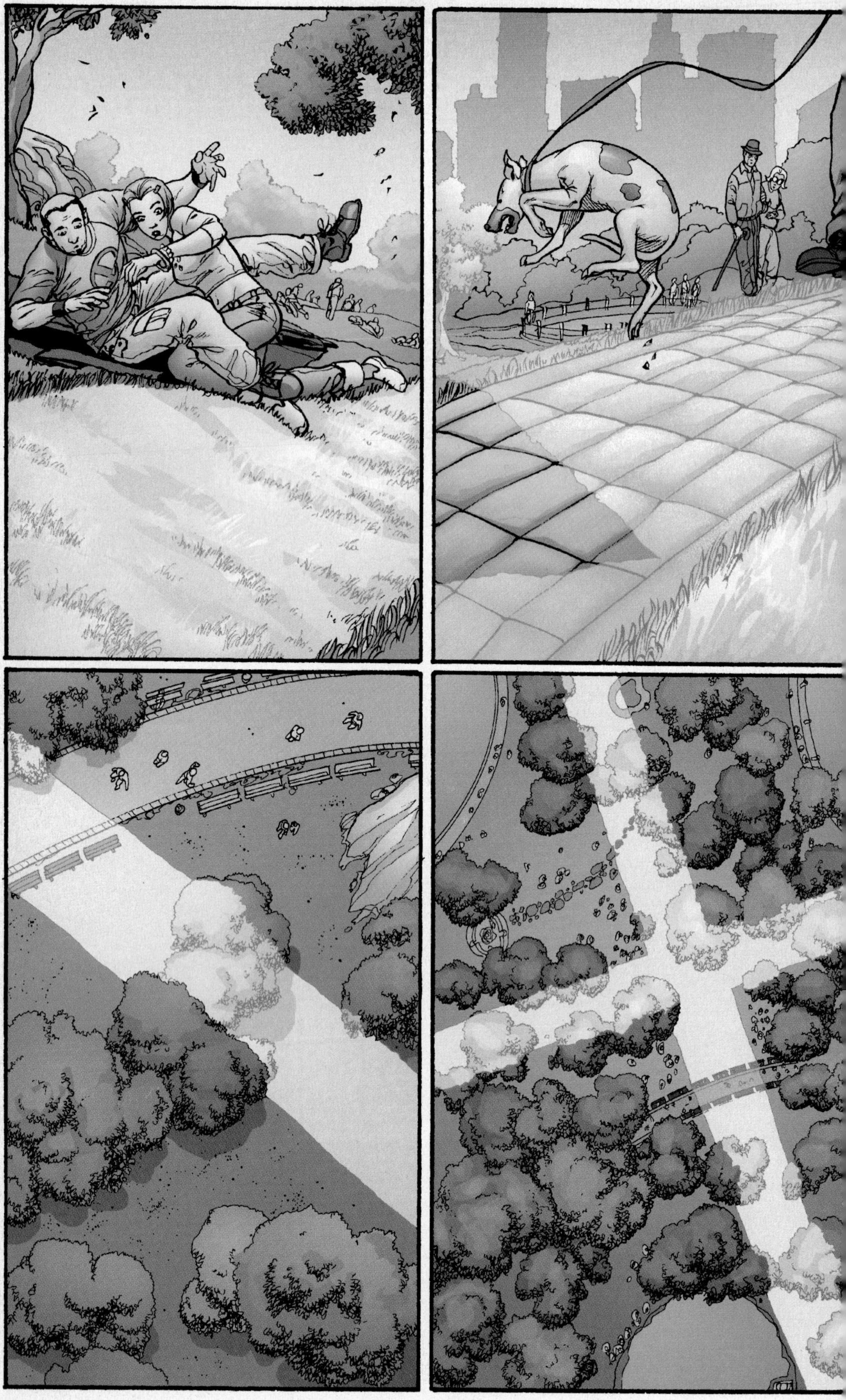

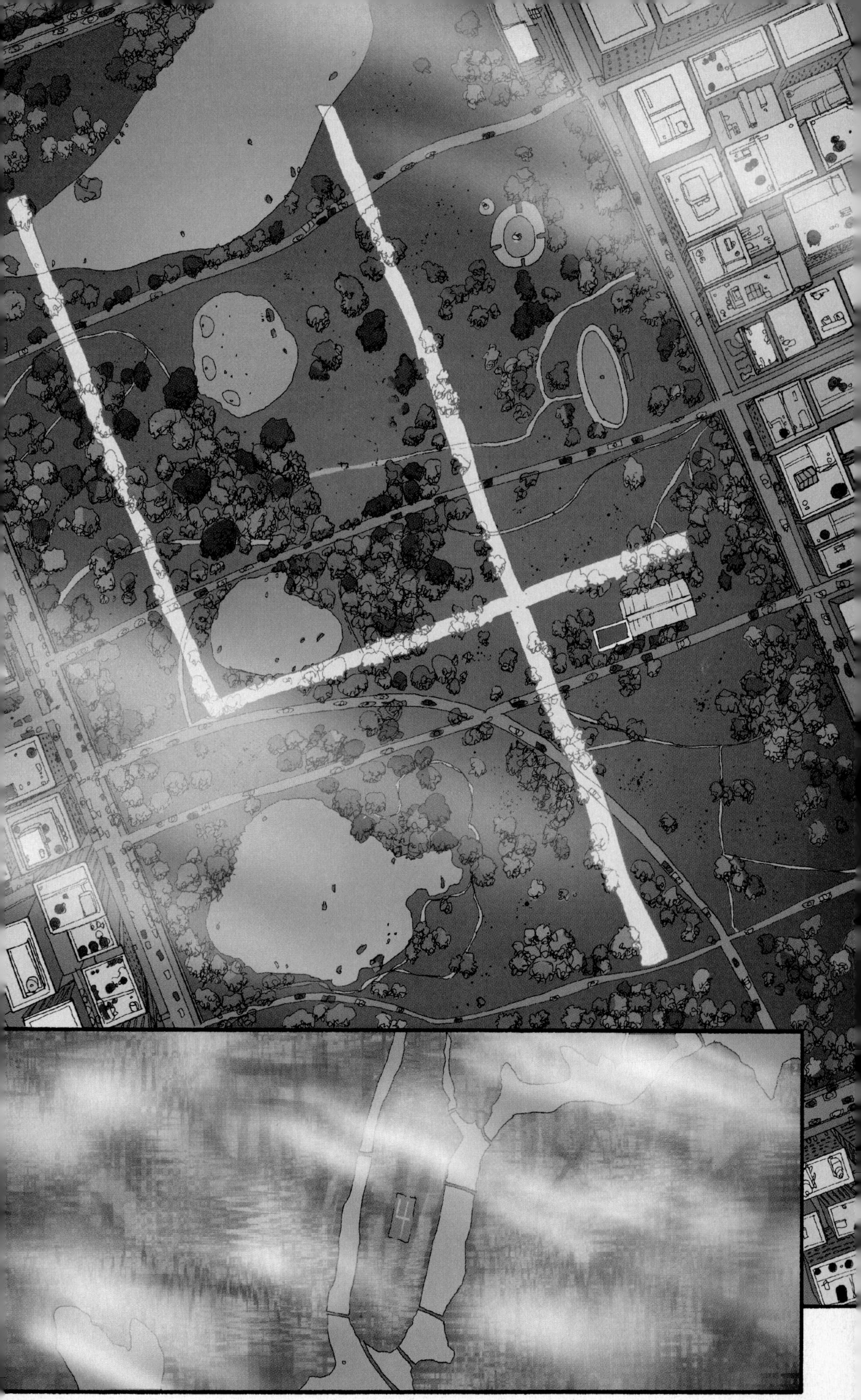

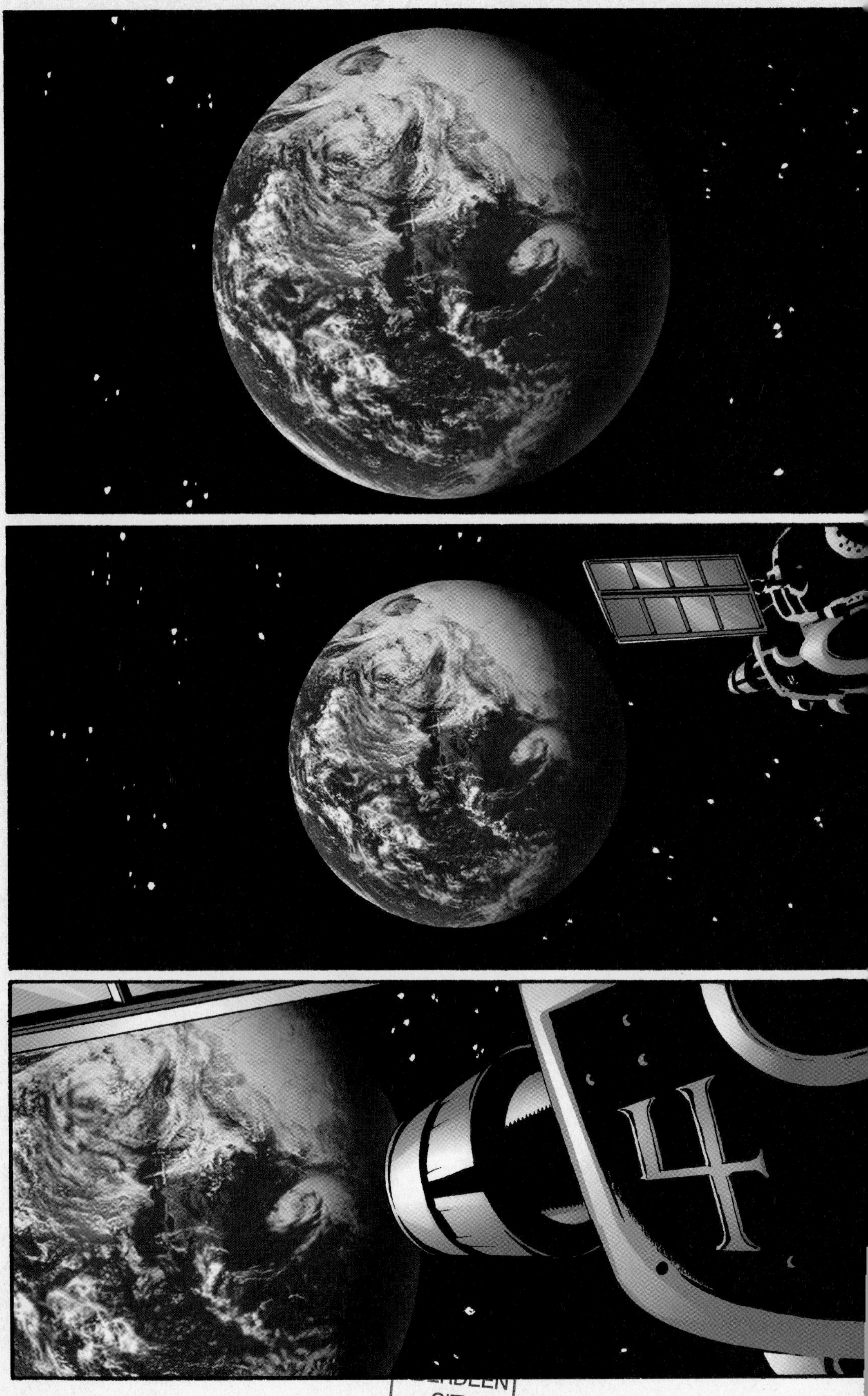

WARREN ELLIS has killed over forty people in single combat over the last two years. Eight of them died by Ellis' bare hands and teeth. So let's have no more smart comments about the English and their bad teeth. He ripped out their throats and bit their hearts in half. That takes good teeth. Hearts are hard. Dense and chewy. You couldn't do it. No. Warren Ellis lives in England with his girlfriend and daughter. And they could bite your hearts in half too.

JOHN CASSADAY has a Venus/Jupiter/Sun Trine, which is very rare. It means he has a unique and special personality. It's a combination of being very genuine, romantic, easygoing and very successful without having to be a "cutthroat" type. The two best careers for him would either be as an artist or in TV as an announcer. His chart is extremely positive. The only conflict is an internal struggle between a belief of science vs. religion. John is capable of producing such works as *X-Men/Alpha Flight*, *Union Jack* and the critically acclaimed Western DESPERADOES.

LAURA DEPUY, in addition to being an award-winning colorist, is also a Nouveau Barrista. Among other coffee delights, Laura has designed *Café Sushá*, for Californians who want their sushi on the go. Laura divides her time between coloring PLANETARY, JLA, *Universe X* and *Ministry of Space* and her fiancé Randy.

DAVID BARON said he would like to do one of two things when he grew up: be a pro wrestler or make comic books. He decided upon comics. For now, anyway. Career highlights include working on PLANETARY and THE AUTHORITY. Future career highlights will include headlining stints on *WWF Smackdown*.

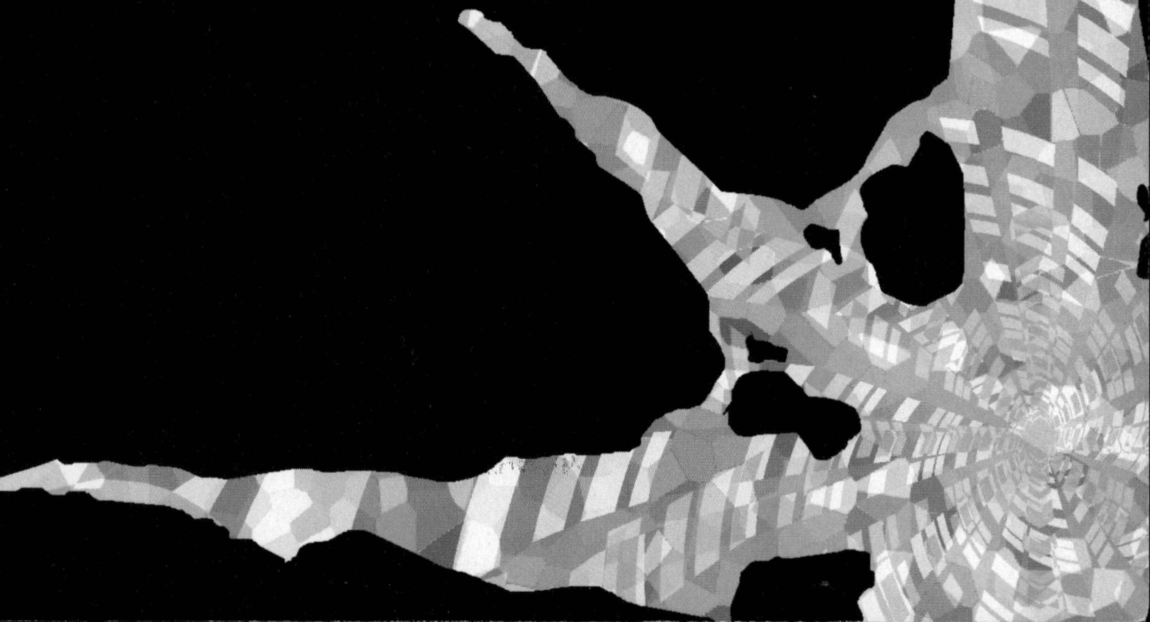

Look for these other great books from WildStorm and DC Comics:

WILDSTORM COLLECTIONS

The Authority: Relentless
Ellis/Hitch/Neary

The Authority:
Under New Management
Ellis/Millar/Hitch/Quitely/Neary

Crimson: Loyalty & Loss
Augustyn/Ramos/Hope

Crimson: Heaven & Earth
Augustyn/Ramos/Hope

Crimson: Earth Angel
Augustyn/Ramos/Hope

Deathblow:
Sinners and Saints
Choi/Lee/Sale/Scott

Danger Girl:
The Dangerous Collection #1-3
Hartnell/Campbell/Garner

Divine Right:
Collected Edition #1-3
Lee/Williams

Gen13
Choi/Lee/Campbell/Garner

Gen13: #13 ABC
Choi/Lee/Campbell/Garner

Gen13: Bootleg Vol. 1
Various writers and artists

Gen13: Grunge the Movie
Warren

Gen13: I Love New York
Arcudi/Frank/Smith

Gen13: Interactive Plus
Various writers and artists

Gen13: Starting Over
Choi/Lee/Campbell/Garner

Gen13: We'll Take Manhattan
Lobdell/Benes/Sibal

Kurt Busiek's Astro City:
Life in the Big City
Busiek/Anderson

Kurt Busiek's Astro City:
Confession
Busiek/Anderson/Blyberg

Kurt Busiek's Astro City:
Family Album
Busiek/Anderson/Blyberg

Kurt Busiek's Astro City:
Tarnished Angel
Busiek/Anderson/Blyberg

Leave It to Chance: Shaman's Rain
Robinson/Smith

Leave It to Chance: Trick or Threat
Robinson/Smith/Freeman

Planetary:
All Over the World and Other Stories
Ellis/Cassaday

Wetworks: Rebirth
Portacio/Choi/Williams

StormWatch: Force of Nature
Ellis/Raney/Elliott

StormWatch: Lightning Strikes
Ellis/Raney/Lee/
Elliott/Williams

StormWatch: Change or Die
Ellis/Raney/Jimenez

StormWatch: A Finer World
Ellis/Hitch/Neary

WildC.A.T.s: Gang War
Moore/Various

WildC.A.T.s: Gathering of Eagles
Claremont/Lee/Williams

WildC.A.T.s: Homecoming
Moore/Various

WildC.A.T.s/X-Men
Various writers and artists

Wildcats: Street Smart
Lobdell/Charest/Friend

Wildcats: Vicious Circles
Casey/Philips

WildStorm Rising
Windsor-Smith/Various

STAR TREK COLLECTIONS

Star Trek: All of Me
Isabella & Ingersoll/
Lopresti/Emberlin

Star Trek:
The Next Generation
Embrace the Wolf
Golden & Sniegoski/
Hoover/Hubbs

Star Trek:
The Next Generation
Gorn Crisis
Anderson & Moesta/
Kordey

Star Trek: Voyager
Elite Force
Abnett & Lanning/
Moy/Carani

Star Trek: Voyager
False Colors
Archer/Moy/Carani

Star Trek: Voyager
Avalon Rising
Young & Young/Roach

Star Trek: New Frontier
Double Time
David/Collins/Roach

OTHER COLLECTIONS OF INTEREST

The Batman Adventures: Mad Love
Dini/Timm

Batman:
The Dark Knight Returns
Miller/Janson/Varley

Batman: Faces
Wagner

Batman: The Killing Joke
Moore/Bolland/Higgins

Batman: Year One
Miller/Mazzucchelli/Lewis

The Golden Age
Robinson/Smith

JLA: New World Order
Morrison/Porter/Dell

JLA/ WildC.A.T.s
Morrison/Semeiks/Conrad

Justice League of America:
The Nail
Davis/Farmer

Kingdom Come
Waid/Ross

Ronin
Miller

Watchmen
Moore/Gibbons

For the nearest comics shop carrying collected editions and monthly titles fr
DC Comics, call 1-888-COMIC BOOK.

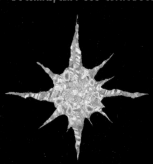